RETURN STROKE

RETURN STROKE

STROKE

essays & memoir

DORA DUECK

CMU PRESS
WINNIPEG, MANITOBA
2022

CMU PRESS

CMU Press
Canadian Mennonite University
500 Shaftesbury Blvd.
Winnipeg, MB R3P2N2
www.cmupress.ca

Editor: Sue Sorensen
Proofreader: Micah Enns-Dyck
Jacket and interior design: Matt Veith
Cover image: "Converging" by Anneli Epp Photography
Author photo by Paige Fraser
Interior images courtesy of Dora Dueck

Versions of some essays have previously appeared in periodicals; see Acknowledgements page for details.

Printed in Canada by Friesens Corporation, Altona, Manitoba.

ISBN 978-1-987986-10-5

Library and Archives Canada Cataloguing in Publication

Title: Return stroke : essays & memoir / Dora Dueck.
Other titles: Works. Selections
Names: Dueck, Dora, author.
Identifiers: Canadiana 20220189137 | ISBN 9781987986105 (softcover)
Subjects: LCSH: Dueck, Dora, | LCGFT: Essays. | LCGFT: Autobiographies.
Classification: LCC PS8557.U2813 A6 2022 | DDC C814/.54—dc23

Table of Contents

for Helmut

1951-2021

Preface

I DID NOT SET OUT to write a collection of personal essays and memoir. Each piece was written for reasons of its own—some compulsion or question that tugged at me until I tried to work it out on paper or, perhaps, an invitation to contribute to an anthology. The essay written most recently, about my husband's death, was provoked by an overwhelming sense of narrative within that grievous event and a matching desire to contain it, as if this would make it possible for me to carry it. The longest part is a memoir of two-and-a-half years our family spent in Paraguay in the early 1980s. I had long wanted to return to that time—me in my young thirties then, still finding legs as mother and writer and desperately wanting to belong in that unfamiliar environment—so I scoured letters, journals, and memories and set down what those years were like and what they meant to me. The result was longer than an essay but too short as a stand-alone book, hence the inclusion of other nonfiction writing.

All of this is to say that, having come together arbitrarily, this collection pursues a variety of themes rather than an over-arching one. In my fiction, I "make up" stories to explore matters such as suffering, secrets, and shame, but here, the ideas are diverse; the quest for meaning bows to the experience as it was. But, if there *is* a thesis poking through the parts, it is probably the notion of change. I think I imagined, as a child, that once people finished growing up and were adults, their minds more or less ran on the spot. How grateful I am to have lived long enough to discover otherwise. The essence of life, it seems to me, is change—sometimes difficult, sometimes joyous, sometimes chosen, sometimes uninvited, but change nevertheless. Growth, turn, turnover, conversion, adjustment, deconstruction and reconstruction, loss, gain, whatever name one may use for change, the very process of living creates a story full of plot.

How wonderful too that these bits of existence, no matter how ordinary, are available for further consideration. I find that change occurs in the process of writing as well. I don't mean change in the therapeutic sense necessarily, for healing, although there may be that, but more broadly in gaining understanding, seeing patterns, facing into inevitable death, enjoying the playful circularity of *then* and *now*. The book's title, *Return Stroke*—the title of one essay, where it literally refers to lightning— suggests such a dynamic, such a dialogue. When I send inquiry into my past, it sends something back to me.

I like to read books that make me lift my eyes from the text occasionally to contemplate some aspect of my own life. That, dear reader, is what I hope will happen with this one. I hope that in offering you glimpses of myself, partially and with some vulnerability, I mostly give you yourself. Please feel free to read the pieces in any order. After a scan through my life via memories of food in "Notes toward an autobiography," the rest appear in roughly chronological order, though huge swaths of my biography are not represented. Paraguay shows up in several essays and is the main location of "In the house of my pilgrimage" (which time-wise would fit after "Learning my geography"); thus there are instances of repetition, which I have retained for the integrity of the individual essays. The parts of this book were written at various times; information about provenance or previous publication appears on the acknowledgments page at the book's conclusion.

My warmest thanks to the editors of journals or anthologies in which some of this writing first appeared, to the Manitoba Arts Council for a 2015 grant to write a first draft of the Paraguay memoir, to my truly wonderful editor Sue Sorensen and her crew at CMU Press for everything concerning this collection, and to my late husband Helmut and our children for letting me talk about them.

Notes toward an autobiography

1. S HE'LL HAVE TO SAY that her mother wasn't much of a cook. Not a good cook, she means, the way others use the phrase in obituaries of their beloved moms. This grieves her a little: the accolade's absence in the list she and her siblings will soon compile for their aged parent, how their mother kept up with the news, daily CBC no less, how she sat evenings in the big chair in the living room and read (rather than tidying the kitchen to a shine or baking something nutritious for the next day, letting her children stir up another round of margarine, sugar, and syrup for puffed wheat cake instead), how she started projects and programs wherever they lived, a girls' club in one town, a thrift store in another.

She didn't recognize her mother's culinary shortfall at the time. The cinnamon buns at her best friend's house were stickier and yummier than anything she got at home, but her childhood was happy and she adored her mother, looking so intelligent and pretty evenings in that chair, reading. Still, she hardly remembers what they ate—beyond hasty meals, that is, rice cooked in milk, fried bread dough, bologna, and *Ruehrei* (a type of scrambled egg)—though she can easily recall, down to the press of linoleum

3

on her knees, how they knelt around the chairs by the table to pray, a ritual as burdensome as porridge but binding and strengthening too.

Will it seem a betrayal to speak critically, or sadly, of what she missed? And then to claim, further, that she herself has been somewhat more accomplished in the kitchen?

But where else can she begin? "For we think back through our mothers," said Virginia Woolf, and surely this applies to everything in a woman's autobiography, even though Woolf was speaking of women who write.

2. SHE WAS THIRTEEN when she made her first buns. She made them on a day when she stayed home to babysit while her mother went off to substitute teach. She was smart in school, it was said; she could easily miss a day or two or three. She watched the little ones and she baked the buns. A constant supply of buns was required because there were eight children in the family. Her mother made wonderful buns, this must be acknowledged; they were large and light. She, the oldest daughter, did the buns, and she was proud of herself, for they turned out well enough. Her mother earned thirteen dollars for a day of teaching and gave her three of them for staying home in her place.

But the anecdote could mislead, could imply she was a child prodigy of domesticity. The truth is, she left home with a huge ignorance around cooking. She liked coming in from the rigours of study to eat in a college cafeteria. Even now, if she considers the life she might have wanted instead of the one she's led, she thinks of a library and large tables covered with books, up the stairs of a hewn-stone building with dark interiors and a pale sun through narrow windows, Oxford let's say, though she's never actually been to Oxford. She thinks of strolling blissfully to meals in the refectory, where bread is eaten warm from the oven and the soup is hearty and thick. (She also likes the word refectory.) All day the mind has hungered and fed itself and then the body takes its turn.

In this vision, improbable as it would be, she's accompanied by her husband and her three children. Her imagination bends its will into the life of a woman who has it all.

3. SHE GAINED WEIGHT during her so-called further education because she was homesick and ate too much. Perhaps she can blame the educational institution as well, its towers of toast to be spread with jam, its mounds of mashed potatoes.

She remembers the trudge of the long narrow hallway, the dim weariness of her quarters, the aroma of popcorn coiling from someone's room. Popcorn! The allure of it: that smell, those kernels so white, so winsome, so unassuming and tender in one's mouth, that comfort of butter and salt. Popcorn could be nibbled at slowly through entire afternoons or seized in handfuls against the gnaw of loneliness. In dormitories, one could make a meal of popcorn.

One day she stole something—a square or a cookie, she thinks—from her roommate's stash of food from home, and when she finished the sweet, she ate the gall of a stricken conscience. She was angry with herself, and with the other girl who could make the goodies last so long, who kept them in plain view and accessible.

Such were the temptations of her youth, and just one of those to which she succumbed.

4. SHE'S NOT ASHAMED to say she learned to cook for her husband, and always tried her best at it because of him and because of the children they had together. She knew how to read, after all, and there were recipes to-read-and-follow galore.

But some kinds of reading are harder than others. She began with the cookbooks of her own tradition: *The Mennonite Treasury of Recipes* and *The Mennonite Community Cookbook*. She put eager comments in the margins when something turned out well: *Aug. 24/75 With our own apples! Yummy, and my first platz!* Later she added, *Also nice with rhubarb.*

In time, it annoyed her that most of the women who'd submitted the recipes identified themselves through their husbands—they were Mrs Jake Krahns, for instance, or Mrs Sam Detweilers—but well before that she was frustrated by their all-knowing vagueness. They left out baking times and other vital information. They said things like "enough flour for a firm dough." What was a firm dough compared to a soft one?

Betty Crocker saved her. In Betty Crocker's cookbook, no one cared about Mr Crocker's name, or whether Betty was even married, or if she went to church. The language was English, the ingredients available in any regular store. The amounts were precise. Every single step was explained.

The recipes succeeded. With Betty as her guide, she learned to make cream puffs, tall elegant cakes, puddings from scratch, stroganoff, and turkey pie. She hung on to that cookbook long after its cover had torn off and its pages were ruined with grease and gobs of batter. Long after her dependency on Betty Crocker had ended, she loved Betty's book best.

5. SHE WON'T RUN on and on about meals she made over the years. She read a diary once in which the writer recorded the contents of lunches and suppers and she found these parts so boring, she skipped over them. She *could* mention some of the failures, however. Surely every autobiography needs comic relief. The time she put rice on to simmer, for example, and forgot about it and stepped out for a walk, thus discovering the acrid smell of burned rice and how many days it lingers in the air.

Or the time she invited her editor boss and his wife for supper. Since he was tutoring her, as it were, in the ways of Mennonite history, it being a church magazine, she'd decided on a menu of *Glums Wareneki*, those quintessentially Mennonite dough pockets filled with cottage cheese—as if *she* had something to offer about Mennonite foodways!—and decided too, after perusing the eight *Wareneki* recipes in the *Treasury*, upon that of Mrs J. D. Letkeman's. Well, and why not make them ahead and put them in a casserole to warm up on the night of the guests? She was a working woman after all.

When the evening was over, she noted the date and occasion beside the recipe and also wrote, *Very good*. But how can this be, when memory overrides these words and reminds her it was embarrassing, the pockets *klebed* together like gumbo or glue? When she desperately wishes she could do it again, properly, slide those *Wareneki* freshly wet and glistening out of the boiling water and onto the plates of her editor boss and his wife, the lovely pockets quivering (individually) for a moment before being smothered by smooth rich gravy made of cream.

There was also the time she tried to enlarge her family's palate and cooked up a concoction of lentils. She wanted it to find favour with her children, so she told them lentils are nutty in flavour and that it was lentils Jacob of the Old Testament prepared for his brother, who desired them so much he sold his birthright for a taste. The children listened politely. They knew the story. Her older son took a bite. He asked if this was Jacob's recipe. If it was, he went on calmly, Esau was even more of a fool than he'd previously thought.

6. SHE'LL WANT to brag about this, that she breastfed her babies. Unlike her mother who was made to recuperate in a stiff white bed for up to ten days after her birth events, as if mortally ill, and then succumbed to the enticements of bottled formula when the infant was brought to her, by the clock, from a sterile bassinet in the hospital nursery. Which was true for many of her mother's generation. She and her peers took birthing classes with their husbands, practiced breathing techniques for the natural labours they longed to experience, rushed home soon after delivery. They insisted they would nurse—on demand. They felt they'd discovered something wonderfully old, something wonderfully new.

She recalls this feeding like an ache, how she stilled her babies' hungry howling with her body. Just like that, she stopped their cries. She heard them suckle and gurgle while she traced their perfect features with her fingers, while she floated coos into their ears like primal lullabies. She'd had trouble at first, yes, with the latching, the let-down, the nipple pain. Her mother and aunts were no help, of course, they of the easy bottles, but her books and her friends and a sympathetic doctor said she could certainly manage if she persevered. And she did. She launched her offspring naturally.

It was her generation's version, she thinks now, of eating local; of going organic.

7. SHE'LL HAVE TO confess she half believed the adage, "the way to a man's heart is through his stomach," though she made it thoroughly inclusive, pandered to the cravings of her children too. Subtly to be sure, but pandered nevertheless. She knew what they liked, what coaxed them into happiness, and she didn't mind when they peeked into pots or grew impatient for the meatballs sizzling in the pan, when the youngsters turned the kitchen upside down to make double batches of chocolate chip cookies or leaned into slices of her freshly baked bread and nearly groaned in their awe of it. She saw the affection there, how the food she—or they—stirred together brought them into proximity. She refused to analyze these moments; she knew well enough how partial they were, how silly-momish she could be, trying to tug her nestlings back again through food while they were always going away.

Sometimes, as they began to leave for good, she sat on the bed she shared with her husband and gave in to despondency, missing the first child, then the second, then the third. At these times, she wished she'd done a better job of things, and she wasn't thinking of the cooking; she was wishing she'd been a better mother. She knew her children had experienced a sizeable portion of the ten thousand joys of which the Taoists speak, but a portion of ten thousand sorrows as well. She sought to comfort herself with the good she'd been, how she'd read to them, one book after the other, and how they'd eaten together, once a day, most days, how they'd conversed while they ate. She kept reminding herself, they'd eaten together.

8. As FOR THE marriage, she'll have to confess that each of them tried to change the other. She'll have to weigh which examples to share. There are many from which to choose. For balance, she'll make a list of what she appreciated about their relationship. She'll say, for one, that his compliments of her cooking were as warm and reliable as sunrise, for he enjoyed eating and his pleasure easily found voice. For another, that they were traditional about who was in charge of the cooking and she didn't mind a bit. Not for them, in the words of bardster Leonard Cohen, "the homicidal bitchin' that goes down in every kitchen, over who will serve and who will eat." When she heard someone say that what mattered in marriage was justice, not equality, she felt happy, and vindicated too, for in this respect, their marriage was just: most of the time, she cooked.

There was an important exception, of course, a kind of kitchen art he practiced, and practices still. He woke early, well before she did; he set the kettle to boil. He transferred the hot water into a thermos. He filled a horn-cup called a *guampa* with *yerba* leaves, pushed a metal straw-like strainer called a *bombilla* into one side of it, and poured a bit of water over the leaves. He sucked up the first infusion and then, at six, he woke her. For half an hour at least, they drank the Paraguayan tea called *maté*, taking their turns. He poured, he served, and within this familiar gentle ritual, nearly every morning, she emerged to the day.

9. HER HUSBAND was raised in Paraguay, so they went to visit. Then they moved there for two years. Living in a Mennonite colony in Paraguay was the most unusual, most interesting, thing she's done. It may take up a disproportionate number of pages. It was a kind of travel through time, for she'd landed inside her family's distant origins in Russia, to customs and tastes and a manner of being she'd read about and felt in her genes. At the same time, it was a place without precedence, beyond her ability to

comprehend. She created a fictional character who'd been set down into the Chaco too. Researching and writing this other woman's life eased her own habituation.

Of course there were real women she learned to know in Paraguay as well, women like her sisters-in-law who, though not that much older than she was, seemed because of their vast competence ancient in the way her grandmothers had been. They knew what to do with chickens, how to kill and strip and eviscerate them in no time flat to be fried or cooked into soup. They made the noodles by hand. They milked. They churned butter. They raised vegetables, by the acre it seemed. They harvested berries, fruits, and even leaves for delectable fruit soups called *moos* and pies-by-the-yard. (She herself fell madly in love with mulberries, and her children did too, returning from their roaming with hands and faces stained red and blue with the evidence.) These women knew how to whitewash, how to slaughter. They seemed to know everything.

Then she realized—and it dismayed and startled her—that here where roles were rigidly prescribed and the burgeoning women's liberation movement of North America merely a distant rumour, the women competed over food. She heard the off-hand remarks and she saw them watching, slyly and surreptitiously, whose cakes and plates of pastries at the church coffees or family gatherings disappeared first. Those who went home with empty pans and platters were the winners. And no wonder: they'd taken the time and had the decency to slice their cakes evenly in half, horizontally, and fill them with cooked vanilla or citrus pudding, and they'd iced them, sprinkled them with nuts!

One woman who worked like a dervish against poverty, selling eggs, vegetables, and watermelons, plus milking twice a day and doing everything else in the household, always lost the competition. This woman offered chocolate cake as plain as an unplanted field, merely dusted with powdered sugar, still in the old black pan in which it was baked. This woman always went home with her cake half eaten.

She noticed these things and pitied that woman and wished to defend her from disdain, though what she hated most was the limited range from which self-esteem could be drawn, that small platform of permissible contest. But she's not sure she went so far with her pity and beliefs as to eat a piece of the woman's cake instead of the prettier ones beside it. She remembers that she put some effort into what she brought to the gatherings herself, and she's never forgotten how good it felt to be asked for her coffee cake recipe, that deceptively simple but moist and tasty cake with cinnamon and brown sugar layered into the middle and baked crisply into the top.

10. THE TELLING won't be complete without a mention of the smallest meal of them all, which she began to eat when she was baptized into the church. She was twelve. It was called the Lord's supper. She sees herself on a photograph of the day, still as flat-chested as the proverbial pancake but wearing a grown-up lemon-coloured two-piece outfit and short white gloves. She looks serious and solemn. She knows she was precocious.

She learned more about communion cookery later. She read a Joseph Bayly parable about a family whose son and brother John had died and how they used to talk about him over bowls of steaming porridge at breakfast, enjoying themselves, until it occurred to their mother that it wasn't nearly respectful enough and they began to remember him Saturday mornings in the parlor instead, tiny plates for the oatmeal, tiny silver cups for the milk, and laughter disallowed. The parable gripped her. She tried to be more attentive at the meal, but also less, by which she meant joyous, not staring at the wood grain of the pew in front of her and straining for anguish. She wrote an article on the subject and some readers misunderstood what she was trying to say, but their pushback was not enough to staunch what had opened inside her like a bubbling underground stream.

Still later she wondered if the insistence that the Mass wasn't really body, really blood, but simply remembrance for which her sixteenth-century Anabaptist foremothers were martyred was conviction big and risky enough for contemporary appetites. Perhaps, in fact, she *was* eating body, blood; hadn't Jesus stood up in the middle of a crowd and cried, "Eat me, drink me?" But really, what did it matter, who cared about that? About any kind of literal and metaphorical fighting to exhaustion in theological battles? Other kinds of subversion and courage seemed necessary now, new kinds of foolish truth. A wider church table, wider love, new orders of out and in and down and up, people of any race or ethnicity or sexual orientation welcome, that's what she wanted, and eating like a child, the pulled chunk of bread a compulsion, the gulp of wine a surprise.

11. SHE'S UNSURE how the autobiography might end. Now cooking and eating builds on memories like a seven-layer one-pot, the hard work of feeding children over, the torrential hormones that once rose and fell firmly

dammed behind her. She'll never be known by what she did in the kitchen. She's a better cook than her mother, true, but it doesn't amount to much; they've both been a-typical. She and her husband have reached a lovely rut in their quiet house, too easily satisfied, she sometimes thinks, with *maté* in the morning and simple suppers of chicken, fish, pasta, or hamburger, side dishes of noodles or rice, vegetables or salad, usually strawberries for dessert. The only remaining ambitions concern her vocation to write.

But the notes she assembles as an outline of her life are less tidy, more complicated, than they look. And then to sit down at a desk, write breath into them? What a flurry of peeling and mixing and stirring that would be! What clouds of flour and heat! Long days of it, and a great deal of reading—and re-reading—to grasp the genre of subjectivity. The ingredients must not be mistaken for nostalgia. There would have to be a summons, a *Come to the table,* a huge expenditure of honesty, poured into a one-chance feast.

To live is daunting enough, she thinks, never mind trying to describe it. Or eat it all over again.

But who knows? She may be lucky, she may be tenacious. What if she tries the thing—the crazy untested memoirish recipe that serves up the past? Maybe, if she's *really* lucky or tenacious, her concoction will be delicious. And if not delicious, provide some sustenance at least.

The knot at the beginning

I'M LISTENING to an interview with cartoonist Lynda Barry on *Writers and Company* and immediately recognize what she's on about when she says she thinks of her childhood "all the time," when she says she goes there for memories of early "aliveness" and "vividness" that motivate her art, for answers to what made her who she is. I've gone looking too. Gone often, peering at my childhood like a stranger in search of an original me. Wondering who I once was and how it connects to who I've become.

When I learned to sew by hand as a girl, I learned the critical anchoring function of the knot at the start of my simple seams. That's what I'm after, I think: the knot at the beginning.

I remember the small grey house tucked into one of those mild hills and valleys that lapped away from the Rocky Mountains in Central Alberta. I remember awful earaches, the itch of pinworms, falling asleep in my parents' bed only to waken on the sofa because I didn't have a bed of my own. I remember the living room with sofa and chair, the two tiny bedrooms, my brothers sleeping in one and my parents, with the latest baby, in the other, the aisle between bed and crib just wide enough for me to crouch in while I soothed or sang to him, my hand pushed between the slats like one wee bird twittering to another.

I remember sitting in the shallow creek, waving at trainmen as the train clattered by. Balancing on the rails. I remember the joy of the Christmas Eve's goody bag with its mandarin orange, peanuts, and candy, and the tape recorder, huge reels of shiny brown ribbon emptying and filling as they turned, Handel's *Messiah* pouring mysteriously, majestically, into all the air of the house.

I can move about that house perched against a hill, run through the yard, wander to the creek or nearby grain elevator or church where my father was minister, even walk the road into the village about a kilometre away. My feet shrink, wear girl shoes, know the way. It's wonderful, such a reprise of my geography, that row of trees, vast sky, billowy hills, winding creek, long prairie grass, a landscape that's still my default position for what I find most beautiful about the earth. But I'm disconcerted too. Most of the content of living in those spaces has disappeared. The geography may be graphic, nearly touchable, but I have no bounteous scenes or page-turning episodes or conversations in their entirety like other memoirists seem to scoop up. My list above is a list of fragments. I stretch them every which way, try to widen their edges, make a story out of them, but there's not much to work with. They're like billboards passed at high speed: a sliver of information, an impression, a whiff of emotion.

Perhaps what fascinates, as Patricia Hampl muses in *A Romantic Education*, is the phenomenon of memory itself. The fact is, childhood amnesia affects us all. Memory is capricious, unreliable, unyielding; it frustrates the endeavour of writing one's life. (Which is why diaries, journals, letters matter.)

But why do we remember one thing and not another? And why do we assume, as Lynda Barry and I and countless memoirists assume—perhaps ironically, given memory's flaws—that what we *do* remember is germane to our most essential selves?

And why do some people remember a lot, and I remember so little?

It's not quite true, however, that I possess nothing of substance from my earliest years. I do have a memory—a cluster of memory, actually, like a twist and loop holding fast in the fabric of my fragments. And I've always believed that, somehow, this is the one that accounts for me.

My strongest, fullest memory involves four books, which my mother read to me.

Not *my* stories, in other words, but the stories of others.

THE FOUR BOOKS were *Nobody Loves Me, Christie's Old Organ,* and *A Peep Behind the Scenes* by Mrs O.F. Walton, and *Pilgrim's Progress* by John Bunyan. The latter was a children's version of the Bunyan allegory, the others were pathos-ridden Victorian tales: a poor organ grinder on the streets of London; a girl actress in the glittering milieu of a travelling theatre troupe whose mother lay dying in their caravan; a miserable woman called Old Grumpy who lost first a cat, then a child. These books took me into worlds of misery I had no experience of or context for—*Christie's Old Organ,* for instance, which Dickens-like led me through the crowded, distressing lanes of London's poorest districts, where thousands of children passed days and nights beside open drains and trash piles, hoping for pity and a few pennies to survive.

We were somewhere in the middle of Old Grumpy's losses in *Nobody Loves Me,* perhaps at the point of the child's death, when I pressed my face, crying, into the comfort of my mother's arm. It was a trying-to-be-soundless weeping, I think, the way one cries when it's not for defiance or drawing attention or on account of falling or getting hurt but something welling up inside, sorrow and commiseration like a cloudburst, hoping my mother and her arm would soak up the flood of what I felt. Old Grumpy was bereft and so was I. Since nobody loved her, she'd resolved to love nobody either, but there remained "that old, hungry feeling . . . in spite of herself." I might have been five or six and my world was secure but I felt—along with her—"that old, hungry feeling."

It could have been evening but I'm not sure of that, for my mother was someone who would stop housework to read to a child. She was a teacher before marriage and a keen reader herself, so she read well, she let the emphasis down on the right words. I see the scene as if from behind: Mom in the middle, me on her right, one of my brothers on the left. I see the backs of us on the pale brown sofa—a hard nylon nubby fabric, wasn't it? I think my mind creates this perspective—behind myself—to keep me truly there; if I climb back into my body, where I'm facing the book, I disappear (tears tumbled Mom-ward notwithstanding). I disappear because immediately I'm inside the story and it takes over and the memory becomes the memory of Mrs O.F. Walton's narrative. *Those* characters, *their* landscape, *their* emotions. Vivid impressions that pressed and stayed.

I've worried this memory cluster over the years, I've tugged on it, tried to loosen it, feeling proud, then ashamed. Then proud and ashamed again. Proud because I'm a reader and, though the four books were read *to* me, I trace myself as reader to that point, and it's the beginning of a line of literature decades long. And reading is good for us, isn't it? Assumes virtue, and brains? Wasn't I one of the students "skipped" by my teacher from Grade One to Two in my first year of school?

And useful too, reading is, isn't it? By vocation I'm a writer, and writing learns and grows from the writing of others. An *avid* reader, to use the preferred adjective, etymologically from *crave;* reading for the continuing desperate requirement of it, like air and water and food. Hearing these four books (and the Bible) matured into a steady exercise of apprehending words and sentences and stories and books, into eventually putting my own pen to paper.

But ashamed: that too. In her memoir *Time to Be in Earnest,* mystery writer P.D. James referred to childhood books like Mrs O.F. Walton's *A Peep Behind the Scenes* as "depressing piety." Who wants to own up to that?

"PSYCHOLOGY, WHICH is somehow *our* science, the claustrophobic discipline of the century," Patricia Hampl continues while discussing memory in *A Romantic Education,* "has made us acknowledge the value of remembering—even at the peril of shame."

"At least," she carries on, "shame is interesting; at least it is hidden, the sign of anything valuable."

Interesting? Valuable? Considering shame this way is provocative to me.

If I mention to others with an apologetic laugh that my earliest memories were the Mrs O.F. Walton books—I may even rattle off their names—no one seems alarmed. Or particularly attracted either, not as I'm perpetually attracted and alarmed. Can't they tell I became embarrassed about those books and their power over me? I'm not embarrassed about the Hardy Boys or Nancy Drew books and other tales of their ilk which I gobbled down regularly like warm cookies and milk, pure filler, entertainment, harmless reading rituals of repetition. I'm pleased about *The Diary of Anne Frank* and Pearl Buck's *The Good Earth* and Somerset Maugham's *Of Human Bondage* in my teens. And about Brontë, Hardy, Austen, my education being mainstream Canadian, which tipped heavily at that time to the literary Brits.

John Bunyan's *Pilgrim's Progress* gets a pass because it's a classic. Even if a shortened children's version with the characters made young, the storyline was there and the names retained. Discretion, Prudence, Charity, Formalist, Hypocrisy, and more made their appearance, proper grown-up names for things, and via the story and charming line illustrations I learned the sites and progress of a Christian pilgrimage, crossing a plain from the City of Destruction to a shining gate opening to life, hills of delight and castles of despair, paths and stiles along the way, Vanity Fair of course, and eventually, many trials and learnings later, the Dark River and the Celestial City gleaming beyond it. I still have on my bookshelf the tattered copy of *Little Pilgrim's Progress* my mother read to us, this first manual of challenges I might expect in life—any life, really, not just the Christian one.

It was the Mrs O.F. Walton books that wrenched me. Someone was always dying, it seemed, there was always wretchedness. I'd not been rejected or unwanted or mistreated. Apart from a bed, I had everything I required. But I was a child and I assented to what the stories said: the tragedy of human existence apart from God's love and salvation within the rubric of the cross. The dying died but the endings were happy anyway, for just in time they heard the good news.

In 1978, when I was the young mother of a toddler and pregnant with our second child, I took a one-semester course in children's literature at the University of Winnipeg. In that course, and then later in reading to my children, I encountered the range of books I'd missed. *The Wind in the Willows* and *Alice in Wonderland*, the works of Rudyard Kipling and Jack London. The Narnia books and *The Little Prince* and *The Hobbit* and *The Railway Children* and *The Little House* series. I was sure no one in that university classroom had heard of the Mrs O.F. Walton books, had I been brave enough to mention them. Those books belonged to the subset of culture called evangelical Christianity, which I must have imagined that I alone, in the class, had inhabited. In the sprouting critique of my late twenties, Mrs O.F. Walton represented Feeling of the most maudlin kind. Slight, badly written, inferior, I was sure, in spite of their remembered sway.

When I spotted a new release of *Christie's Old Organ* in a bookstore, however, this "Victorian classic for children" now "revised and updated," I bought it. Some time later I came upon a worn copy of *Nobody Loves Me*, the original version, at a thrift store. I found myself secretly pleased to own artifacts linked to my childhood. I read the toned-down *Christie's Old Organ* to my boys, in fact, like a small bow to my past; one Mrs O.F. Walton volume, I thought, couldn't hurt.

Then I was surprised how good her writing was. Here, for example, is the opening of *Nobody Loves Me*:

> The great church clock, in the most crowded part of that crowded city, was striking eight.
>
> It was a solemn old clock, and it spoke very slowly and distinctly, as if it thought that the people who lived round the church were not able to count quickly, and as if it were afraid they would make a mistake, and would lay the blame on the clock.
>
> One—two—three—four—five—six—seven—eight!
>
> The children heard it; and they left the mud pies they were making in the gutter, and ran to their different homes. The bricklayers, who were mending the old church porch, heard it; and threw down their trowels, and hurried away to their breakfast. The milkman, who was driving down the street, heard it; and he whipped his horse, and drove quickly, that his customers might be supplied in time . . . .

Clearly Mrs O.F. Walton had not become a bestselling author in her day without some narrative skills. Her style was musical. Here's her description of the old woman:

> Old Grumpy was a thin, bony old woman, with a hard and cross face. Even the children ran away from her as she passed through the court, for she never smiled at them, or spoke to them, but stalked on, with a determined step, and with her lips tightly pressed together, as if she had made up her mind to be the Ishmael of the court—her hand against every man, every man's hand against her.

Ishmael? In a children's book? The inference is sharp and smart.

This writing had been good enough to hook me on the marvel of language. On that point I could be at ease.

BUT THE CONTENTS of those books!

One afternoon, in the late-1980s, while my mother and I quilted a blanket for my daughter, I asked her why she'd read us those books. I was middle-aged and assessing my past. I felt I'd carried something too intense, too heavy, away from Mrs O.F. Walton, perhaps because of the misery and death, but more likely because I was spiritually attentive as a child and took on the responsibility for others' salvation these books imposed. I took it on with a seriousness beyond the measure of my age. I could not have articulated the weight of that obligation at the time but I grasped it in retrospect.

"They probably *were* too much for you," she said. "I realize that now. But that's how it was then."

That's how it was. Then. When missionaries from Africa or India came to our church, we children sat in the front rows during slide shows and stared at lepers with their hideous oozing wounds, stared into the wide eyes of children from other countries who were described as needy, poor, heathen. Although my parents didn't stress hell, we were certainly presented with reminders of its fiery torments in other settings, as well as repeated instructions on what to do about it.

Too much for you. Indeed. One day at school, my best friend and I lingered behind in the classroom after everyone had gone out to skate, in order to "witness" to our teacher. For some reason, we'd decided she wasn't "saved" and we loved her and of course desired that she should be. Our teacher must have reassured us about the state of her soul; at any rate we were sent out to skate with the rest of the class and I recall no further anxiety over her.

I've since journeyed to a better place in my spiritual convictions but I cringe over that scene; I want to soothe and draw those two young girls away into another conversation about the human condition and salvation; I want to tell them this isn't their job.

Perhaps in the mingling of their piety and pity, however, these books also fastened something in me that literature stitches forward to this day? Dare I call it compassion?

On a road trip in 1997, coincidentally the day Princess Diana died in Paris, my husband and I listened to Martha Nussbaum, author of *Poetic Justice*, in radio conversation with Eleanor Wachtel—about the importance of fiction, I think. I had my journal open. "Nussbaum said fiction allows us to imagine the value of other people's lives," I jotted. "In reading novels we're learning to go behind appearances . . . to go beyond the shape of the person we see." Imagining the value of others—a vital step in learning to love—started for me within the vigorous, complicated memory of the Mrs O.F. Walton books. Yes, I'm quite sure, and it's no less a default position than the prairie landscape is to me.

I CHASE AFTER Mrs O.F. Walton on the internet. There's not much information, no biography, it seems, which surprises me, considering how many books—more than thirty—she wrote and how well they sold. According to Lamplighter, which still publishes some of her archive, Mrs O.F. Walton's most famous book, *A Peep Behind the Scenes* (1877), sold two and a half million copies when first published.

She was born in 1849 in Hull, England, the daughter of a vicar, and died in 1939. Her birth name was Amy Catherine Deck; the O.F. stood for Octavius Frank Walton, a minister she married in 1875. The British Library Online says that in her first book, *My Little Corner: A Book for Cottage Homes*, the narrator is a young mother who describes life in the new terraced streets of a place like Hull "where the town has expanded rapidly into the countryside and destroyed it." The story gets personal and moralistic, however, tracing the young mother's "backsliding from church-going and her re-conversion after her daughter is burned to death while she was gossiping in the street." The same article notes that in her later life Mrs O.F. Walton enlarged her scope and style, focussed more on story and drew on other genres such as adventure or mystery stories. "While her evangelical themes were not neglected, they no longer dominated the story so entirely." The Mrs O.F. Walton books of my childhood fall into the middle section of her career.

Another site describes the author as "plump and homely," but I find a photograph that reveals a cheerful, kindly face, certainly no you-are-lost scowl which her plots might indicate. It relieves me. She and her husband, living in the vicarage, would have been among the more educated in the community, would have been considered of respectable social status. The couple had seven children and took expensive holidays, it's said, because of Mrs O.F. Walton's earnings from her books.

I wish I knew more about her and her family, how—besides the holidays—she and her husband and the children managed her fame, and what happened to them all. I can glean from my searches only that a daughter died at eight and a son in his youth, that one daughter married in Uganda, one remained single and lived with her widowed sister whose husband had died in India, and I can't help thinking that if I were younger and had the resources to poke about in Britain for a year, with a side scoot to Jerusalem where the O.F. Waltons lived in his first church assignment, I'd be tempted to research and possibly write the missing biography myself.

IF I'VE MADE my peace with their style and their fervent, melodramatic religiosity, the memory of four books confronts me with another challenge: the peculiarity of stories not my own as my strongest early memory. What does it mean, that other characters and tales swallowed me, stand in for memories of myself? I'm reconciled to being a lifelong reader, but I would definitely prefer to be knotted at the start to a solid consciousness of myself rather than Old Grumpy, or Treffy the organ-man, or Rosalie and her dying mother in a tiny caravan.

In a story I once wrote, "The Act of Reading," a woman named Ruth joins a book club upon her retirement, only to discover the club is in the midst of an odyssey of re-reading. This dismays her, for there's still so much she hasn't read once. Nevertheless, she soon becomes enmeshed in the group because of the women's friendship. She fears, though, that they'll discover who she is, or isn't:

> . . . Then I lay awake, looking back at myself, and I was like a paper chain, one of those long paper chains of cutout girls, the same girl over and over, and there were pages of text open on every figure where the heart would be. I'd been a lonely child, always hunched hungrily into a book. Only stories made me thick enough to exist. I couldn't understand why this was so. This sense of my insubstantiality had lessened over the years but had never entirely disappeared, which was harder to admit than anything else about me.

Ruth isn't me but I resonate with her. A sensation not unlike panic occurs if I leave the house knowing I'll have pockets of empty time but forgot to bring something to read. As if that time will thus barely exist. As if, like my fictional Ruth, *I* will barely exist.

Artist Moyra Davey, in her essay "The Problem of Reading," sets the scene of a woman—herself, we presume—moving about her book-filled home, not finishing up domestic chores, browsing a page here or there, trying to decide what to read next. "It is not just a question of which book will absorb her," Davey writes, "for there are plenty that will do that, but rather, which book, in a nearly cosmic sense, will choose her, redeem her. Often what is at stake, should she want to spell it out, is the idea that something is missing, as in: what is the crucial bit of urgently needed knowledge that will save her, at least for this day? She has the idea that if she can simply plug into the right book then all will be calm, still, and right with the world."

Moyra Davey likes Virginia Woolf, who champions "voracious, indiscriminate reading," who advises to "[feed] greedily upon books of all sorts." Avid readers cannot deny, however, that there exists at least some menace in this demanding and compulsive habit of the deepest self—*what am I calling for? what's calling me?*—by which we fall under the spell of the printed word. Russian poet Osip Mandelstam, for example, disdained "omnivorous" reading and "the demon of reading" that "plays havoc" with our minds, "the mechanical absorption of incompatible things." There are many, many compelling reasons to read, but the need is relentless for some of us; Mandelstam is right about that. Surely reading requires the same discernment as any other "need" or obsession; whatever valid reasons one summons, or snobbishness one wishes to claim for being a reader, these must be tempered with the entire reality of its practice.

So how shall I understand this knot, this essential me I catch sight of in my earliest memories and the curious way in which I still find myself existing and not quite whole unless I have something at hand to read? How do I accept this strange dependency?

The truth is, the mechanism of our first shaping continues to shape, even transform. If there's something fixed at the beginning, there's also change. I have dozens of adult examples of that—books that have altered and grown me. Shall I feel badly then about reading, about the practice started by four books read to me in a small valley house so many years ago? About wearing the subsequent requirement for books like an undergarment, silk or sackcloth as it will? Or, it might be more accurate to say, wearing it like skin?

No, I won't. It's who I was, who I am. Thomas Merton said, "For every man is his own Jacob. He wakes up at the foot of his own ladder and sees the angels going up and down, with God at the top . . . ." My ladder of ascent and descent from the earliest years was stories, set into lines and pages, set into books. Impossible to switch to a different ladder now. What I mean is, while I gather—in this strongest clump of memory—clues to how I was made, and who I became, I won't boast of it, or be ashamed of it either, but eagerly read on, knowing that stories continue to fill the aching gaps in me. I'll keep reading, to see what happens. I may stand at a distance. I may get involved. Feel alongside or identify. Push back against. I'll be there. Absorbed. And whole.

I adopted the John Bunyan and Mrs O.F. Walton books with unreserved receptivity; I was formed by them. I remembered them, later viewed them with legitimate suspicion, decided some of what I'd consumed was wrong, decided some was much too much. I probed and re-interpreted, and loved again the girl who opened herself to those books, then grew out of them in all the ways one grows beyond childhood. I reach back still, to find the motivating "aliveness" in childhood Lynda Barry talked about. I finger the steady, complicated line to and from the knot at the beginning of my memories, touch the impressionability of being young. Touch the joy and abandon of it too, the pure emotion spilling into a mother's sleeve.

Learning geography

This is a kind of grieving—to discover
the falseness of beliefs I didn't know
I carried . . .

(Joanne Epp, "On Finding a Friend's Obituary")

THE KNEEHILLS CREEK begins in the gentle bosomy terrain of central Alberta and, on its way eastward toward the Red Deer River, curls past the village of Linden where I grew up. On internet satellite imagery I see how sinuous the Kneehills is, how almost picaresque its intentions, but as a child I glimpsed its character only briefly and in parts, around a curve or from a rise perhaps. One of its most extravagant oxbows was visible from a point on the road that weekly bore us home from piano lessons in a neighbouring town and I always looked when we passed it and always it seemed remarkable and beautiful.

But my direct experiences of the creek were at ground level. The Kneehills was a mild and sluggish thing much of the time, more bank and bed than water. My brothers and I often played in the hills outside the village and sometimes we scouted as far as the creek. I recall a summer's day when we were able to cross it, jumping from one dry hump of dirt to another, while the water slid lazily between, just deep enough for us to consider our accomplishment a feat but not so deep as to make us truly afraid.

Sometimes, though, depending on the rains or the amount of snowfall or the quickness of thaw, the Kneehills became river-like, with enough frozen water to skate on during winter and deep enough to drown you in spring. And so it was in 1966, the year I was sixteen.

On April 1 of that year, the creek was running high. Its frigid stream, mustering from snow melt, moved as swiftly and impatiently as a wild animal let out of a cage. Several friends were shooting gophers that day and then they got the idea of putting a rowboat into the creek for a ride.

We'd had graduation ceremonies at our small high school the night before. The three friends were graduates. In those years, we wrote "departmentals" in June and wouldn't know whether we'd actually passed until well into summer. But we celebrated in anticipation of success or, for those who wouldn't make it, to bid farewell.

The school was small, twelve in the graduating class, four in my Grade Eleven class. All of us in the upper grades knew one another. All of us were involved in almost everything. I was vice-president of the student council so I presented thanks and a gift to our visiting speaker after his speech to the graduates. I wore a knee-length, short sleeved dress of a pale yellow colour, which I paired with short white gloves and, since I had a date, a red rose corsage. I felt myself elegant, perhaps even fetching.

Ours was a conservative, church-going community—two kinds of Mennonites predominating—so our speaker, Dr. John B. Toews of the University of Calgary, felt free to compare the twelve graduates to the twelve disciples of Jesus Christ, "who didn't rank high in possession of talents." Yet each, he went on, by doing their individual part, "turned the world upside down."

Shooting gophers and boating that first day of April continued the graduation celebration for the three friends, something fun and physical after the serious, formal ceremony. The school year wasn't finished; no need to turn the world upside down just yet.

It was the boat that capsized, however, and E, one of the three, drowned.

THIS WAS MY most significant encounter with death to that point.

Years earlier a woman in our church had a car accident in which her child died. I was part of a young girls' ensemble that sang a children's hymn at the funeral. Our sweet voices added poignancy to the service but all I could think of was that the mother had, reportedly, lifted the car by herself to free her pinned daughter. Such strength seemed superhuman.

I'd also been at my grandmother's funeral as a youngster of eight and remembered the house and farm and my pretty dress in black and white but little else. The sadness seemed adult in nature and didn't adhere to me. She was old, after all, and I hadn't known her well because we lived in another province.

But E was close to my age, he was part of my cohort, his death was an astonishment. Confusion. Another kind of encounter altogether.

FOUR DECADES later, I find myself meditating—even obsessing at times, I confess—about E and his untimely departure, though I'm not sure why. It was a shock at the time, yes, but we weren't close. What I mean is, I knew him well but also barely knew him, for even in small communities, youth form into groups, and E chose "rebellious" which in our context meant not joining his church and smoking, and I chose "good" which meant the opposite and several months after he drowned my family moved to Manitoba and after a year or so I lost touch with most of my friends and acquaintances in the village and environs of Linden, and being away from the place, also lost touch with its traumas. There was nothing to remind me of what had happened to him.

I assess our photos in the yearbook—his and mine and everyone else's who was there at the time. Calculating the years that have passed. Reaching back and touching as much of who we were as I can touch through photographs. Our faces seem impossibly young and weightless but his—good-looking, unsmiling, his curly hair combed halfway down his forehead—seems older than it should have been for eighteen, more substantial than the rest of ours. I suspect this is illusion, though, simply the fact that he died and the rest of us kept going and are still alive.

I read what he wrote in the literary pages of the yearbook. His contribution was an untitled thirty-two-line poem.

> Last night I had an awful dream.
> In fair competition, but with selfish means
> I built, from nothing, a national empire
> With sweat, brains and self-determination.
> With all this wealth I became a playboy
> And in my middle years, I toyed

With all the pleasures I missed before.
Oh! A better life never existed, as the one
I lived; I became young again, and none
Dared trespass in this vale of sweetful bliss . . .

It goes on in this vein, a tale reminiscent of Ecclesiastes or the farmer in Jesus' parable who built himself bigger barns and decided to eat, drink, and be merry, with the same conclusion.

Came the last day,
My name and wealth and pleasures were unable
To comfort me. And Oh! On THAT final hour
I faced eternal insecurity!

If E had lived to also peruse the yearbooks of our youth, I think he might be pleased to see what a good writer he was. He used words like interdict and intercluding. And the clever play on "eternal security," a theological concept most of us had heard about.

He might be amazed too—or squirm—at his bravado. At how much he already knew but how little. Which is exactly how I feel about my diary entry of the time of his death.

V, M, and E were boating on the creek. They had come quite a way to their destination, the bridge. The day was quite windy, the water was very high and running swiftly. It was cold, cold water.

Suddenly, for an unknown reason, the boat capsized. M was under the boat.

E and V couldn't stay with it. M, a powerful swimmer, got the other two boys back to the boat. It was so cold, they couldn't speak. M and V swam to shore. It was very hard swimming but they made it. Then E tried. The boys yelled, "Swim, swim." He had cried, "What shall I do?" M yelled, "Pray!" He lifted his head up. Then he went under. M had gone back to try to reach him when he saw his difficulty but his hand couldn't make contact. E went under. In eternity.

M was barefoot, V had only tennis shoes. E had had the truck keys and although the two tried to cross the wires they were unsuccessful so walked about a mile to [another] farm, and took their truck to [E's] place . . .

. . . When [E's mother] saw the boys drive up alone, and all wet, she knew something had happened to E . . .

No one can say whether he was ready at the last moment or not. But, oh, the despair in that household. "Why did it have to be my boy?" [she] cried.

Both pieces of writing could be picked apart and scrutinized in any number of directions. They could be criticized or defended. The point I see is this: they are typically high school. Straining for adulthood, they suppose they have to step away from the personal. Both of them take distance from their subjects, perhaps to cope with the questions they have, or the way real death—not literary death—has suddenly come to call.

Both of us fit the details we had into a bigger, religious narrative. Mine hints at, but ultimately hides, my thoughts about a community's rush to judgment about E's relationship with God. It privileges soul while the search is on for his body. It's a report instead of grief, as in the details in the diary entry about the night before.

Thursday was graduation. E stood there, tall and handsome. When he was introduced by the [vice-principal], he said E liked Science and Math, he had many hobbies. When someone asked him what his plans for the future were, he had replied, "It depends on the weather."

But I've had the opportunity to live longer and will allow myself to feel the grief of it now, and so I grieve. I feel the sadness and incomprehension that comprises grief, the loss of him to family and friends, the longing for reversal that grief contains as well, not preoccupied now with destiny after death but human absence. I can't help thinking as well what a joy it's been to be alive these years since high school. To grow up some more and to better comprehend as a mother how one could lift an automobile off a child. To learn as I get older that my grandmother wasn't actually that old when she died and to read her love letters and diaries and know what I missed by not knowing her. To have no idea about E's mother's question, "Why mine?" but to fervently hope she found peace about it in the intervening years.

I pity E. Looking at our photos, I mean. Pity him that he couldn't journey further in life as we did, because sometimes the joy of living is almost uncontainable. It was heady then, but continues to be, that mad mix of not knowing and knowing, but most of all the chance still being here provides to fill in one detail after another, to make our stories bigger and longer. And to trace them back to intimations of possible futures glimpsed in, say, a diary or a yearbook poem.

Not that I think he requires my pity. I still believe the big truth of "in eternity" (though I like the German word *Ewigkeit*—foreverness—better) and I believe that God, beyond the lowered curtains of our deaths, does all things well, that E is safe within that wellness. So he won't require my pity. Perhaps pity is what the departed possess and reserve for those of us left behind.

I WAS IN ALBERTA for other reasons but one of the friends I've kept up with agreed to spend a day driving around Linden with me, to the places our family and hers and our mutual friends once lived, by stores and houses and churches and views of the creek. The landscape was pre-spring beige and brown, monochrome, and it was cool and overcast, but I knew again my memories of the area weren't merely the rosy hues of childhood. What gorgeous country, the boundless rolling terrain and big-sky feel of it! We stopped so I could take a photo of the remarkable oxbow but my camera lens wasn't wide enough to get it all on one shot. We drove by the section of the creek where E disappeared, got out at the bridge where they hung netting in hopes of catching the body. I stared at ground that had swarmed with vehicles and searchers some four decades ago, but there was no one here now and no transport back to those days. We were two middle-aged grandmothers with memories, still friends, standing in a sweeping, colourless, heartbreaking landscape, talking about our lives. Then and *now*.

After our gallivant through the countryside we drove into town to get gas. Another friend of mine from childhood was working the pumps. An unusual job for a woman her age, I thought, but she seemed happy. Happier than I remembered her, actually, and lovely-looking too. She wore her curly grey hair long. It suited her.

At the same service station, I had another serendipitous encounter. Once, in a kids-of-the-neighbourhood feud, I picked up a stone and threw it at the boy who lived across the street. I hit him in the mouth and the stone chipped an inverted V out of his two front teeth.

Now here he was, a man. He hadn't forgotten the rock in the mouth either. But I saw immediately that his broad smile was fine and he was fine and the missing bit was smaller than I remembered. "I'm so sorry," I said, and he said it was no problem at all. I wouldn't have recognized him if my friend hadn't known who he was but now, because we met again, the memory confronted us and we had this opportunity to add a warm and friendly brew of apology and assurance to the narrative. It felt as if we'd given each other a blessing.

E WAS GONE, drowned, and there were crazy rumours. The broad valley where the three boaters tipped into the water filled with cars and the creek filled with other boats and divers and the banks of the creek filled with onlookers. But they never found the body. So perhaps it was just an elaborate ruse, E's rebellion against church so well worked out he was in Mexico by now, and laughing?

Of course he'd drowned, it was clear enough. The police did their investigation and eventually, after weeks of waiting and hoping for some miracle, some evidence of him, a service was held. A funeral of sorts. I recall sitting on the women's side in his family's church, glancing through the plain windows of the plain white building to trees that surrounded it, feeling the wooden bench, but I don't recall what was said.

He drowned, of course he did. The water had been cold and very swift. People murmured that for all we knew, he was at the ocean already. On clear days the Rockies were visible on the distant horizon so I pictured him slipping through mountain valleys, over falls and along the white-green stream, sliding past salmon, mile after mile, making that rushing dangerous journey to the Pacific. Stupid of me to dwell on this, surely inappropriate, but the mind does tumble to such terrifying places.

I also hate to admit how long it took me to learn my geography but I've finally also lived long enough to know that E couldn't have entered the Pacific. The Kneehills Creek flows into the Red Deer, which empties into the South Saskatchewan, which pours into the Nelson basin of Manitoba—where I would move the next year—and on through the port of Churchill and out the bay and into the eastern ocean, the Atlantic. His body—the outer wrap of the person he'd been, which is what I'm speaking of now—was not recovered. I'm grieving him at last and everything, yes, everything he was and might have become. We all eventually moved on, but he was gone before we'd even written our departmental exams or found out whether we passed.

Return stroke

While he was speaking there came a vivid flash of lightning
which lit each of them up for the other.

(George Eliot, *Middlemarch*)

MY FATHER-IN-LAW died before I was part of the family, so all I
had were photos and second-hand stories by which to form him
in my mind. What I cobbled together was a kind of effigy stuffed with
impressions. A placeholder. At the beginning, it was the best I could do.

I did not realize that I had become a biographer, that informally and
privately I had embarked on capturing a version of his life.

The first story, the most pressing and important while my future
husband Helmut and I were getting acquainted, concerned his father's
death. It was recent. New. Heinrich was only sixty-seven. He had died
alone. He dismounted his horse to rest beneath a tree and was overtaken
by a fatal stroke. He had crossed the reins neatly over the animal's back.
Helmut's older brother, who was at the ranch, installing a fence, felt uneasy
and went to look for his father. He discovered the horse waiting riderless,
and the peaceful, lifeless body.

The death took place in Paraguay, in the semi-arid Chaco, where

33

Mennonite refugees from Russia had settled in the early 1930s. This is where Helmut, this boyfriend of mine, grew up. In 1970, adventurous and somewhat rebellious, he migrated to Canada, which is where we met. The news of his father's passing reached him by short wave radio and there was no possibility of attending the funeral.

A letter followed with additional details. It was dreadfully hot and humid; there had been no wind; it started to drizzle as the older brother searched. That morning, before Heinrich—Helmut's *Papa*—left the house, he stroked Mama's back and when she said, as she always did, "*Lass gut gehen* (May it go well)," he replied with "Thank you" instead of his usual "It will." Retrospectively, this seemed significant.

I was given these bits while we dated. One evening over coffee, Helmut talked about his father and suddenly he could not go on; tears welled up and began to run. They seemed to run a long time. I was touched by his loss, by the fact that he cried. I wished to share his sorrow. Perhaps I was not expressing it properly, though, for he was embarrassed. He feared I thought him weak, that I may not have liked his breaking-down. No, no, no, not at all, I told him, I really cared. But it was the good-looking man I had fallen in love with who was the object of my concern. *Papa* was a word, only relevant because of this other, younger man I wished to get to know. I had never met Papa; how could I miss him? Since he had never appeared to me, how could he be as one who had *dis*appeared?

Still, the older man *had* appeared in a way. I had unwittingly launched myself on an endeavour regarding him, Victorian in character as it may have been: sentimental, sad, focussed on the subject's death. Finishing him off, that is, before he had even been alive to me.

Is it possible to know someone you have never met? This is the question beneath the practice of biography, at least for those working with persons of the past. And the common answer? Yes, it is possible. This is assumed, implied, and announced in biography after biography written or published every year.

The answer will be qualified, of course, by statements regarding the many difficulties involved in reaching conclusive truths, by acknowledgements that the narrative at hand is the best approximation an honest investigation can produce. And yet the answer is heard as Yes, is believed, is devoured by readers as inevitable. Surely "approximation" means close enough to leave no gaps; otherwise, why bother?

Distinguished biographer Hermione Lee's conversation with Louisa Thomas on the art of biography at *The Paris Review* (2013) is just one example of the strong confidence that lovers of the genre express. Lee's tone is one of joy. Hers is such a lovely, intimate, and persuasive way of explaining how she wrote biographies of Edith Wharton, Virginia Woolf, and most recently Penelope Fitzgerald, it seems her methodology must be rich and reliable too, as well as her books. Her understanding of biography is not without its nuance, of course, but she definitely projects an impression of assurance about what can be known and conveyed of another's being. While you're working, she says, misgivings must be mastered; "you have to feel that she [the subject] is yours and you alone understand her."

Over the years, I made occasional notes in my journal about what I encountered of Helmut's father, just as I made notes about many other things that interested me. He was not a formal project, as already indicated; he was not intended to be written. He *was* the work of biography, however—I see this clearly as I look back—and in that respect, my earliest answer to the possibility of knowing someone I had never met was also Yes. I married Helmut, his late father became my late father-in-law, and in the elation of our newly sprouted vows, I let myself be pulled backward from Heinrich's death into his previous sixty-seven years. I eagerly scooped up more stories about the dear, departed Papa. About Helmut's entire family in Paraguay, in fact. It made me happy.

But again I found myself working at the biography out of order, for I researched and comprehended the stage upon which Papa's life had played—the historical chronology, landscape, culture, worldview of Mennonites in the Fernheim Colony settlement—before resolving him clearly as an actor. I read about the Chaco region and its people, and I lived there a while. I learned about the drama of the Mennonites who were the last to escape the descending Russian terror en masse, more than ten thousand of them thronging together in Moscow in 1929 and less than half finally permitted to leave, but then, once safely in Germany, directed not to Canada, the country they desired above all others, but to Paraguay or Brazil. I learned about their struggles while pioneering in the inhospitable Chaco, about the heat, the poverty, the typhoid that claimed a swath of victims the first year, the surprise of escaping one place of violence only to land on contested ground in another during the Chaco War between Paraguay and Bolivia. Not to mention insect plagues, lack of markets, daily temptations to despair. And the howling north wind, hot, thick with fine yellow sand. Recalcitrant oxen. A continual need for rain.

HERMIONE LEE warns in *The Paris Review* interview against starting a biography with a concept, with any kind of a straitjacket for the subject. Yet she also acknowledges that one is inclined toward certain people for certain reasons, not least of all for qualities within oneself as biographer. In her case, it was subjects "who are individualistic, who don't like joining movements... who have remarkable minds, and whose marriages or partnerships, when they work well, work as forms of companionship." She is a writer who likes to write about writers. She is a woman who writes about women, though not exclusively. More specifically, in her work on Virginia Woolf, Lee was drawn in because the very challenge of it mirrored the challenge Woolf had wrestled with, which is, how in the world do you tell the life story of a person?

Carolyn G. Heilbrun, the biographer of Gloria Steinem in *The Education of a Woman*, began from the desire to write the life of a woman who became "the epitome of female beauty and the quintessence of female revolution." In *Margaret Laurence*, a small book about that Canadian writer, Noelle Boughton says she was intrigued by what had been left out in other work on the author. She looked for, and found it, calling the result Laurence's "spiritual biography."

For me, pushing backward from death into the life of my father-in-law, one incident grabbed me in particular, and held me hard. It happened in 1931, March 18, when Heinrich was twenty-four. That day he was struck by lightning and knocked unconscious. His mother, standing beside him, was killed. They were inside their first crude wood and clay house in the village Schoenbrunn (which means *beautiful well*), and somehow the lightning had found its way in.

When Helmut told this story, he always mentioned that the lightning melted the chain of the clock into a solid rod. The clock was important. It was carried out of Russia when hardly anything else had come along; it was an icon of status and the so-called golden years for Mennonites before everything went bad after the Russian Revolution. (He could not remember, however, if it was a Kroeger clock or one of the slightly lesser names like Mandtler.) He would also say that his father was immediately buried in dirt to the neck to draw the electricity out of his body. These details fascinated me.

This story—so exotic and terrible—appealed to my sense of drama and tragedy, to my curiosity, to my tenderness. I could surely be indicted by Dominick LaCapra's warning in *Writing History, Writing Trauma* against the "appropriation of particular traumas by those who did not experience them"—typically, LaCapra goes on to say, "in a movement of identity formation." But I could defend myself against the charge, I think, by countering that surely this is what marriage involves, taking on a second family and culture. It's a complicated process, this taking on, this *movement of identity formation*, and without pause I believed that every accomplishment, and every sign of suffering too, was mine to claim. I freely stepped as near as necessary, to stare or embrace.

MUCH OF WHAT I gathered came to me orally, but the lightning story is found in a published source as well. (Textual sources are a biographer's paydirt.) The Mennonite colony's fledgling news sheet, the German-language *Mennoblatt*, carried a report in the March 1931 issue.

The article begins with the weather, as so much in the Chaco does, beginning with how there had been days of heat and humidity, how the clouds had racked up on the horizon. The writer informed his readers that clouds like that move from north to south, churn up "until there's such a tower of them, they seem not to have room" and "roll angrily" in the opposite direction, "one flash of lightning barely finished before the next appears." He noted that in storms of this type, "the nervous observer ducks cautiously and looks for cover."

But then to the real news of the piece, which happened in Schoenbrunn. Translated, the article reads:

> The elderly widow Johann Dueck, formerly of More,
> Crimea, stood with her son Heinrich in the house, not far from
> the window. The other son stood by another window while the
> three daughters were in bed. A sudden lightning flash lit up the
> house and there was a clap of thunder. The four siblings saw their
> mother and brother lying on the floor. Soon they concluded that
> the mother's life had vanished, though Heinrich showed signs of
> still being alive. He was paralyzed, but is already quite recovered.
> It was a terrible shock for the family, the village, and the whole
> colony. Evidence indicates that the shaft came through a bolt
> that held the rafters together, and split from there in various
> directions. It passed also through the large Mennonite clock and

the chain is partially melted. It was 10 o'clock in the evening and the hands stopped on account of the jolt. One of the sons, Peter, returned from the train station to find, to his great sorrow, only his dear dead mother, his paralyzed brother, and his disconsolate siblings.

Besides the human elements in the story, I was fascinated by the lightning. Until then I had not known anyone struck by lightning, never mind killed. Growing up in the foothills of Alberta, I witnessed many storms. I loved to watch them. I have a strong brief memory of perching in front of a second-storey window with my brothers, all of us rapt to the pierce and display of a summer disturbance in the sky. Lightning was beautiful, the way it exploded in sheets of light, the way it jagged down, zigzagged, divided. Every flash was huge and stunning. I probably exclaimed, over and over, "Wow, did you see that?"

We were told of the dangers, we were taught the rules—if in a storm, do not seek shelter under a tree but crouch low in a ditch or field, and so on. And we probably learned the science of it in school, that lightning is a giant electrical spark in the sky, that these sparks can manifest from cloud to ground, cloud to cloud, or cloud to air. The electrical discharges that strike the earth are called *strokes* and the bright light seen in the flash is called a *return stroke*. The major forms of lightning have expressive, pictorial names: forked, streak, ribbon, bead, or chain. Lightning travels at about the speed of light and releases about 100 million volts of electricity. Return strokes heat the air and produce waves of pressure called thunder. Sheet lightning, which seems to fill the sky, is actually lightning whose flashes are hidden behind clouds or too distant to be seen clearly.

I was never afraid of lightning. In my memory of watching with my brothers, the tumult was a show's length away and we had perfect ringside seats. I also knew that death by lightning is relatively rare. As luck would have it, Heinrich's mother was the only such fatality among the Mennonites in the Chaco. The same *Mennoblatt* that reported her death published at least seven articles in the years following about near-misses or other damage done by lightning. I looked up (and translated) these references at an archive where the periodical is stored.

The language of the articles is fervent, storms described step by dramatic step. In 1943, for example,

> Heavy humidity weighs over the region. In the evening, a thunderstorm masses in the west. The sky is soon covered as by a leaden veil. Flash lightning in its natural-divine and wonderful power sears the darkness, accompanied by the dull rumble of thunder . . . . Stroke after stroke cracks nearby and reveals for a moment the surroundings, which otherwise are covered in deepest darkness . . . .

I was moved by various descriptions and images: three horses killed, "their heads pulled together as if to a point," witnesses to lightning speaking of "sheaves of fire" spraying about a yard along with "the sound of crackling." I wondered what my late father-in-law thought about when he read them.

The Mennonite community in the Chaco was deeply religious, so everything, no matter how beautiful or calamitous, was eventually linked to divine will. God was the beginning and end of every event. Following the report on Heinrich and his unfortunate mother, a poem expounded on its pathos and referred to it as "this, which the Lord of the earth has done."

It is not the biographer's place to judge, professional practitioners will say, their job is to observe how and what the subject may have judged. But I find myself recoiling from the hideous cause-and-effect drawn so specifically in the statement of that poem. I admit that my judgment colours the story, the biography. I think of God's bent and creative finger reaching humanward in Michelangelo's "Creation of Adam" on the Sistine Chapel ceiling and suddenly it seems a crook of lightning earthward. I imagine the flash, hear the boom, see the young man with his deep eyes and curly dark hair falling and the mother stiffening in the millisecond wake of that capricious and powerful current. Two struck, one taken. If this was deliberately ordained for that woman and her son, it seems cruelly unbearable.

THE BRILLIANT essayist and journalist Janet Malcolm is much more skeptical than most of her peers about the possibilities of biography. In *The Silent Woman: Sylvia Plath and Ted Hughes*, Malcolm exposes how variable and deeply compromised the versions of poet Sylvia Plath have been, how brutal the hunt for details from and about those still living, like Hughes, even as Malcolm herself engages "in the chase that has made his life a torment."

Says Malcolm, "The transgressive nature of biography is rarely acknowledged, but it is the only explanation for biography's status as a popular genre." In her book *Reading Chekhov: A Critical Journey,* she writes that letters, journals, and impressions we have made on others "are the mere husk of our essential life. When we die, the kernel is buried with us. This is the horror and pity of death and the reason for the inescapable triviality of biography." In *The Journalist and the Murderer,* Malcolm is even blunter, saying that what journalists—biographers too—do to their subjects is "morally indefensible."

Malcolm has written profiles of dozens of people, and knows she is also on the hook when she complains about the meanings biographers foist on their subjects and how they hide their motives as they write. "The writer, like the murderer," she says, "needs a motive." These motives must be recognized.

I am troubled by the possibility of treachery within the practice of biography, no matter how modest my practice may be. Is it there, I wonder, within the quest to know my late father-in-law?

Following our marriage, Helmut and I had three children. We visited Paraguay several times, as well as living there for a stretch of more than two years. This is when I filled in, by my reading and experience, much of the set of Papa's life. I continued to listen for stories. My motivation was the children. I was daughter-in-law but our offspring participated by blood in the life of the old man who died alone at the ranch and the young man struck by lightning and everything he was in between.

I wished for them some knowledge of their origins. I wished to hone their honour of elders. Perhaps I wished to mediate as well, protect them from his faults, which along with the stories, I had also become aware of. What is it that traces down through bloodlines? Two rivers—mine and my husband's—meet in our children and flow there as one, and since they could hardly prevent what they inherited, I felt I had to help. It was their Pandora's box but I was the researcher, the storyteller, and I would help them open it, and if tales flew out that bothered them, I would try to capture these tales and explain.

Helmut usually spoke admiringly of his father. As youngest children often are, he seems to have been treated more leniently than his nine older siblings. He remembers creeping into his parents' room Sunday mornings, curling up with them, absorbing their favour. He returned home from Canada for a visit the year before Papa died and felt his father's gladness and a welcome as generous as the Prodigal's. The affection and humour of that visit comforted him later.

They had been riding together at the ranch one day, through the bush. Helmut had grown his hair long in Canada, longer than was acceptable in the conservative Mennonite colony, but nothing had been said until that day, when Papa wryly called, "Be careful that what happened to Absalom"—the biblical son of David who got hung up in a tree by his flowing locks—"doesn't happen to you!"

These stories were good for the children, but I felt I had exhausted the fond store of Helmut's memories. Papa required articulated form, more presence, if I were to pass him on. I asked Helmut's older sisters and brothers about their father. What was he like, this Heinrich?

I got a story or two, a few descriptors. Not, in truth, that much. They were not unwilling, but it seemed difficult—onerous even—for them to portray in words someone they had known for as long as they could remember. Well, they said, he was hardworking, gifted at anything mechanical, the head of the colony's industrial plant for years. He played with them when they were small. He was a strict boss, a strict father. He had a temper, some of them said uneasily. The stresses of a large family when finances were tight made him lash out. When forced to close a business he had poured his mind and time and money into, to extract oil from *palosanto* trees, because the colony authorities deemed it competitive to their own, he was embittered. He had forgiven, he said, but still referenced his grievance.

I had to be careful in the asking, and maybe these exchanges were more shadowed than I realized at the time. Some spoke more freely than others, or mainly of the negative, as if finding my questions convenient for processing their childhoods. Some explained with cautious speech that suggested they wished to play the same mediating role with me that I wished to play for my children.

I knew from photos that Heinrich was a handsome man. I knew that my mother-in-law had loved him absolutely. Depended on him. Then Helmut's sister told me she had seen Mama crying in the *Kammer*—the walk-in pantry—because of Papa. Every story seemed a counterpoint to something else. ("Biography has so much to do with blame," Hermione Lee says. "It is not a neutral zone.") And, in spite of my efforts, or perhaps because I was only adding layers of the same, my sense of Papa remained as indistinct as ever. His presence in the family seemed concrete, robust, but for me he shifted and wavered. I lost interest in pinning him down for my children. Let them cobble him together themselves.

JANET MALCOLM proposes revenge as the motive in some biography and perhaps she is right. I confess that I used the flaws I discovered in Papa against my husband. Brought them out to say that *his* biography of his father was hagiography. Used them to probe at weaknesses Helmut may have inherited or learned in his home. I stated that if I ever felt he was not being fair to me or the children, I certainly would not hide in the pantry and cry. I would speak up, defend them or myself. I challenged some of his stories. That bit about his father being buried in the ground after the lightning? It seemed preposterous. I felt I had gained some rights to knowing Papa too. And I wanted credit for my diligence in combing the sources.

Still, I do think I took it easy with secrets I uncovered. My probing of Papa's personality and character had yielded mixed results, but I was sympathetic to the man. I tried to braid together failings and virtues. I know what a complicated mixture I am too; I believe in—and rely on—grace. I remembered the extenuating circumstances. Ten children and the endless daily pressure of keeping body and soul together, and the bodies and souls of those for whom he was responsible. Heinrich was nothing if not responsible. But he had no parents to consult, to lean against for love or support. He and his siblings were orphaned by that lightning strike; their father had died the previous December of heart failure. Apparently he never ruminated in front of his own children on the impact of his parents' deaths, four months apart and he in his early twenties. I was sorry about this, for the deaths must have shaped him, shaped him irretrievably, even though the shape itself remained, for me, amorphous.

IT WAS ABSENCE, rather than presence, that firmed and hardened in the next phase of my bid to know my father-in-law. My store of stories about Papa had enlarged but it was the fact that he escaped just before I stepped into the family picture that frustrated me now. The space where he should have been was palpable, it attracted my constant eye by its emptiness. I would comment to his other children or Helmut that I was the only one in the family, even among the spouses married in, who had never met or known him. They heard this but did not seem to understand. Perhaps they thought I was feeling sorry for myself.

I was.

I was also ashamed that he actually mattered one way or the other. Father-in-law? Surely the role carries no psychic freight, has no cultural potential, not the way mothers-in-law serve as the brunt of jokes or sources of contention, veering too closely to the wicked stepmothers of the Grimm brothers. Are there wicked stepfathers? Does the pantheon of gods truck in fathers-in-law? Are there notables? Moses' father-in-law Jethro, perhaps, with his excellent recommendation that the younger man should delegate instead of carrying the burden of leading a nation alone, but the example seemed obscure. In fairy tales, fathers are fathers-in-law in the wings, true; they set contests for those who desire the hand of their child. Once the hand is won, it is happily ever after, and the new father-in-law fades from the scene.

Fathers-in-law might be wise, but they also seemed benign and harmless. They could fill some vital grandfatherly role, but as far as daughters-in-law are concerned, they were dispensable. Papa and I never coincided, I missed him by that much, and those were the facts. And since I had a lovely, accepting, non-interfering mother-in-law, what more did I want?

More. I wanted more. I reached mid-life and was assessing my past. Re-evaluating. I was going through some inner tumult, some festering phase. I critiqued my own parents in new ways, separated from them again, as it were, though yearning toward them too as if they ought to compensate me for whatever remained unaccomplished within me. I noticed, with a budding discontent, how few older men there were in my life. I had scarcely known my grandfathers on account of geographical and language barriers: they lived in distant provinces, they were German-speaking immigrants and I was thoroughly English. For a variety of reasons, I ended up rather short on uncles. My father was a good man, but quiet and mild and uninitiating. And I had never had a father-in-law!

"Do you think Papa would have liked me?" I asked Helmut more than once. He always said Yes. He had no doubt of it whatsoever. I doubted in spite of him, figured he was trying to protect me.

There was a day in my bedroom then, me alone on the bed, the mirrored closet doors tossing the smallish room with its pale rose wallpaper back to itself and the Chinese elms outside the window rendering the air shady and green, when I reached an impasse. I wept. I prayed. Who else but God could I tell about this strange ache? Although I did not know how persons might continue after death, I found myself begging that Papa be informed of me. Be given a greeting. I threw this as if to the wind, just in case, though I certainly would not be telling anyone else of the weird request sent heavenward. But I had made it, because the hole of his absence had widened, seemed more conspicuously yawning than ever, and I saw that it was filled with grief.

THAT STAGE passed. I entered a wider field of reconciliation to how life unfolds, in gifts and losses. People come and go, or never come; missing is common to human experience. I resolved some childhood slights and let go of others. Acceptance and calm lightheartedness were the wisdom I sought to accrue. Our children grew up and made their own lives away from us.

Helmut and I visited Paraguay again. Mama by now was also dead but the siblings and their spouses still lived in the Chaco. We stayed with a brother and his wife and enjoyed reconnecting with the larger family, and since it was July, which is winter in the southern hemisphere, the weather was temperate, and this was a bonus.

One pleasant evening as we relaxed with our hosts, Helmut's oldest sister showed up bearing a coil-bound 8 1/2 x 11-inch book of typed pages with a pale blue cover. "Papa's diaries," she said, handing me the book.

Diaries?

She was transcribing his notebooks into the computer, she said. These were the years 1929 to 1932, and would I like to have a look?

Would I like to have a look? Oh my.

Once again, I had landed in the wrong order in the enterprise of biography, finally arriving at the place where biographers usually begin. When interviewer Louisa Thomas asked Hermione Lee how one learns to notice that there is a gap to be filled, Lee answered that you don't, but first "you get to know the archive. You go through the whole archive."

Now here was this archive I had never seen, or even known to ask about. I recalled vague mention of some notebooks, but the extent of them had never registered, nor had I heard that they had been saved all these years in a wardrobe.

Casually Helmut said, "Oh yes, I remember as a boy, evenings. Papa sitting and writing." He and his brother seemed unaffected by the blue bound book, the evidence of their father's years of words. Perhaps they thought because they had seen him at the table making his notes—in a thin ruled book not unlike those they used at school—and had lived that day in his vicinity, they had experienced what he had written and did not need it rehearsed.

"An astonishment and treasure!" I exclaimed in my journal later. That *this* existed! That Papa's *sitting and writing* came to this much!

As soon as I could, I stole away from the conversation and began to read. My excitement would not abate. I read in a tremble of surprise and ecstasy. I heard his voice. For the first time, I kept thinking, I am hearing his voice!

The diary opened in the refugee camp in Hammerstein, Germany. "Because I tore many pages out of my diary in order to prevent problems while crossing the border from Russia to Germany," he began, "I will now think back and record again." (He wrote in German; the translations are mine.) He proceeded to recap how he ended up in Moscow with his family, how they were among the fortunate to leave. Then the diary continued, day by day, through the crossing by ship, the arrival in South America, the settling into their designated land in the strange and isolated Chaco, in the settlement they named Fernheim, meaning *far home*.

I jumped ahead to find the day in 1931 which had always beguiled me. March 18.

> As I came inside the house again, the wind had torn the
> canvas cover partly off the window and the rain was driving in.
> I moved the pan with bread to the side and . . . that's as much
> as I remember. The lightning had struck! I heard, ever more
> persistently, calling and crying: "Heinrich, Mama, Heinrich,
> Mama," and then praying and crying for help. Kornelius came
> very close and asked, "Hein, what's the matter?" But I was unable
> to speak, I had no air. My throat was full and I couldn't empty it.
> And my limbs were completely unresponsive. I could only move
> my right leg a little. After painful stammering, I finally managed
> to get out a few words, namely, "Help, pray for me. This is not
> our final home," for I didn't think I would survive. How heavily
> thoughts of my dear [fiancée] Suse pressed on my heart in my
> wretched situation. We prayed; I was able to pray as well. Mama,
> however, had blinked once and after that there was nothing, no
> movement, no sound.

[The neighbors] were called to help. Also Mr Balzer and Mr
Loewen came with alcohol. They did everything possible for me,
washing me and rubbing me with alcohol, until my limbs finally
began to move. But every effort made with Mama was useless:
she was dead!

The next day, Heinrich noted that many people visited, to look at what
had happened, at the house "chaotic, the beds lying about the room and
covered with earth that had shattered from the walls."

"The path of the lightning, it was all there to see, how it had been," he
said, "but to experience it is much worse." With his practical, engineering
mind, Heinrich set down in his notebook the lightning's course. It struck
the house gable on the street side, one ray scratching along the wall and
upward toward the window and into the cutlery, running along the rafter,
down the brace, breaking a wooden bench he had just set to the side and
rippling through the lamp hook, under which his mother was standing,
"which probably killed her." The lightning travelled also to the back gable
and down into the clock and through the longest chain as far as the plumb
weight, into the wall and then the earth.

He wrote about the funeral. The sermon used biblical texts focused
on divine power and judgment: "Listen, my people, and I will speak. I will
testify against you . . . I am God." I read this with dismay; I could not be
objective. Why, with a Christian theology as wide and manifold as the
Chaco itself, would they choose this emphasis for such a day? Why did this
terrible circumstance, close on the heels of the typhoid fever which had
ravaged Schoenbrunn village, need to be heard as an exhortation? Why not
"my God, my God, why have you forsaken me?"

At the graveside, Heinrich wrote, one of the ministers addressed him
by name. He was still not feeling well; he had also been struck and yet was
alive; he was the oldest of the unmarried children of the family. They were
orphans. "There is more laid upon me now," he confided to his diary. He
had been told by the minister that he must fulfill the duties of head of the
home, lead the household's religious rituals.

He stated this without chafing, it seems. He must have been in shock.
He simply lowered the weight of the minister's instructions onto the page.
He said he was glad and comforted by the presence of his Suse and that,
at the graveside, before the final look at the mother's face, before the coffin
was nailed shut, there were copious tears. Family Penner, he wrote, sang "a
wonderfully appropriate song."

Later, Helmut's sister sent us an electronic copy of the 1929 to 1932 diary transcriptions. Still later, I assisted in typing the remaining notebooks—up to 1934 and about eight years of the 1950s and 1960s. (The records he kept at the industrial plant stayed with the colony.) As I transcribed Papa's daily accounts from his quite elegant handwriting, I kept hearing his voice. He mostly recorded the details of work—sowing the crops, pumping water for the cattle, cleaning the well in the early years on the farm, and then, after he and Mama moved into the centre of Fernheim Colony to head up the industrial plant and later to undertake his own business, about progress and setbacks there. He wrote of stressful village meetings or situations that vexed the administrative oversight committee he was on. Occasionally there were comments about the family—care and concerns for his children, love for his *liebe* (dear) Suse, expressions of homesickness when he travelled to Asunción to make purchases for the industrial plant. I read and typed and felt glad with him when something in his *palosanto* extract operation went well, got angry when he was cheated in the same operation, had to remind myself that it was a long time ago and did not matter anymore.

When I first started to construct Papa's life, I believed it would be possible to reconstruct him whole. I thought, yes, you can surely know someone you have never met. As the decades passed, it seemed I was wrong. Now, having heard him speak on the page, I feel I have, in fact, come to know him. Partially of course and with a very different intimacy than I would have gained from seeing and hearing him in the flesh. But some kind of satisfaction has been achieved; he's not quite real but he's not an effigy either. Somehow he has entered my narrative as a rounded character, as a person with presence.

But there is one more thing. It is probably off the radar of the conventional art of biography. It probably contradicts my criticism about assigning events to Providence. What I mean is, the following may seem mystical. But I include it to remind myself that if the practice of biography, per Janet Malcolm, is murky in many ways, it is certainly also, per Hermione Lee, a surprise and a joy.

Helmut and I were eating breakfast. Cold cereal that day instead of the usual oatmeal, although this detail is unimportant. He mentioned that the robin was back, but only one, and though singing, it sounded unhappy. We had been thrilled when the robin pair chose to nest in our yard and when three aqua eggs appeared in the nest. We were dismayed in equal measure when we returned from a camping trip to find the nest and eggs abandoned.

Some minutes later, as if unhappy birdsong was segue enough, Helmut said, "My father used to document the sadness of pigeons. If they lost their mate or something."

Used to document the sadness of pigeons. It struck me as a fine memory, and beautifully put, and then it came to me, a thought like a jolt that zigzagged away from his meaning. If I have come to know my father-in-law, I thought, in some mysterious way he has also come to know me. For a moment, in a flash, I felt that Papa and I had met.

As peculiar as it was, this brief meeting seemed convincingly real. My late father-in-law's impulse, like mine, was to write. He documented; he spoke in notebooks as I do. Fellow scribblers, we two, recorders of escapes and daily tasks and joys and heartaches. Perhaps now and then while writing, he had considered, as diarists do, that someday someone might read his sentences. He must have hoped that whoever did so would hear the uniqueness and complexity of him, but hear his integrity, his love, as well. Now and then he must have sent some recognition flowing forward. Sent it to a future relative or stranger. In the curious way that longings and prayers transcend chronology, I felt he must have received my greeting and returned it.

On the memory set

IN 1984, WHEN I was thirty-four and living in Paraguay, I decided to write a play.

I'd never written a play. I'd studied Shakespeare's *Hamlet* and Peter Shaffer's *The Royal Hunt of the Sun*, I'd seen a few plays, yes, but in fact I knew virtually nothing about theatre. But there'd been a notice in a Mennonite magazine forwarded from Manitoba of a contest "seeking an original play to be performed by the Mennonite players group" and the prize was five hundred dollars.

I was working on a novel, though keeping this fact a secret from everyone but my husband and closest friends. I'd written articles and done journalism for a Mennonite church magazine in Canada but I wanted to be more of a writer, and a different kind of writer. Besides secretive, I suppose this desire made me venturesome. If trying a novel, why not also a play? And five hundred dollars was a shiny lure.

While I debated with myself about the contest, potential play-plots pushed into my head. Stories teemed like the heat in that place in Paraguay where we lived, a Mennonite colony in the intemperate Chaco, relatively closed and isolated, where gossip—salacious or tragic—was entertainment, though generally more by way of tantalizing hints than full flesh; presumably everyone knew everything already and a reference could suffice. The professedly upright Mennonite man sneaking off to a nearby Indigenous encampment, watermelon under his arm to exchange for sex, for example. The two girls who may have been accidentally exchanged at birth because their mothers delivered in the small local hospital at the same time and each girl resembled the other's family. The post office worker who hauled bags of mail into the bush where he opened letters and extracted the money sent to his poor compatriots from their richer relatives in Canada. And since the colony was barely fifty years old, many people still remembered Russia and how it had been over there and how they escaped. There were a great many stories of that.

The story that eventually seeded in me and began to grow for a play concerned a woman in a neighbouring colony formed by refugees of the Second World War. Years earlier, back in Russia, her husband left her for another woman. During the war, she reached the West ahead of the retreating German army and was eventually re-located to Paraguay. Decades later, her unfaithful husband, who'd managed to get out of Russia into Germany, discovered where she was and wrote to her that his partner had died and he was unwell and would she come and live with him again?

I reminded myself I was embarked on a novel and was totally inexperienced in writing for theatre but that woman's story was like a camel who, getting his nose in the tent, soon follows with his body. It was building in me, taking over, and then another issue of the magazine arrived with another round of the contest advertisement and its five hundred dollar prize. Our monthly income in Paraguay was the barest of bones. I took the story, fictionalized it, and, in the bits of time I could squeeze away for myself as a mother of young children, set to work.

The dilemma at the heart of the piece would be how the woman, whom I named Margarethe, should respond to the letter from the man who'd abandoned her.

The stage would be divided in two. One half would unfold her current life and quandary, Margarethe's granddaughter coaxing "yes, it's so romantic," her daughter declaring "no, absolutely not." Her son-in-law would seek to mediate these options. The other side of the stage, which I called the memory set, would reveal the backstory, enacted by a younger version of Margarethe: her wooing by the charming Herman, his betrayal, the war and flight, her re-settling first in Paraguay, then Winnipeg.

I added in children and the tragic disappearance of her sons during the madness of the trek out of Russia. Because one of the plays I'd seen live on stage was an ancient Greek one, I decided to feature a chorus in mine, intoning Margarethe's thoughts like wind in the background of everything.

I read the draft to my husband and he was encouraging as always, his eyes moisting-up at emotional points. I also recruited the critique of a fellow Canadian expat, a good and compassionate friend, who knew no more than I did about writing a play but hesitantly offered, over tea, a number of minor suggestions.

But I must back up, explain more fully the context of my writing this play.

I GREW UP in a Mennonite family in Canada. I married a man who grew up in a Mennonite family in Paraguay. Although a mixed marriage in terms of country of origin, we had much in common, namely roots in the Mennonite story going back to Russia, except that my grandparents immigrated to Canada when it was possible in the 1920s and his parents narrowly escaped the Soviet Union some years later when the only options available to them were Paraguay or Brazil.

They chose Paraguay, and in Paraguay, settled alongside other Mennonites in the Chaco. A truly godforsaken place it seemed, but those immigrants put grit to sandy soil and extreme weather and slowly made a go of it, my husband's family among them. He, the youngest, wanted more freedom, more opportunity, however, and moved at age nineteen to Canada.

Now he was married to me and we had two children, and we'd returned to his home country for a two-year contract as development workers with the Indigenous people of the area, offering training in the operation and maintenance of large machinery. This assignment doubled as a chance to reconnect with my husband's family.

We lived in what was then called a "mission station" about forty-five minutes out of the colony centre. My husband did his development work and I kept house, which was time-consuming and laborious in that environment. A third child was born. In between, I tried to write the novel, which I'd set in the Chaco, though secretly, as I said earlier, not quite trusting my ability and not wanting relatives and other colony residents to stop giving me information if they knew what I was using it for.

I had questions about everything. Questions were the easiest manner of discourse for a newcomer not fluent in the local languages. They also became a major method of my research.

At any rate, I interrupted the novel project to write the play. Several months later, just in time for the postmark deadline, I mailed off the fifty-five typed pages. It was gone and I returned to my other writing.

Shortly before our service term concluded, I received a letter from the contest committee. They told me they'd chosen another entry as the winner but I'd been "a very close runner-up." They enclosed the judges' evaluations. Astoundingly, these offered considerable praise, at least so it seemed to me. One urged that the play be produced, another called it the most exciting and daring of the entries, the third liked it too but urged it be re-worked. Their opinions were contradictory in some cases but detailed, so I would know what to fix.

The judges also noted that it was rather short. Which it was. Certainly it was too slight for the weight of the story I'd meant it to hold.

Soothed by these affirmations, I scarcely felt the sting of not winning. Plus, we were returning to Canada soon with the expectation of earning more than a local development worker's salary; the five hundred dollar prize was no longer urgent.

It's DECADES LATER and I'm trying to organize my papers; to reduce them. I come upon the file with a copy of the play, the committee's letter, the judges' notes. I wonder why I'm keeping it. And, I wonder, should I continue keeping it?

I never did anything further with the play. Margarethe and Herman and her lost sons and her daughter had later migrated into a short story, however, which was published in a literary journal and then included in a collection of my short fiction. I altered some names and deleted the situation of the letter in order to focus on the events of Margarethe's life. In the short story version, the unfaithful husband didn't contact her again so there was no reply for her to agonize about.

I flip through the file. Surely these characters have been given their development, their due. Surely I don't need to hang on to their genesis in this play.

But, speaking of reply, what had Margarethe decided by the play's end about her long-ago husband's strange invitation? I honestly can't remember.

I re-read the play.

Ah, now it comes back to me: the voices of yes and no compete to the last. No decision is stated. The tone is pious, though, and the final words of the chorus and a hymn, "O Power of Love, All Else Transcending," suggest that she'll return to him as requested. I've portrayed her as religious, her faith like a well she draws from to sustain herself through her many painful circumstances. And she's been looking back at her younger self on the memory set of the stage and sees that she didn't heed her mother's warnings about Herman. And she sees her failures and rigidity in their marriage. As religious women often do, she sees the fault lines in herself. She also sees that the war and flight and unspeakable loss of her sons, after nearly breaking her, roused more resourcefulness and strength in her than she'd ever guessed she had.

In the play, Margarethe's accounts of how she sang and trusted in divine providence irritate her daughter but beguile her granddaughter, and they must have beguiled me too, writing it. I must have assumed, even while leaving it open, acquiescence to the letter's request beyond the final curtain.

The reunion would be difficult, I imagined, there would be further indignities, but some tenderness too, perhaps just enough to keep her going. And I must have imagined that Herman, who was sick, would not be long for the world. By returning, Margarethe would have rounded her narrative into a virtuous and satisfying circle.

Re-reading the play, however, I'm less approving of its tilt into pious romanticism. Now I find myself on side with the disapproving daughter. Really? I hear myself saying, you really want to climb back into that old, done-with link in the chain of events?

And by the time Margarethe moved from play to short story, I'd already known better too, hadn't I? What she longed for there was not reprise as much as to be fully known.

> Some bird has flown against the window, believing the reflection
> of clouds and blue. There's a fragment of feather on the glass. I
> search the grass but the bird isn't there. It might be hurt, if only
> I could find it, let it rest in my hands. In the nest of my words.
> I'd say, I know, I know. Yes, I know. Somebody knows what has
> happened to you.

I set the play, and the task of going through old papers, aside and go for a walk. I walk into town, sit on a bench by the small pool in the plaza, listen to the water gurgle. I watch people pass. But my mind is still on the play and the problem of whether or not to keep it. The yellowed pages are quiet and unassuming in a file; they're no bother. On the other hand, I wish to spare my children decisions about my accumulated stuff when I'm dead.

The tug of war in me shifts—unexpectedly—from the question of whether or not to keep the long-ago sheaf of papers, shifts to the time and the place of writing them. Suddenly I wish to be there again and the wish takes over—it possesses me now, this wish to be back in our Chaco house with the husband of my youth and our three young children, the baby girl having learned to crawl and crawling everywhere, so irrepressibly curious she was, and the boys in the fervour and fire of their childhood, sand and sun and constant outdoors life a boon to them! And the feel of the just-washed diapers blowing damp into my face while I pinned them to the line and the fragrance of sun in them after they'd dried. The heat and wind and the daily necessities of food, laundry, and cleaning I accomplished, and our lovemaking, our trifling arguments and unwindings and happiness around a fire, the sensuous silence in a place far from cities, vast stars by night, vast sky by day. Daring to write a novel, daring to try a play.

I want all of this again, desperately, and this time I won't drift into a nap, inattentive while my little girl toddles about and howls, and evenings I'll read longer to the boys because stories matter and their minds are open and beautiful, and once again we'll cry when we finish *Charlotte's Web* and the story of Joseph but, in addition, I'll be much more patient, not a mother so quick to say No.

And once again I'll ask my questions and borrow from the answers but I'll ask more of them, and I'll write in my journal every day, cram it with specifics because I'll know, as I didn't know then, that one *does* forget what one expects never to forget. Living those years in Paraguay was unique, unlike anything I'd done before or would do after.

My wishing overwhelms me.

But something else rises in response, equally strong: the resistance that comes with getting older and knowing how easily but unwisely we may gild the past, me twice as old as thirty-four by now, realizing I can choose to store or shred the file with an unsuccessful play in it but whatever I decide, I'm done with it and with those years. With the experience of the play's creation.

And I don't actually want any of it again.

Not again the brutal heat day after day, that trickle of moisture from my baby's head mingling with mine on my arm as I nursed her. Not again the dust that settled in tiny dunes inside the house on account of a gale force wind just after I'd spring cleaned every room, not again the busyness, exhaustion, relentless needs of children. Not again the overbold dreams of playwriting or the identity I'd imagined for myself when we set out to Paraguay.

I'd believed I could become a *Chaqueña*—Chaco girl—but I couldn't, I was always a Canadian with faltering German and non-existent Spanish among Chaco-dwellers with their stalwart souls and hardiness, striving to prove myself capable of managing a household where nearly everything had to be done from scratch but unable to kill or eviscerate chickens or manage an acre of vegetables or keep up with the weeds or bear the patriarchal expectations put upon women.

I was never really one of them. Never entirely at home. I was immigrant, expat, ultimately stranger who came and went. I took that place into my heart, embraced it, poured it into my first novel. I was greedy for its stories, but if it's true that in every relationship one of the parties loves more than the other, then in this one, it was I who loved the more. But even that love was shot through with complaint and a standing apart. Love declares one thing and reality another, so I can't—and will never—live there again. And this is true for stories. Whether failure or success, past stories are made and done and all that remains are the words once written. As if, like author Ben Lerner says, "all the real living were on the page." And even the pages of that living may be tucked away or disposed of entirely.

Mother and child

THAT DAY, THE end of May and her twenty-sixth birthday, she came over and we had waffles with white sauce and strawberries, and the meal was delicious and the conversation warm and pleasant, but I've forgotten other details that writers seek for their narratives such as the weather and the table setting and bits of dialogue and gestures or if we lit a candle for lunch. She asked for what she called "story time," simply sitting and talking, I do remember that, and the fact that she fiddled at the computer, writing something, until we sat down to eat instead of hanging about the kitchen as she usually did when she visited us.

I don't recall the details of the next hour either, only the broad feel of it, the three of us seated in the living room, she in the chair in the corner, her father opposite, and me in the loveseat kitty-corner to them both, and it was the feel of Andrei Rublev's Trinity, the most famous of all Russian icons, which I purchased as a souvenir reproduction on a small block of wood while on a tour to Moscow and St. Petersburg. Also called The Hospitality of Abraham, the icon portrays three angels who showed up at the old patriarch's home to tell him that he and his wife would have a son. I love the fresco-like blue green brown tones of the piece, its muted but palpable unity, the understanding that seems to ripple within the circle of figures even though the scene is utterly still. Each head tips downward and toward the other in a powerful humility.

In my memory, our being together that afternoon had the same solemnity, the same leaning in. We two parents listened as our daughter told us her stories—fragments, really, of her childhood and youth—and how they formed an arc to an identity we'd not known about or expected.

Queer, she called it. Though she didn't particularly care what word we used. *Gay* was fine if we preferred.

We assured her of our love. We said, We loved you before, we love you now. *Maybe even more, certainly not less.*

But if I claim the icon's gravity and harmony for the occasion of our daughter's coming out, I certainly cannot claim its serenity. She was nervous. She spoke slowly and carefully, consulting her papers where she'd typed parts of this announcement, and beneath my held-calm exterior, my guts were roiling as I grasped what she'd said.

That evening, my husband and I had to attend a barbecue with friends at Birds Hill Park but it was impossible for me to make cheerful party talk. I was heavy with thought and the need to be alone. I wandered away to Pope's Hill, as it's called, where John Paul II conducted a celebration of faith decades earlier, in 1984. I saw that someone had left a bouquet of white roses at the hilltop's commemorative altar. The flowers were fresh. They seemed intended for me. I broke one rose off its stem and held it. It felt plump and cool in my palms, it was spectacular in its perfection. *Oh my dear dear beautiful girl.*

And its creamy whiteness—hadn't she always seemed in her essence like alabaster?

I cradled the rose, then pressed it into a crevice in the grey altar stone.

I'd released the matter with a rose and a prayer but then I took it back with me too, and that night I slept poorly, my stomach worrying over our daughter's news, hurting over what *gay* must have meant for her during its long secret existence in the Mennonite environment in which she'd been raised, not to mention our home's blithely heterosexual assumptions. It ached over what her truth—now finally spoken aloud—might mean for her, for us, for me.

I'D REALIZED immediately that her coming out, as well as our affirmation of her, would put us at odds with our church community. The branch of Mennonites to which we belonged wasn't even fully persuaded of women in ministry leadership, never mind same-sex attraction. Even worse, I was filling in for the editor-on-leave of the denominational magazine that year, I was part of the church's institutional bureaucracy.

Since she'd decided to come out gradually, first to us, then siblings, then friends, her identity could remain my secret too for the rest of the year and I mostly kept quiet when the so-called homosexuality issue was raised at work. But I was now keenly alert to what was being said. Discussion on the matter generally involved a defensive doubling down on the traditional church position in the face of culture's growing acceptance. There were reminders to be kinder to gay people, yes, but the dreadful word *abomination* still swirled like oily backwash in their wake.

One leader declared that if the denomination ever affirmed same-sex relations, he would leave. Another told me, almost breathlessly it seemed, about a young pastor-theologian who'd written a paper with a progressive re-interpretation of the Book of Romans verses that belonged to the Church's seven-text anti-gay arsenal, and it was going to be published in a theological journal, and what in the world could be done about this? I was struck by his agitation, his near-panic.

An irrevocable wedge opened between me and the formal apparatus of our church on account of our daughter's news. While I experienced a crisis of church, however, there was no crisis of faith. Not this time. I'd had several such crises already, as I moved through an evangelical Mennonite upbringing into adulthood, through a pilgrimage that both embraced and let go. I'd (mostly) relaxed into more ambiguity. Mystery. I'd discovered practices not learned as a child. Practices like Lectio Divina in which one considered Scripture—*the Word!*—not as rigid theological superstructure, but alive and whispering and intimate, fresh for today, individually specific. Practices like listening in prayer, rather than just kneeling and jabbering on and on, then getting up with high expectations and another daily duty done.

It may seem surprising—even ironic—that I now drew my profoundest consolation from the very Book usually wielded to condemn people like my daughter. But my maternal energy—fierce, protective, stubborn— had geared into overdrive. I studied the seven bludgeon texts, quickly accepted better interpretations, then left them alone. Arguments about them seemed as useless as the question of how many angels dance on the head of a pin. Theology might be a magnificent endeavour in the abstract but it was personal now, autobiographical, as author Frederick Buechner once remarked. I grabbed for the deeper, wider truths I'd learned from my earliest memories, heard them with other ears, seized them—for her, for us—with a certitude approaching vehemence.

The psalmist had written, *You knit me together in my mother's womb . . . I am fearfully and wonderfully made . . . How precious to me your thoughts,* and I heard no distinctions there, the words were surely inclusive.

And the womb being referenced was mine.

When our daughter said, I had to be willing to lose everyone and everything to be who I am, I thought, that sounds like the gospel's notion of conversion. When I read at Sacred Space, an online prayer site, *The narrow gate is the gate of love which leads to life,* I thought, yes, of course, this is the meaning of the narrow gate! And, *When we enter into the world of love, we find that it is a wide world, with its own energy, strength, and beauty.*

Don't interrogate her, my husband cautioned, but I did. I had so many questions. I needed to hear our daughter's stories again, as if by absorbing them I could enter the past, be present with her there, but wiser than I probably would have been if she'd voiced her intuitions as a child. I longed for her to be, say, four again, so I could gather her onto my lap. Longed for her to be in junior high, in high school. I wanted to hold her through university and her architectural technology studies. I could hardly bear the pain of knowing she'd been alone in the unique complexity of her coming-of-age. If I'd failed her by ignorance then, I would *not* fail her now.

Like many gay kids raised in a religious community, she'd agonized before God. She'd pleaded, she told me, for a way to reconcile her feelings and the negative attitudes of her environment.

And, she said, God never answered. So she'd reached a place of self-acceptance, and now that was answer enough.

But I was her mother and I would continue to plead on her behalf. My parental assignment, after all, flew at me from the pages of Isaiah when I was reading chapter 58, where it says that God's acceptable fast is justice—to break yokes, free the oppressed, clothe the naked, and *never turn away from your own flesh and blood.*

And one day I'd looked up from my computer in my home office at the painting of the Madonna and Christ-child hanging in front of me. I hadn't really noticed it for some time, as tends to happen with the pictures on one's walls. The Madonna stared at me, her expression formidable, earnest it seemed, and I stared back and her gaze continued steady and penetrating, as if to say, *Yes, be mother.*

ONE EVENING after tea at her house, my daughter and I sat and talked on the floor because she didn't have a sofa. I ended up crying a little and she comforted me. I asked if I could hold her, and she said I could, so I put my arms around her and rocked her retrospectively for all her twenty-six years, for everything she'd borne on her own.

The floor was hard, the position uncomfortable, the rocking could not be sustained.

You need some furniture, I said.

Both of us burst out laughing.

IN DECEMBER I booked a weekend retreat at Saint Benedict's Monastery near Winnipeg to mark the end of my editorial stint at the denominational headquarters. Besides my responsibilities at the magazine, besides the knowledge about our daughter that brooded inside me, there'd been other challenges those months: the deaths of two sisters-in-law to cancer; another relative's suicide; my elderly mother's surgery and subsequent immobility and her needs and demands; the relentless toll of my father's Alzheimer's disease. (He would die less than a month later.) I'd travelled to Paraguay to cover the Mennonite World Conference, I'd done final edits on my upcoming novel. I needed to re-group.

On the morning of the retreat, I made the mistake of checking the denominational online forum, where I encountered a rant about the "slippery slope" from women in ministry leadership to homosexuality in the church. The writer's language, bluster, confidence distressed me. Once again I felt myself defensive, and in turmoil with this community. I borrowed a line from the psalms, wrote *My bones burn like glowing embers* into my journal.

But evening arrived and our daughter dropped me off at the monastery and I slipped into the circle of retreatants, ready for whatever. A song played in the background. I couldn't catch the words except for a line about the loveliness of my soul and before I knew it my eyes had filled with tears and I thought, uh-oh, I think I'm going to be crying again this weekend.

I was assigned to Sister Catherine as spiritual director for the retreat. When she asked what I'd come about, I said the future, the switch from outside employment to writing at home.

I paused.

No, I admitted, it was actually about our daughter and what she'd told us. And the church, I continued, isn't really good with that.

We need to pray for the church, the Sister said. Her voice was soft but very sure and the sentence startled me with its recognition and sympathy. The church wedge was a pain but she was on my side of it. With her I would be safe.

She gave me a text from the prophet Zephaniah and told me to ponder it, pray it, record any movements—of spirit and Spirit—that I experienced.

I left her and read the passage. It disappointed me. I tried again but I couldn't rouse any mood to respond to it. I was too wrung out, too tired. I went to bed.

The next morning I found myself a cozy room facing south, the best light possible on a bleak wintery day, and I read Zephaniah's words again.

> Shout for joy, daughter of Zion,
> Israel, shout aloud!
> Rejoice, exult with all your heart,
> Daughter of Jerusalem!
> Yahweh has repealed your sentence . . .
> Driven your enemies away.
> Yahweh is in your midst . . .
> Have no fear . . .
> [Yahweh] will exult with joy over you . . .
> dance with shouts of joy for you
> as on a day of festival.

I could not shake my resistance, however, could not surrender to the joy. My head ached. I talked to God about being a mother, the *standing between* it involved. Then I was prompted to speak the Zephaniah words over my daughter as if she were in the room.

She was a gift, it was as simple as that.

I went for my second meeting with Sister Catherine and she blessed what I'd done in praying the motherly love of God upon my dear one. But she probed. What did *I* want?

Suddenly I knew. Mother was inescapable. Necessary. Praiseworthy. Mother was me and I could never—would never—abandon it. But I was at the end of my strength with mother. I was exhausted with mother. I wanted to be *child*.

What is it like, Sister Catherine asked me then, to be a child?

Not worried, I said. Happy.

So ask, she said. Ask to be a child. Joyful, trusting, without concern.

The gentle Sister sent me off with another text to ponder and pray: the Magnificat of Mary in the Gospel of Luke. She told me to notice how much the Lord desired me to have what I wanted.

I did what she said. I came to the text as a child and this is what I heard: *Mother God is mighty. Is merciful. Lifts up the humble. Sings over me. Quiets me. Delights in me.*

Relief. Release. My dormant joy gave way. I felt like John, who'd been wild and unfettered even as an unborn child, who'd leapt in her womb, his mother Elizabeth exclaimed, when Mary had greeted her.

How DISTANT they seem by now, these events of many years ago. Our daughter flourished, and her father and I did too, I think, in our roles as allies and advocates, and if I've written here of the churn of beginnings rather than the contentment of endings, it's because those early months were intense and spiritual. Too much carrying and wrestling, I notice, but spiritual nevertheless—*soulish*, I would call it—where strongest memory sits down and resides.

Looking back I see the delicate play of giving and receiving within— and between—my daughter and me, and I also see the triads, shadowy imitations of the Trinity in our story time unity. And if we never achieved the delicate serenity of the Rublev icon, there was certainly a bending toward the other, and a current of love. She and her father and me that afternoon. Then she was tucked along with me, as it were, into my St. Benedict's retreat, both of us a child and both of us wombed in our Mother, we three leaning, listening, leaping, laughing.

Burial grounds

I DON'T THINK of myself as morbid but I've always been grateful when reminders of mortality come my way. Second-century theologian Tertullian claimed that victorious generals in triumphal processions had someone stand behind them to hold up a crown but also whisper in their ear, "Remember you're only human, look to the time of your death." This may be apocryphal but I like the idea of it, that whisper like a mosquito around one's head. We don't get enough provocation to proportion nowadays, not in a culture obsessed with youth and skittish of negative truth. Signs of *memento mori* are generally so rare they ought to be received as gifts.

Which is why, I think, I got as attached to Elmwood Cemetery as I did. Elmwood Cemetery lies alongside Henderson Highway in Winnipeg at the point where it turns into the Disraeli Bridge over the Red River into the heart of the city from the northeast. We lived in Winnipeg some forty years and I passed it many times—by car or bus or foot. It's a beautiful old-fashioned graveyard with vertical stones rather than markers flush to the ground, which the newer places favour. Those cemeteries, outside the city, vast green lawns pocked by narrow vases of probably artificial flowers, irritated me on account of their resemblance to golf courses. They were mute on the topic of mortality. The stones of Elmwood Cemetery, however, stood up, insisted as I glanced at them in passing that I was destined to die.

In that case, was I living well with the time I had left? Being decent? Kind? In other words, those vertical stones were a help to me.

Now and then I walked inside. Elmwood Cemetery comprises thirty-eight acres; it's much deeper than it appears from the street. Its magnificent canopy of trees (ash, maples, elms which gave the place its name), curving roadways, and dense vista of gravestones rendered me pensive, introspective. I would not have to walk far before quietness closed off the babble of city, the pitch of traffic. This astonished me, this powerful hush, this peace, and how quickly it surrounded me.

One walk happened in winter. Now boughs were bare, a gnarled, spectral canopy, as if the dead had roused themselves to construct a trellis of bones to hide the sky. Then it began to snow, and it snowed and snowed, fat patient flakes that wrapped the branches as with skin, a tender net of indiscriminate flesh like infant arms and legs and tiny voices squealing that they were newborn and alive. It was beautiful, nothing to be afraid of, and all this too, this teeming soft silence, was a reminder that *only one life, 'twill soon be past*.

Elmwood Cemetery's inaugural burial was an infant, Grace Eveline Lemon, nine months old. March 8, 1902. The cemetery was built for 25,000 persons, was non-denominational, Manitoba's first of that kind. Its beginning was dogged by controversy, however, because the Council and residents of the municipality where the thirty-eight acres were purchased alongside the river felt the cemetery had been forced on them without consultation. Land owners in the vicinity feared it would diminish the value of their property.

No value, it seems, was placed on *memento mori* in their midst.

Several years later, the southern part of that municipality was annexed into the City of Winnipeg. What had previously been known as Louise Bridge District or Kildonan Village was now Elmwood. That is, it took its name from the cemetery. And perhaps Elmwood residents eventually felt satisfaction, perhaps even pride, as the place came to reflect the history of the city, *their* city, important personages and ordinary folk resting together: the remains of two former premiers, for example, and *Winnipeg Free Press* editor John Dafoe, journalist and feminist E. Cora Hind, a couple of professional hockey players, and among the ordinary, Lola Cowan, fourteen, made known because of her tragic death at the hands of serial killer Earle Nelson. Also among the ordinary were my uncle and scores of other Mennonites, whom I considered "my people."

In 2016, for family reasons, my husband and I left Manitoba for British Columbia. Our friends hosted a farewell party. They said nice things about us and then we had a chance to respond. "I always thought I would die and be buried in Winnipeg," I began. "In Elmwood Cemetery."

Had I ever uttered this before? Somewhere along the decades of our residence and my inevitable aging, this wish must have gathered and firmed, the cemetery must have shifted from a generic, generous prompt about death to death's personal specifics. My mind must have crept into the borderlands at the end of my existence to make some plans. But at the farewell party, our friends laughed and I laughed too.

Of course we laughed. I laughed when a friend said his dying mother resisted his suggestion of where she be buried because she didn't know anyone there. I'd laughed at my parents' excitement over the purchase of plots at Glen Eden Cemetery, north of Winnipeg. Close to relatives, they said, and—my mother rushing on with obvious pleasure—near two pines! "Mom!" I chuckled with a touch of disdain, "what difference will it make?" One pine, two pines, no pines, you'll be dead, I thought, and you really won't care.

In B.C., we settled into an apartment in lovely Tsawwassen, near children and grandchildren. With my husband retired, my work as writer slipping to part-time, I became acutely conscious of having reached the last third, possibly last quarter, of my life, a stage in which *memento mori* is no longer an occasional warning but rather known steadily and solidly as impending reality. I found myself startled in retrospect by what I'd blurted at the farewell. In the moment it seemed a clever opening line but the thing was, it was true. I *had* expected to be "laid to rest" in Winnipeg.

Now I remembered the comment and the companionable laughter and told myself it was silly to grieve over burial grounds. The grief of it persisted though, like an unanswered question, like a problem to be solved. When I read what Gloria in Colum McCann's novel *Let the Great World Spin* had said, that "everyone knows where they are from when they know where it is they wanted to be buried," I realized what was at stake. We'd re-located ourselves and I no longer knew where I was from.

But no, I knew where I was from! I was from Winnipeg. Even as a girl, born and raised in Alberta, I'd pined for it, that city where immigrant Mennonites clustered in large numbers. And at twenty-three, I'd finally arrived to it. I lived at the Mennonite college on Henderson Highway and my first job was at the Mennonite magazine and printing press, two blocks north, and between the press and college stood a fine-looking Mennonite church. I placed myself into the history of Winnipeg Mennonites and then into the bigger multi-ethnic history of the city, and our overlapping histories were tangible in those buildings, in a row on that road, and all of them facing Elmwood Cemetery.

Surely I could return when dead. I checked the cemetery website. Elmwood Cemetery holds more than twice as many persons by now as originally planned, many graves with two burials. But plots and columbaria spaces are still available. There would be room for me.

As the months passed, burial in Elmwood felt increasingly impractical. It felt lonely. We had no children, siblings, or parents left in Manitoba. We would not be moving back. It could, after all, be years and years before my death and ties to our former city would only weaken further with time. When I talked about this with our children, I sensed incomprehension. Or amusement.

"Write your wishes down," one said with a scratch of impatience as I raised the subject again.

But what wishes should I write?

The dilemma wasn't that there are no cemeteries in this part of British Columbia. There's one right here in Tsawwassen: the Boundary Bay Cemetery, small, rising on a bit of a slope, most markers of the flat stone variety. It's close to our son's house. I'd already made memories there with the grandkids, playing hide-and-seek among the cedars and firs next to the parking lot or following them on foot while they rode push or pedal bikes along the cemetery's narrow paved roadways. (All of us using our best graveyard manners, of course.) Once, armed with large sheets of paper and crayons, I showed them how to do gravestone rubbings.

But I never imagined it a place for me.

Maggie Nelson, writing in *Bluets*, said, "It calms me to think of blue as the color of death." I don't think of death as a colour but it does calm me to think of death as shade: the way colour itself deepens under the cover of trees or the advent of dusk, the way it disappears into a rich, comfortable dark. At Elmwood Cemetery, shade is abundant. It muffles the noise of living, which cemeteries ought to do. Boundary Bay Cemetery wears, in spite of scattered trees, an impression of treelessness; it sprawls open, sun-lit, insufficient of shadow.

I combed through swaths of Thomas Laqueur's huge book, *The Work of the Dead*, which probes the "exquisite consciousness" of our own mortality and "the cultural significance of human remains." Was I looking for alternatives, or better thinking perhaps? I copied one sentence after the other: "Bodies in a landscape matter," and we "endlessly invest the dead body with meaning because, through it, the human past somehow speaks to us."

If practices around burial ease the dead into memory, into speaking, was my obsession with my remains a stubborn quest to be remembered? To still have voice, to secure the meaning I've wrested for myself over my adult life? Or was it simply an overwrought case of micro-management, a failure to let myself go, let others choose how to invest in the meaning of me?

I wasn't the only one beset by forethought, of course. Burial wishes are ubiquitous. Biblical Jacob ordered his bones returned to his fathers. My parents purchased plots. Writer John Bentley Mays, originally from the American South, left ten pages of instructions in event of death, including "one important directive: To remain in Toronto," specifically, he said, among the trees of Prospect Cemetery where he liked to walk. Reading the biography of P.K. Page I noticed that she ordered half her ashes to her late husband's Ontario burial spot and half to the sea off Victoria. Even Bill Norrie, former mayor of Winnipeg, who founded the Friends of Elmwood Cemetery group when the cemetery fell into disrepair, in order to restore "glory" to the place where his parents and grandparents were interred, was not thinking only of them but also of himself; he intended to be buried in Elmwood Cemetery too.

I also read *Smoke Get in Your Eyes and Other Lessons from the Crematory* by Caitlin Doughty and concluded that I don't care whether I'm body or ashes when dead. Either is a remnant. As long as it or they are attached to my name. The commitment "we as a species have to the names of the dead," Laqueur notes, "is . . . an even more remarkable feat of imagination than that which we mobilize to care for their bodies."

But my problem about burial wasn't resolved by insisting on my name. Even a name, I thought, needs a somewhere.

One day I walked by the local cemetery to our children's house and spotted faded red flag ties pinned near and between the trees where the grandkids and I played hide-and-seek. A large sign announced "Boundary Bay Cemetery Capacity/Beautification Project." It further explained that the cemetery would be upgraded with additional plots, columbaria structures, a memorial wall, and a scattering garden, added in the area of the trees near the street. I'd never regarded this area as part of the cemetery itself, but I was wrong. It is. Already the grass between the trees had been cut, one curving path in place. I felt strangely elated, as if an inner knot had come undone. Though not yet at home with the history of this corner of British Columbia, though not yet yielding prairie and sky in my spirit's core to water and cedar, these trees—so wonderfully broad and tall they presented to my eye primarily as trunks, as a congregation of solemn convictions—produced quiet. And shade. Generous shade. I can live with this, I thought; my remains, my name, here. Yes, here will be alright.

Some months later, over supper with a group of new friends our age or older, the conversation turned to burial. The oldest, a widow, charmed us with stories of how she disposed of her late husband's ashes, one portion where he golfed, one along the bed of a dry Australian river, another dug with a spoon into his foster parents' plot, and one on hand for herself. This drew tales of other family burials. The exchanges were serious but lighthearted too and we laughed, and laughed some more, even if half-nervously at times because the talk was on death. I was grateful for these friends and recognized again that we enjoy life here in B.C. How we carry on in the afterlife is one matter, I thought, but along the human plane we continue inside the memories of the living who cherished us. I said nothing that evening about my struggle on the topic but driving home later it seemed a long while ago since I'd turned the loss of my previous home into anxiety over the ground of my burial.

Nevertheless, the next day I tucked some tentative wishes into the file containing our wills. Nothing as bossy as instructions; merely a suggestion or two for the inevitable prospect of my final ruin. *Ashes, sure, and here where I've landed, in Tsawwassen, will be fine. But you might separate a tablespoon or two into a little baggie and if one of you visits Winnipeg, walk through Elmwood Cemetery, won't you, and remember that I loved it, and the city and the past it reflects, and when you find a pretty spot that's veiled by shade, slip (surreptitiously) the last baggie-bit of me into that earth.*

Reunion

You know how it is when you travel, you want stories and photos for your social media crowd, and you post the usual, the most flattering. You don't have the nerve to say what lingers most, and why, and how whenever you go where you've not gone before something small and odd is sure to surprise and double you up, clap together past and today. You'll keep it to yourself because this happiness is sly, and childlike too, and they might chuckle and spoil it. This: sitting in a bed with very white linens in the Antalya hotel, two large windows open to the Mediterranean Sea, and you can hardly bear the joy of it. Tourists from everywhere are sunk into the scene of this resort but for you it's a sighting of stories that raised you, the biblical Great Sea journeying Paul and his companions (*from thence they sailed*) to points of their world, tipping them into roil (*being exceedingly tossed with a tempest*) and almost certain death (*but they escaped all safe to land*). It's that vast miraculous crayon blue between countries of pink and lilac and yellow and green on Sunday school maps, and you remember crowded basement rooms, a spinsterish teacher and all of you neatly in a circle, compelled to be there. That cheerful blue like a womb you crawled into Sunday by Sunday through the boredom and the drone, and here it is for real this touristy day beside the huge impenetrability of geography and history rushing into cliffs, a gleaming sapphire now, the Bey Mountains in the distance, low, hazy, and serene. Palm trees, oleander flowers, those tall grasses with their creamy plumes, and you're in the midst of the pleasure of crisp white sheets and you look and look at the Mediterranean Sea and your husband beside you falls into a nap, still and strong as a tree, and when he wakes you go down to the water, to the rocky shore at the base of the steep shore ledge and you stretch beneath a blue and white umbrella, you listen to the swell and it's like the rhythms of the King James Version, and soon, being hot, you decide it's time to get in. A skiff blows by, sunlight scissors trails in every direction. Your log of a partner is now a frog while you're cautious because it's deep and you're not a swimmer, but you can't come this far and miss immersion in the blue of long-ago stories. You lower in, get completely wet as if baptized again, and never has a bit of a paddle felt so necessary, extensive, forever. You clamber out and salt water dries on your skin, you taste it on your fingers. You cannot plan for this, you never know in advance—when away—where you'll discover reunion with yourself.

How I got old

I WAS FIFTY-EIGHT and my father eighty-seven when I made him laugh hard for the first time. He'd always been austere, a minister and teacher, not someone we children joked around with. Now he grinned at me and giggled. And giggled.

I'd been making a speech, basically "Use your walker!" because he kept trying to get around without it. He was in continual danger of falling and Mom urged me to get into his head our need for him to use the walker.

But when I asked him what I'd just said, he replied "I've forgotten already." This seemed hilarious to him.

My father had Alzheimer's and there was nothing to do except repeat and emphasize and laugh along. Mom looked on and smiled but I could tell she was embarrassed. She struggled to understand and accept what was happening to her husband. I would have to coax her along too, into their altered reality.

It felt strange to me, this bossy new role, me drilling him as if he were a child and he acting like one, me insisting to her it wasn't Dad but the disease that made him silly and forgetful. It set me above them both. Nevertheless, I was still their daughter. And, while my own aging was beginning to be obvious to me, relative to them I felt myself young.

My mother said, "You're so comical. Dad enjoyed that." Being praised by her in this maternal way made me feel younger as well.

Younger, yes, but besides their care I was busy with work and many other responsibilities and the rush and busyness and duties of my days felt heavy. *I want my life to be about writing but seems it's about my parents,* I wrote in my journal. *I struggle to accept the interruptions, demands on my time, the weight of Dad's loss and Mom's burden.*

Eventually we got my father into a personal care home. At the end of 2009, he died. This allowed me respite from the oversight I'd taken on in relation to his care but in the meanwhile, my mother grew increasingly reliant on my help, physically at first, on account of surgeries and subsequent immobility, then cognitively as she developed dementia. Since I was the only one of her eight children who lived nearby, much of the ongoing decision-making and assistance, in her suite and later a seniors' facility, devolved to me and my husband. It was a privilege to be close to her, and I loved her, but I can't deny I often chafed at the ongoing requests, from buying peanut butter or a bra or a bed, to coming over for visits, to sorting and disposing of things when she moved. I felt restless with it, like a teen longing to get out from under the thumb of the parental home.

This went on until 2015, she aging and me aging, but me far less aware of my aging than hers, for I still had many plans for the future—when things would be easier with an elderly parent, when I would finally have more time, when the pressure of life would soften! My husband planned to retire; I planned to complete writing projects I'd begun or dreamed of.

We also dreamed of moving closer to family. Our adult children had left our city and put down roots in Ontario and British Columbia.

Two of my sisters, residents of Saskatchewan, knew of our wish to be nearer family after retirement. They also knew I wouldn't leave Winnipeg as long as our mother was there and alive.

One day, one sister asked, "Why don't we transfer Mom to a nursing home near us in Saskatchewan?"

"Really?" I gasped. "Is that even possible?"

She replied that it was; she'd checked.

"It's our turn," the other sister said.

I heard these words and something long-held in me released. *Oh my, oh my my my,* I breathed. The lift was palpable and for days I felt the joyous gift of it, something coming true for me not because of Mom's death but because she and I could go on with life in other places.

We settled our mother into her new residence and my husband and

I decided to re-locate to British Columbia. We put our house up for sale. We began to downsize our possessions. This took months for we had two floors of house with three guest rooms and two offices, three bathrooms, bookshelves in three rooms with hundreds of books, as well as a detached workshop loaded with a lifetime of construction supplies and tools. Essentially, we Marie Kondo-ed our entire existence, selecting what we needed for a retirement household and what sparked enough delight to keep. It was a great deal of work and the memories attached to what we owned gripped us like a claw at times, but every item that left the property, from rakes to towels to extra tables and beds to our second vehicle, was another breath exhaled, another lightening.

At the end of our labours, the furniture and objects of our future life had been packed into an 8 x 8 x 10 container. We felt pleased with ourselves. Now we could drive away from a good past in one place and meet up with the container and our future in another, ready to unpack it into an apartment. I'd been freed of responsibility for both parents. We'd shed a house and a lot of stuff. We'd transferred property concerns to a landlord in exchange for a monthly cheque, and disentangled—by moving—from myriad connections and obligations and expectations. Our close friendships would be strong enough to continue via emails, phone, social media, and occasional visits; the rest of it—committee work, for example—would be a welcome break.

Then I was startled by something I'd intuited but knew now with unexpected certainty, with force: I was old.

Old is as old does. Old cleans up. Old lets go.

Old is lightness.

Some of this was circumstantial, in the move up the generational ladder, neither parent physically present any more. Some was a surprise, in my sisters' generous gesture. Some was chosen, in facing and paring material accumulation. Those first months in B.C. I would stand at the apartment balcony doors late evenings, staring over the parking lot below to the far street and wall of cedars beyond it, awed at where I'd arrived. When it rained, the streetlamps gleamed in the wet, and it all seemed magical to me, a vista of happiness.

I vowed to embrace my latest locations—both the geographical one and the life-stage one. I would claim the word *old* as modifier, *older* as preferred noun for what I am. I began a blog called *Chronicles of Aging* to observe and express who and where I was, kept it up for a year as if to root myself.

I found myself increasingly conscious of death, statistically the next big event of my life, and that prospect had a kind of lightness about it too, a quality of lift and ease. I certainly wasn't pining for death, nor was it discernibly imminent, plus I still had all those plans, but the awareness of it, sooner rather than later, was an invitation to clear emotional garbage, to downsize at the psychic level. Ironically, while aging depleted my body energy, the inevitability of my end supplied energy for a vision of how to use my remaining time and resources.

In *This Chair Rocks: A Manifesto Against Ageism*, Ashton Applewhite states that people are happiest at the beginnings and the ends of their lives. The hardest prejudice, she says, is "prejudice against myself—my own future, older self—as inferior to my younger self. That's the linchpin of age denial." When I met older people who seemed resistant to the very idea of aging and death, I wanted to tell them that in my experience, acceptance was blessedly lighter than denial.

Soon after my husband and I moved to B.C., we travelled to California where we volunteered for two weeks with Mennonite Disaster Service. We worked on a crew building a house for an uninsured couple who'd lost theirs in an area fire. We slept in bunks set up in a church hall, ate communally, showered in a trailer outside the building. One crisp morning I stepped out to walk to the showers. The air was cool, the stones under my feet rust red, and a thought popped into my head as if from outside, unattached to anything I'd been thinking. It was *you're almost done!*

Not done as in our volunteer assignment. Not some dissatisfaction with life. Just a glimpse of having done, imperfectly, and surely not yet finished, but done nevertheless, what I was born to do. I felt affirmed; glad. This too felt light, like the rise and wave of a kite in perfect wind.

Almost done. Old. Less now, but more than enough.

The moment was crystalline.

I could, of course, write a completely different narrative about aging than this one, and it would be true as well. I could write about it sneaking up on me, about the challenges I've experienced or can anticipate as an *older*. The wrinkles, the grey, the arthritic ache. Hearing loss, already underway. My fear of dependency, of dementia like my parents'. The small and not so small forgettings and less than stellar physical capacity. The subtle ageism, also in the writing world. Loneliness and envy. My husband's cancer and my sadness with—and for—him. We have our troubles and I see that other people who are old have troubles too. Yes, I could dump everything I've said so far on its head and say, persuasively, that life is as full and heavy as it was before I got old. Even heavier. I could say that aging is a load to carry.

But I can't convince myself. Not so far at least, on account of how aging settled into its identity in me. I got lighter, discovered myself old, and the process felt backwards but exhilarating.

At sixty-nine, I like the time-place I'm in. And in spite of his health challenges, my husband says he likes it too; he's amazingly reconciled to his life. For now, I have the companionship of a partner. He volunteers at a thrift store and Habitat for Humanity; I write. We share the housework. He's nourished by the sight of eagles; I find my zen in reading or jigsaw puzzles. We walk. We feel at home in a local church. Our children are good people, independent and caring. We live simply but have enough money to do so. We have these advantages.

And there's a final argument in this for me. If old is as old does, which means letting go, dropping what's too heavy, there remains what's always been portable. What's been joyous to carry. Words, for example, as they find their way into poetry or stories or even lists. Art and music and nature and beauty and love. These have no weight, but nevertheless fill and expand into every cavity where they're received. Laughter too is light and ineffable, and in spite of the grim diminishment my father's Alzheimer's forced on him and us, I think fondly now of how he laughed that day about my fake-stern scolding. He was old and he laughed, and I'd laughed along, as if reaching toward an odd but beguiling lightness he'd already achieved.

As he lay dying

THERE WERE nineteen beds in the hospice, that's what I heard, most of them occupied, but I paid no attention to them. When we first arrived, yes, I'd glanced into the room next to his and saw a tiny woman in the bed, tucked up like a newborn and the next morning the bed was freshly made and empty. There was a stained-glass butterfly lamp beside the book where we signed in every day because of the Covid, and they put the little memorial cards—like place cards—with the latest names in front of it. There was always one new card, it seemed, sometimes two. But it was true what a character in Brit Bennett's *The Vanishing Half* says about death: "Only the specifics of it hurt. Death, in a general sense, was background noise."

He was the one who mattered, he was the specifics that hurt.

His room, though, was an awful disappointment. I must have fantasized dark woods, thick fabrics, soft lighting, hushed voices for his end. He was delivered to the hospice by the hospital transfer service, and I followed, and our daughter came too, from another direction, and what we found was our husband and father lying in a bed in a room with bare beige walls, a mounted television, a window. And the only other furniture was a squat bedside table and a mini-fridge in the corner. His bed was low like a stretcher and he was lying flat. They hadn't raised or maneuvered it yet for his comfort and the room was colourless and bleak. I felt an enormous loneliness about it all. A nurse told us the couch that was usually in the room had been removed for cleaning. Since there was nothing for us to sit on, she went and got us some chairs.

I fed him some of the broth and jello brought in for his supper and he began to cry: what did his daughter think, her father so weak, and being fed? She soothed him. It didn't mean he was weak, she said, just his body. Afterwards, we talked about this and that, and he said there wasn't much he still wanted to do but he wished he could sit by a fire. Maybe fry up some burgers. I murmured sympathetically, for he'd always loved making and presiding over fires and he was good at it too, and we had wonderful memories of sitting around them with each other, with family, with friends. But our daughter said, "Sure, I can get you a fire," and moments later a beautiful one was burning on her laptop, complete with wood crackle and pop. We sat companionably around this YouTube miracle, enjoying the sight and sounds, and you could even say we were warmed by it.

STRICTLY SPEAKING, he'd been palliative since the time of his diagnosis some two-and-a-half years earlier, of prostate cancer metastasized to his bones. Meaning there was no ultimate cure. But quality of life, some quantity too, was possible, given current advances in cancer mitigation. His oncologist accomplished both the quality and the quantity with cheerful alacrity, using several courses of radiation to alleviate pain and various medications to suppress further cancerous growth. During those years we planned and prepared for what we knew would come. He built his own ashes box out of walnut and maple woods. But all that while, though dying, he was living—until dead, he was alive—and I learned that and experienced it thoroughly, though it seems almost too obvious to state.

The things people said to us about our situation were often doleful, as if they imagined us perpetually sad, but we slept and ate and talked and did our household chores and connected with our children and grandchildren—carefully or virtually during the pandemic—and we read and watched movies or the news. He tended his balcony plants and a garden plot at the apartment complex and kept the bird feeders stocked. He continued to volunteer at Habitat for Humanity and a local thrift shop. Eventually his mobility lessened and independent walking turned into walking with a cane, to walking with a walker, to needing a wheelchair. But the balance between living and dying was weighted on the side of living.

Until it shifted, that is, and to my mind tipped heavily to dying, the mid-October day his pain was so excruciating he couldn't rise from his bed and in the wake of that had to be hospitalized to get it under control. And then we were told that options for "treatment" had finally run out and from now on, back home, it would be strictly management of his pain.

"Well," he said to me, in the wry uncomplaining way he had, "they're not going to bark up a tree where there's no cat."

But even then. Even then, back home with his family doctor and palliative team in charge instead of the oncologist, and hydromorphone doses steadily increasing to confront his suffering, he lived. The seed catalogue in the mail excited him. He loved our Christmas drive to view the lights. He kept doing what he could.

I asked, more than once, "Are you scared?"

And he always said "No."

On one occasion I remarked it didn't seem fair; at sixty-nine, he was too young for this. His eyes filled with tears, as they did so easily those months, and we hugged. He said I smelled good.

"Well," I said, pressing in for another embrace, "smell me again."

But the diminishments of function continued. "His body's breaking down," our son told me bluntly, gently, when I phoned him in distress about his father's latest bodily humiliation. "Reverting."

"I know, I know," I said. The scale had tipped—drastically—toward death. Now I tried to remember our conversations. I tried to remember and record his sentences because all of them seemed last words.

THE MISSING couch never re-appeared and after a week someone pulled in two large wing chairs from the lounge area, which was nicer for us than plain hard chairs. We'd mounted photos on poster paper and tacked up words about his roles and qualities and our daughter painted a hummingbird—which was, besides the eagle, his favourite bird. We had made the room as homey as possible.

We were governed by rules at the hospice because of the pandemic: only two in the room and the same two all day and no overnight, unless the circumstances were exceptional—meaning, unless he was very close to the end. Of his sixteen days in residence, I attended for fourteen; the children took turns accompanying me. I yielded two days to children-in-law so they could spend a day with him as well.

On one of the days I wasn't there, he asked a nurse to connect us by phone. "Life is upside down," he began. He'd had a bad night. He felt the staff were upset with him, because he'd tried to get out of bed.

"Are you having pain?"

"Not at the moment, but it can come as fast as saying Johnny Appleseed."

Then he said, "I'll have to get out of here."

"You mean out of the hospice?"

"No," he said. "You know I won't be getting out of that."

Oh. I'd skimmed *Final Gifts* by Maggie Callanan: about listening to "nearing death awareness." About listening for what the dying may be trying to communicate. About the message behind the words.

Oh. I told him I wanted to be there but today it was the girls who were coming. I told him I put seeds into the birdfeeder. I told him a hummingbird had stopped by for a drink. I said a prayer and he said thanks and we said goodbye and ended the call, and I thought about his attempted escape and I wailed a little.

The next night he tried again, and this time he succeeded in getting out of bed except that he fell and staff discovered him on the floor. How in the world he got over the bars of that bed in his weakened condition, I will never know. Was this sudden strength an example of what palliative care experts call an end-of-life rally? He couldn't remember why or how, or even that he'd done it, he only remembered being lifted and put back into bed.

"The next time you want to get out of here," I said, holding his hand, "just go, and leave your body behind." I kept my tone light, made it a bit of a tease.

He'd been intermittently agitated those days too. Was this the terminal agitation or restlessness that hospice sites discussed? I had plenty of time, while he slept, to google everything I wanted to know about palliative care and hospice life. In his periods of agitation, he would adjust—over and over—the position of water glasses on his tray, spread and organize tissues on his lap, ask for one glass to be emptied and the other to be filled, fold and unfold the edge of his blanket. His eyes would close, then flare open. I grew agitated myself, watching and trying to satisfy his requests.

"Stop fiddling!" I ordered, and then was sorry I'd been annoyed.

I spoke with the doctor and she wondered if the meds they'd given to calm him were actually having the opposite effect. That can happen, she said; they would halve the dose, or try something else perhaps. The children and I also advised the staff that his pain wasn't properly controlled yet either; we saw him flinch, jerk, grimace. When a nurse told me they tried to balance pain control and lucidity, I figured they could go ahead and err on the side of comfort, he'd said everything he'd wanted to say. He'd told me as much over months by now, that he'd had a good life, that I'd been a good wife, that he loved me and everyone in our family. Told us there was nothing, as far as he was aware, that he needed to clear away. He'd said goodbye to his brothers, spoken to the children and grandchildren of his pride in and love for them. Reminded them to love each other. We had spoken our love to him as well, said he'd been a good husband and father, promised to remember him.

They moved him that day, into another room, into a bed with an alarm, in case he tried to get out again. This room, though essentially the same as the other, felt better. This room, I thought, would be okay for his death. It had a couch, long and blue, and outside the window, the branches of a small tree reached across the pane. It was winter and they were leafless but hung with droplets of rain water that glittered like tiny lights. He said he liked the branches too. We moved the photos and posters and the hummingbird painting over.

He spent his last six days in that room.

"Do you think about the apartment?" I asked. We'd sold our house, downsized, moved across country to be nearer our children, and lived in a light-filled corner apartment.

"No."

"Do you miss it?"

"How can I miss it if I don't think about it?"

I had to laugh. He was such a logical man.

IT WAS AN up and down, inhabiting that fraught space of waiting and uncertainty. A rollercoaster, we called it. We knew we were observers in the midst of his dying but no one could predict for us how long it might take. He'd bled rectally at the hospital and, early on, at the hospice, and then we were told it could be a matter of days. The bleeding stopped and the nurse said he seemed stable, and—since he was still talking—it could be a while. "The body," she said, as if to warn us, "has a lot of reserve."

I checked the internet for "average stay in hospice" and found numbers like seventy-six, twenty-four, and forty, and I was astonished. All seemed interminable. Our out-of-province children had flown in, Covid notwithstanding, and they couldn't stay that long. As for myself, I felt I'd nearly reached emotional capacity.

I returned home exhausted at the end of each day. I was on the tail end of months of being support and carer—done gladly, I'm truly relieved to say in retrospect—and because it had been intense and intimate, I didn't want it to be over yet. But I wanted to be done with it too. For his sake— he'd suffered much—and for mine.

He sent me off with a "go in peace" one evening, and I had supper and settled into a Netflix movie. When the credits rolled, I felt a jarring sensation, for during the entire time of the movie I'd forgotten my dying husband a forty-minute drive away, and it felt something like guilt, but sorrow piled on to it too because now I remembered him and how we used to enjoy going to movies—we preferred the big screen—and we would never do that again, and besides that, the smallest and worst thing of all, his toothbrush was still in the cup in the bathroom and though he would never need it, I couldn't bear to throw it out. And every time I brushed my teeth I saw it and I wanted to back up and beg for a re-do. Not of the suffering, not of the pain, not that, but even to have him well enough to look at his phone and tell me the weather for the day, to make the breakfast porridge, to shuffle behind his walker. I couldn't keep up with this event, I couldn't process it. And besides being at the hospice, the children and I were making cremation arrangements—the hospice office needed to have them decided—and composing his obituary, planning an online service, setting up a memorial site. And my role as chief information officer—so many messages coming in, so many people wondering how he and we were doing—was in overdrive. ("Note to self," I wrote in my journal, "don't ask questions of those in this situation. Questions want to be answered. Just say, 'thinking of you and no need to reply.'")

Most nights I slept well and woke re-energized and eager to get to the only place I wanted to be. At the hospice. In his room. Beside his bed. When I wasn't there, I prayed, and tried to trust he wasn't alone.

"Do you feel God's presence?" I asked.

"Has he ever left?" he said.

There was no fuzzy spiritual radiance in the room, that would be entirely the wrong impression to convey, for those days were far more difficult and mundane than that, but we'd been married forty-six-plus years and he'd been a father for forty-four and the children and I were drawn to him and his approaching death and it held us like a grip, and in spite of our sadness, I think, we sensed the mystery, the strange tenderness of it all, and some kind of glory too was leaking out of his transition away from us. I brought my sketchbook along one day and sketched him sleeping on a page where I'd earlier put down some watercolour as background. Later I realized that, unplanned, his face had landed in a patch of warm yellow, as if bathed by light.

NOT JUST UP and down, but the days blurred together. I couldn't recall anything in order or proportion. Later, using my journal, I set summaries of each day into a calendar grid in order to grasp and recall how it had been as he lay dying. There was a narrative. It had to be linear. But when I talked of it—and oh, how I wanted to talk of it, as bereaved people do, repeatedly (and so they should, palliative physician Kathryn Mannix says, for it moves the experience from "parallel reality" into memory)—it never kept a tidy, chronological line. It behaved more like the murmuration of starlings I often enjoy at the nearby bay, swarms of birds adhering and rising and turning and swooping; it was a cluster of anecdotes and recollections that changed shape according to a rhythm the particular telling required. What I said was true, so what difference did it make what day it was he'd greeted me happily with "You're here. I nearly sent out the search party," or days later, with only a grunt? What difference when or how many the episodes of agitation or his flare of frustration ("I'm not a cow, I'm a person!") at nurses thrusting thermometers into his sore mouth because of the pandemic?

In the early days it seemed he felt obliged to visit with us, and I remember how ecstatic he was to see a granddaughter, newly arrived from Toronto, who was briefly allowed in by pleadings and special permission, but, I see, checking the calendar, that was nearer the middle. And the day he croaked my name and said "I love you" and, maybe minutes or hours later, started croaking the children's names before giving up to say, "I love you all," that was soon after being moved to the new room, wasn't it? No, it was the day before he died. And the time after not drinking for days he suddenly pulled a glass toward himself and gulped thirstily, as if in fact, he wasn't ready yet to quit. This was the last day, though I thought it had been earlier than that.

LATER, I READ Kathryn Mannix's wonderful book *With the End in Mind: Dying, Death, and Wisdom in an Age of Denial.* I'd heard her first on the CBC program, "White Coat, Black Art" with Dr. Brian Goldman, explaining the process of dying, how people get more tired, need to sleep more, how their sleeps get longer and longer, how they may slip into unconsciousness, how their breathing changes, becomes "an automatic reflex cycle." How slow breathing may alternate with regular and steady breathing. How the noisy breathing of the last days doesn't hurt. How it eventually slows and stops. How death is "usually okay"—that is, painless and peaceful.

I could put everything we experienced into the patterns Mannix describes in her book. At least three, maybe four, times we found ourselves holding his hands and speaking or singing or not speaking, but sure it was the end, his breathing slow, lengthy pauses between. And then, as if picking up steam, carrying on again. In the last four or five days he didn't eat or drink, except for that gulp of water. Mostly he slept, breathing in, breathing out. Breathing out, and in.

Later our daughter showed me a short video she'd taken of him in hospice. The ticking of the clock in the room was loud and obvious on the video. "Ticking away the time," she remarked. But when I'd been in the room, I never heard the clock. The only sound I really heard was his breath. How it grew louder and raspier, how it played with the phlegm building in his throat, how it slowed and seemed to stop. How it continued.

That's how it had been the last Saturday morning too, us thinking "the end," but no, not yet. The day passed. We got supper and ate it beside him in the room.

Should we stay? The nurse on duty couldn't advise us either way. "He's still breathing from his diaphragm," she ventured. So, we might surmise he would last the night. On the two days previous, our sons—not sure their turn in the rotation would come up again—had said their private goodbyes. Now our daughter did the same. We left.

I went to bed early. I had just sunk deeply into sleep when the phone jangled me awake. It was someone from the hospice on the line. My husband had died.

Peacefully, said the nurse who witnessed it.

Peacefully, of course. The last breath is an exhale.

This phenomenon—dying when family have left—is also a pattern, Mannix writes. It occurs "with such regularity that we often warn families, especially when the dying process stretches over several days, that it may happen." Is it the presence of people they love that keeps dying persons hanging on? Are they choosing? "We don't know the answers," she says, "but we recognize the pattern."

One of our sons and I drove through the dark—a great kindness, it seemed, that dark—back to the hospice. Back to the familiar room, now utterly quiet. Entering it, I was pierced by the quiet, by the surely impossible absence of the sound of him breathing.

We connected virtually with the other children and together participated in a small ceremony of washing and dressing the body. I'd forgotten a comb so his soft silver hair got fluffed. We had a psalm and a prayer. When we were done, I stayed a while alone in that impossible stillness and heard myself keening, as if I'd tuned into some ancient and continuous high-strung note, desolate as smoke. But then I had to leave his body behind, just as he'd left it behind.

At the far end of the hallway, by the sign-in book and the glowing butterfly lamp, stood a new "in memory of" card. The name on it was his.

In the house of my pilgrimage

I. Back

WE RETURNED into the howl of wind. It was August, late winter in the Paraguayan Chaco, perhaps the worst time of the year, *Nordsturm* blasting out of the distant Andes with a vengeance of heat and dust, the air grey, the landscape coughing up sand as if to choke on its own desolation. The bottle tree at the corner of our street had shed its leaves and leftover seed pods swung from its convoluted branches. A bird's nest trembled in the tangle and the tangle seemed malicious.

We were back.

We'd been there earlier that year. Been there for a visit. Just a visit was the plan, our two young sons in tow, and four months of renting a house and connecting with my husband's mother and family. And then, in the course of the visit, came an unexpected invitation to extend our stay—or come again, since we had return tickets to Canada—in order for my husband Helmut to fill a term as manager of the machine station in Yalve Sanga. This project, sponsored by Mennonite Economic Development Associates (MEDA) of Germany, was one of an extensive array of programs for local Indigenous groups under the auspices of what we simply called the Mission.[1] It trained and employed Indigenous men on large equipment like bulldozers, graders, and tractors, clearing land and doing road work for their settlements as well as taking on contracts within the Mennonite colonies.

The idea first surprised us, then intrigued us, and eventually we said yes, he would let his name stand for the position. Nothing had been decided on the Mission's side by the visit's end so we departed for Canada and carried on living there and more months passed and we figured nothing had come of it after all, which was fine with us by that time, until the Mission called and told Helmut he was the candidate they'd chosen. Would we come? Since we'd said yes before, we said it again. We said we would arrive in Paraguay as soon as we could free ourselves from our house and work.

Once again, then, the long flights from Saskatoon to Asunción, once again the day-long trip by bus from the capital's red soil and voluptuous green, through the swampiness of the Paraguay River terrain, along the straight-line Ruta ever north and westwards into the tight dry thorn bush and occasional campos of the middle Gran Chaco. Once again rumbling along the hard earth roadway into the Mennonite colony called Fernheim, meaning far home in German, once again reaching Filadelfia, the colony's main town. Down Hindenburg Street, past the co-op complex and museum and park, past the elementary school grounds and around the jubilee anniversary monument, turning left down Trebol Avenue. Just a short way now to the lone waving palm at driveway's end. Turning in, unlocking the door, unloading our cases.

I was exhausted from travelling and from looking hard at everything.

The looking of return is different from the looking involved in one's everyday familiar environment. It's different too from the looking done when viewing a place the first time. I'd seen all this before, known it, been

---

[1] Mission: These relationships between Mennonites and Indigenous people in or near the Mennonite colonies in the Chaco were formalized organizationally under Asociación de Servicios de Cooperación Indigena Mennonita (ASCIM), Indianer-Beratungs-Behörde (IBB), and Licht den Indianern. Other agencies that helped with funding and staff included Mennonite Central Committee (MCC) and Mennonite Economic Development Associates (MEDA), the latter having both North American and German branches. For ease of reading, I refer to the whole pie of which we were a slice as "the Mission" rather than by names or acronyms. There was, in any case, a great deal of connection and overlap between the programs, with all of them represented at Yalve Sanga where we would live. MEDA Germany sponsored the machine station and hired us, and locally my husband was responsible to the agricultural arm of ASCIM.

possessed by its strangeness and peculiar appeal, but we'd left and I'd begun to forget what I'd known. Now I gaped and what I'd known came back to me, even as I came back to it. There was effort—negotiation—in the process. *Oh yes, this is where I am, and this—this—this is what it's like.* This looking demanded recognition, as in *re-cognition,* and in every moment of the exchange there was a split second of doubt, which might open to disappointment or to reassurance. But there was no reneging possible, I had to commit to what I saw, and all the while the wind blew and blew some more.

NEWS ITEM IN the local periodical, the *Mennoblatt,* September 16, 1982 (trans. from German):

> The MEDA machines have been managed since 1979 by Mr. Martin Braun. Mr. Braun is returning to Switzerland. MEDA, together with the IBB [Indianer Beratungs Behörde], has appointed Mr. Helmut Dueck to take his place. A house for the machine station manager and his family will be built in Yalve Sanga.

IN THIS EXERCISE of memoir, I am once again there, unpacking those first days back in the Chaco, August 1982, but also watching the young woman I was then as she stepped into the Filadelfia house, which we'd lived in during our visit, which we'd left five months earlier, cool now on account of it having been closed up while we were gone. I see the months of our absence disappear as if they'd never existed, all these rooms the same as before. I see the pathetic eagerness that extruded from their arrangement, wanting me, I imagine, to clap my hands. A curious meekness about that house, as if it realized how inconvenient it was and how impatient I'd become with it by the end of our visit. But smugness too, as if it had always known I wasn't finished with it yet. The house we'd been promised in Yalve Sanga, location of the machine station, was no further advanced than a good idea in some committee's mind. Until it actually existed, we would live in the Filadelfia rental.

We gathered the basics of furniture. We'd left some things behind but they didn't amount to much. The wooden waterbed frame, deflated bladder spread across its bottom, seemed cavernous and unappealing. Waterbeds were all the rage back home in Canada and we'd been proud crusaders of the concept when we came to visit, bringing along a bladder and its paraphernalia, and Helmut built the frame and we slept on the bed those months, intending to sell it later. I wasn't that crazy about sleeping on water, I discovered, but that was irrelevant now; we'd kept it *just in case* and this would be our bed again. Another two watery years at least.

We purchased starter groceries and supplies and then my dear husband, the incoming machine station manager, was off for his on-the-job training, roaring about the Chaco at Autobahn-like speeds with the wiry, hot-headed though knowledgeable Swiss man he was replacing. I settled our things and the boys, three and nearly six, played. Neither wind nor grit bothered them. They circled through the house as if they needed to revive their grasp of every room and dashed in and out, the weather surging in every time they opened the door. The house grew hotter.

When they tired of running about, they sat at the table and coloured or looked at books.

This is a fact, and was important: the boys were happy. They'd flourished during the visit and I was sure they would flourish in this longer stay as well.

I kept the shutters closed against the wind. The *Nordsturm* could sound like water rushing by, but that was just a bitter joke. Hot and dry, this torrent, scooping up fine sand as it went, rattling every loose object in its way. I could never understand how, with me inside and the wind outside, it could so completely sap my strength, make my legs ache. In the sleepy disorientation of siesta, I could have mistaken it for a snowstorm on the Canadian prairies and think myself tucked in cozily, safely, but waking

I would be moist with perspiration and the tiny dunes in every corner of the verandah, on every window ledge, weren't snow but dirt.

The wind, when it moaned, seemed to mutter a single unfriendly and repetitive thing: *This place was never meant to be inhabited, you know.*

But, inhabited it *was*. The Enlhet and other *indígena* peoples had survived here for generations. (Our work in the 1980s was mainly with the Enlhet and Nivaclé; at the time they were called the Lengua and Chulupi respectively.) Paraguay and Bolivia both desired it enough to expend some 100,000 lives fighting over it in the Chaco War, 1932-35. Mennonites hunkered down on the land around the same time and were making a success of their settlements, no doubt about that. Among them was our extended family on Helmut's side.

Various members of his large clan stopped in to say hello. Some brought gifts—produce or eggs, cottage cheese, a chicken or chunk of beef, roses from gardens. They were good folks, this family; they'd accepted me. And even if, as Penelope Lively's protagonist Anne in *The Road to Lichfield* muses—accurately enough I think—that "[h]armony between relations . . . has to be built up of evasions," on any number of topics where there might be disagreement, what this family gave me as I moved from visitor status into the desire to belong of resident status was a close, immediate, vital layer of association and inclusion.

Between the interruptions, I organized and cleaned, dealt with bugs and dust, arranged dishes, pots, and utensils. The house was an old dwelling the owners had enlarged and were trying to modernize. The indoor bathroom was complete with plumbing for toilet, shower, and sink but all the kitchen offered so far was a single cold water tap without a drain, a hot plate for cooking, a small fridge, and several shelves fronted with a fabric curtain. Into this pioneering version of a kitchen cupboard, I placed the cutlery and four-piece set of Corelle dinnerware—Old Town Blue—I'd brought along, as well as a few cookery items I considered indispensable and had tucked into our cases, such as wooden stir spoons and the excellent quality kitchen knife that was a wedding gift.

I needed to set down words as well. Words on paper had always been a help to me. Words I read, words I wrote. They steadied me with the stillness and stability of pinned-down thought. Those I wrote seemed to ensure that what happened had actually happened. They gave to particular moments what those moments may have missed as they hurried past: weight. A proof I existed within them and was, therefore, weighty too. Not that I had time to write myself thoroughly into or out of the motley sensations of the return, the entire startled once-againness of it all. I couldn't afford the luxury of going on and on in search of heft or equanimity, there was far too much to do, what with setting up and meals to prepare and drop-by visitors to greet and the children to tend. Just time for a few paragraphs about the wind and the dust. Then two lines by themselves, one after the other, as if to accomplish a poem.

> The comforting smell of insect spray,
> The triumph of dead cockroaches in the fridge.

And two bleak questions: What are we doing? Are we crazy?

2. Desire

As it always eventually did in the unending duel of the north wind and the cooler *Pampero* cycling from the south, the weather turned. It turned abruptly. Brutally. On Wednesday we'd arrived into high heat and wind and Sunday it felt as if Antarctica itself had floated closer to the South American shore. Temperatures plunged to near freezing. Colony buildings were constructed with brick, stone tile floors, wide verandahs to ward off the intense sun of the semi-arid climate, but in contrarian patches like this, they might as well be tombs.

We dressed in our thickest and layered Sunday-best and trudged across the street to church. Surely we could have excused ourselves this first Sunday but it was the monthly *Gemeindestunde*, congregational hour, when the three denominational strands of Mennonites in Fernheim met separately instead of together as on the other three Sundays. Most of our Paraguay family was affiliated with the strand whose building was nearest. Our presence—or absence—would be noticed. Or so I imagined, being of the conscientious sort. We dressed and went.

But the cold! My mouth numbed in the singing. The prayers and preaching seemed alien, merely gusts of frigid air. And why on earth were the sanctuary windows open?

Gemeindestunde included hot tea and sandwiches at noon because there would be an afternoon service as well, and the meal filled and warmed me, but I was sure ice had reached my bones. I told Helmut that he and our older son could stay if they wanted, but I was taking myself and our younger son to the house. The boy surrendered to my arms and I carried him off, thankful for the excuse of a child. We stripped off our jackets and, still wearing our clothes, burrowed into the waterbed under a pile of blankets. He was soon asleep, his soft breath beside me as sweet as an apple. I felt my body grow placid and sprawling too, as if cell by cell. Only degrees in a thermometer, this change, but a transformation out of all proportion: from miserable to contented.

THIS INTERLUDE, ME tranquil in a perfection of warmth and the tousle-headed boy in the bliss of his nap, is as good as any to answer, briefly at least, the question of what we were doing in the Paraguayan Chaco. The backstory of back, as it were.

It begins with our marriage. A mixed marriage of sorts, because I grew up in Canada and Helmut grew up in Paraguay. We shared the same deep roots, however, roots in Russia, Prussia before that, and even further back, the Low Countries of the sixteenth century. We were both Mennonites—Anabaptist nonconformists of the European religious reformations who, over time, because they lived together as separate communities for long periods, also took on the patina of ethnicity. Which meant we had a lot in common. His parents and mine emigrated from Russia/the Soviet Union.

The Mennonite map lines leading out of the Soviet Union in the 1920s diverged dramatically, however. My parents emigrated in the middle of the decade and crossed the Atlantic in a more or less straight line, latitude-wise, to Canada. Helmut's parents, part of the refugee group that experienced a final and rather sensational release from Moscow at the end of that decade, unable to move to Canada as they hoped, found that fate—or Providence—had angled them sharply southward to the southern hemisphere instead.

At nineteen, adventurous, and seeking better economic opportunity, Helmut made his way to Winnipeg. Which is where we met, some four years later, the lines on a map of our joint story now forming a triangle—Russia, Canada, Paraguay—and both of us Canadian, though one by birth and the other by citizenship.

We soon discovered that when people marry, origins have consequence, and that metaphorically, at least, couples drag their birth families along. Our larger families mattered to us, but how could we make them matter practically with mine being in Canada and his being in Paraguay? How keep the pole of the marital union somewhat balanced?

In 1976, about a year-and-a-half into our marriage, we visited Paraguay for three weeks, and Helmut introduced me to his family. We went in May, a pleasant month in the southern autumn. We stayed with Helmut's mother—Mama—and had a good time. I kept a tourist-like diary: the day's itinerary, who we visited, what we ate, notes on what was unusual for me—palms and cacti, frog music through the open window, the Southern Cross, *campo* or stretches of open grassland, dense brambly treed sections referred to as Bush (though Mama, who'd never forgotten the tall forests of Germany as a refugee, called it Cripplebush). I churned butter and attended a pig slaughtering. I met, it seemed, most of Helmut's ninety-six cousins, or however horrendously many there were. Sometimes I was jealous of the long late hours he and his mother talked in their customary Low German and there were small shocks about Chaco life I kept to myself, but overall I was favourably disposed to the place. Paraguay felt exotic. I could now visualize the who and what of Helmut's earlier years, and this was a gift.

Nearly six years and two children later, living in Saskatoon, Saskatchewan, we decided it was time for another visit to the Paraguayan side of our marriage. Our boys ought to meet their father's mother and relatives, and they in turn ought to meet the boys. A visit of some months, we decided, and living, if we could, on our own rather than as houseguests. Our *Geschwister*, siblings, found us the half-renovated house on Trebol, which would be quite good enough and had the advantage of being just down the street from Mama's. We hadn't saved enough money to be without interim income, but the *Geschwister* assured us Helmut would find short-term work. When we arrived into a prolonged period of drought, someone joked that he should get a truck and haul dead cattle away. He did some carpentry work instead.

Four months in duration, the visit was good for us as a couple and family. It was like playing house in another country. Perhaps it scratched the proverbial seven-year marriage itch and Helmut figured that showing up with two children had finally proved to his older siblings that he, the youngest, was grown-up too. Canadian city-girl me, who thought she detected misgivings about her ability to manage a household in the Chaco environment, demonstrated that she could wash with a wringer washer, open and clip a clothespin, cook from basics. The boys were immensely popular with their grandmother and older cousins and numerous aunts and uncles.

And this is where the opportunity I mentioned earlier was introduced. A brother-in-law who worked in finance with the local Mission began a gently persuasive campaign for us to stay and do a term of Christian service. When Mennonites entered and settled the Chaco in the late 1920s and early 1930s, they encountered the Enlhet, nomadic hunter-gatherers who lived and moved within the region. The Enlhet attached themselves to the Mennonite colonies, and soon other groups began to arrive: the Nivaclé, the Ayoreo, and others. They lived side by side, the Indigenous and the Mennonite, the latter benefitting by Indigenous labour and their acute knowledge of the Chaco environment, and the *indígenas* by the relatively stable food supply and safety from enemy groups. The Mennonites eventually began "mission work" with the *indígena* communities and, with the support of development and church agencies abroad, the local Mission grew to include a full range of religious, educational, agricultural, medical, and land settlement programs.

As a boy, Helmut believed that the missionaries in the colony were very important and he envied them because they drove jeeps and other vehicles while ordinary folks got about by horse and buggy. An older cousin he much admired happened to be a missionary too. My childhood context placed missionaries on a similar pedestal. These fervent warriors of the Word and foreign "fields" travelled to churches with slide shows, artifacts, and heartrending stories which beguiled me.

Both of us had long since gained more realistic understandings of missionaries, and of ourselves—neither of us such a person by talent or calling—but there must have been remnants of the childhood attraction. This assignment would not be missionizing, of course, but service—service defined as motivated by Christian love. Service was a powerful value for us too.

Yes, we could see ourselves in a helping, development role. And Helmut liked machines, he was still drawn to vehicles of all kinds, he could make mechanical and material things happen. And he knew the Chaco and its people. Couldn't he postpone returning to his drywall contracting business in Canada for a few more years? Yes, we decided, he could.

That, in sum, was why we were back: because of a marriage straddling two continents and an opportunity to serve.

Helmut was doubly back, in his former home. A local. Old times on repeat. In his element. I'd been tourist and visitor, now grasping that it was one thing to visit, even for a chunk of months, and another to be an immigrant. In Canada, Helmut had been the immigrant, but it was my turn to pull up roots, put them down elsewhere. Two years for starters, and who knew how much longer it could be.

Two years felt major but I intended to make a go of my supportive role in this assignment, a go of the Chaco. I desired to fit in, to feel at home, even though I was far—very far—from being a true *Chaqueña,* or Chaco girl.

THERE'S ANOTHER reason it was good to be back in the Chaco. I wanted to be a writer. I was a bit of a writer already but I wanted to be more of one. I wanted to write a novel. I believed I'd found a story to tell. A story about a brother and sister, raised in Paraguay, Mennonite of course, the sister weary of a community she thought dull, too conservative, who left, and the brother burdened with the place, its history, and momentum, who stayed.

My plan wasn't entirely a secret, for I'd talked of it to my husband and several friends, but it was *like* a secret since I generally kept quiet about it. I wasn't confident enough to explain desire like this or defend it. It didn't seem the kind of aspiration that would make sense to many women in the Chaco, even in Helmut's welcoming family. I had my roles as wife and mother and homemaker, and that was plenty; that was enough, wasn't it?

Besides, what if I failed? Gave up? The secrecy was my protection too.

I'm not one of those writers who knew almost from the womb that they would write. That ambition evolved for me through various experiences and affirmations and a growing awareness of my interests and gifts. I entered an essay contest in high school and won a trip to Expo '67. I worked at a Mennonite periodical for two years—one year before marriage and one after—where I learned churchly journalism and some editing and proofreading skills. I had done some freelance editing and contributed articles to a number of (mostly Mennonite) magazines. I began to say, if tentatively: *I am a writer.*

Increasingly, however, though still imagining the same Mennonite audience, I wished to tell stories too, to work with the truth of fiction. Not reporting or learnings wrapped in tied-sweet bows but dilemmas, choices, repercussions. When our first son was still a toddler, I set up my typewriter in our duplex basement and tapped out a mid-level children's "chapter book" while he napped. I proposed it to several publishers, received generic rejections, and set it aside even though I thought it quite good. Then I realized—or decided on account of the rejections—it was adult fiction I preferred, and since I'd learned something about scenes, plot, dialogue, and characters, the kids' book had served its purpose. There was so much adult angst and joy inside me and surely inside other people I knew, so many stories from which one could draw to tell fiction that might entertain but also speak profoundly to the human condition.

My mother read novels to us as children. Though an avid reader, she seldom read fiction for herself, however. "I like to read books that are true," she said, by which she meant non-fiction of a religious bent or theological books. Fiction seemed, by her example, something one might mature out of, like childhood. But here I was, an adult, compelled by novels as much as I'd always been, and more than that, longing to write one myself. And even if writing fiction wasn't high on the list of worthwhile options within my community, I kept persuading myself to make the attempt.

I'd made notes for my story during the visit. How heat assails the body. How breezes like mercy lift leaves, play with corn stalks in a neighbour's garden, comfort perspiration rising on skin. How the sky looks in its variety. How wash ripples on an outdoor line. The peanut buttery colour of the Chaco earth. I listened in on stories and conversations for twists of plot and character traits, began to read books about Paraguay and its Mennonite settlements.

Four months of notes was an excellent start. Maybe I could have written the novel in Canada with what I had. The story unreeling in my head was melodious and quite wonderful, after all, though not much of it had landed as evidence on paper. But now I was back at the source and the stimulation of the place was smack in my face. And Fernheim Colony was relatively young; it threw out the thorns and flowers of its history with abandon. To my embryonic identity as writer, therefore, our return to the Chaco was fresh provocation. I had no excuse not to proceed with the novel now.

WHEN HELMUT AND the older son came home from the afternoon service that cold Sunday, we nappers got up. We spent the rest of that day in the back entrance, which also served as *Waschzimmer,* laundry room, with a woodburning stove for heating wash water and cooking the whites. (Not that I ever bothered cooking the whites.) Helmut made a fire. A brother and wife dropped in to drink yerba *maté*—widely consumed in Paraguay and other South American countries as a hot water infusion of crushed yerba leaves in a horn container called a *guampa* and sucked through a metal pipe or straw called a *bombilla.* (Infused with cold water, the tea is called *tereré*). *Yerba* tea is an acquired taste; fortunately, I'd acquired it.

Our visitors left and the four of us ate supper beside the fire as if on a picnic. We talked and recited rhymes and told stories. I read books to the boys. Our familial existence expanded into every corner of the room and the present circumstance like the necessary, welcome heat. I cherished hours such as this, husband and sons pressed inseparably against my life, my domestic aspirations fulfilled and creative longings strong and surely possible. I'd achieved a taste for yerba tea and we were together and the solid simplicity of this seemed enough belonging-in-the-Chaco for starters.

THE BROTHER-IN-LAW who lured us back to the Chaco came by with a plan—passed "in committee"—for the new house. The MEDA Germany group that sponsored us wanted us to live in the *indígena* settlement, nearer the Enlhet and Nivaclé drivers and the station buildings, rather than in Filadelfia where the former manager resided. No house was available in Yalve Sanga, however, hence the decision to build. Besides the fact that nothing had been started, Helmut discovered that he would have to supervise the construction, this in addition to learning and taking over the machinery program.

We bent over eagerly to examine the plan. "It's quite large," I ventured.

"Yes," brother-in-law said. "Someone commented in the meeting that the Mission talks of cutting down, yet when all is said and done they still want to build such a big house."

"I guess if someone else is paying," Helmut said, "it's easier not to cut down."

I put my finger on a bedroom and study with separate entrance and bath at the end of the drawing. "And this?"

"For guests. Or to house a single person at the Mission. One of the *Fräuleins.*"

"Single women. Who would eat with us," I said. He murmured in the affirmative.

A bit of privacy, some separation, but essentially living together. I didn't want to be critical, not this early, especially when it was a Mission house, not ours, and I was here as support. When the expectation of me as a woman would be *supportive, no matter what.* Appear to be so at least. Mennonite communities were patriarchal, but this one was even more overtly patriarchal than I was used to from North America where the women's liberation movement was introducing healthy shifts into the culture.

I certainly had opinions though, far too many opinions probably, and in this situation, resistance that would definitely need to be heard. "Maybe we can look at this more closely, get back to you," I said.

The messenger was barely out the door before I was flying the kite of my panic, winding out line. "Too big," I fumed, "way too big! It will surely cause offense." *Indígenas* in villages around the Yalve Sanga station lived in one or two-room shacks. I knew that gaps between a nomadic but newly settled people and the comparatively affluent, technology-wielding Germanic-Mennonites were inevitable, knew that they were complicated, but we didn't have to exaggerate them, did we? And furthermore, I couldn't have someone living with us, I just couldn't. I was completely willing to host guests, of course I was, occasional guests and for sure a small room with an extra bed, a prophet's chamber as it were, but not someone living with us. Eating with us. Involved with us. Plus, it was the last thing they wanted, the *Fräuleins* who worked in Yalve Sanga. Why did committees of men imagine that singles wanted to live with families, as if under the care of another woman? That they wouldn't want a home—a kitchen—of their own? Helmut had a single sister, a teacher in a Mission school, and she had said as much.

"*That* at least," I said, jabbing the attached rooms, "we've got to get rid of! I won't be able to refuse a lodger in good conscience if that is there."

I grabbed a piece of paper. Houses in the colony were constructed on the basis of simple drawings like the one in front of us. I could provide another on the spot. I sketched it quickly, with unruled lines, the basic outline of the main house similar to the committee's as a sign of goodwill, but with everything smaller and no guest or singles' attachment.

"Here," I said, "our bedroom, just big enough for a bed and built-in-closet, here the boys' room, two beds and built-in closet, small office for your work with maybe a bed for a guest, another bedroom here, for a guest, or"—I smiled—"a baby, and a bathroom in between, open area for a bit of a living room and a table and chairs and a U-shaped kitchen, no unnecessary doors, and back entrance with washing machine. *Schattendach* around the works and there you have it!"

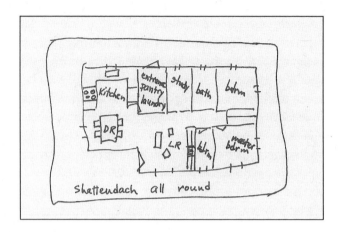

He looked at it, agreed, made suggestions about dimensions. I drew a clean copy with straight lines.

He delivered it the next day to the powers-that-be. "The reaction didn't seem too positive," he told me.

Several days later the committee met again, and switched to our plan. I could have done a happy jig when I heard this news, plus the news that the committee had placed a plan with two apartments for *Fräuleins* on the books for another lot in Yalve Sanga as well.

"I'm just so relieved," I said to Helmut. "I didn't want to be selfish but I prefer to be us, alone." Then, fervently, "Do you think we can be in before Christmas?"

He glanced at me and it was the look that said I didn't have a clue what he was up against. "There's a lot on my plate," he said, exasperation in his voice. He'd been going out to bush-clearing locations with the bulldozer crew, driving in one day, staying the night, returning the next evening. He was pleased with progress so far but he came home dirty and tired and stressed with everything still to be done.

"You're busy," I said. "But ... "

But I wanted to get properly settled. To get on with our two-year permanence.

"Dora," he said. "I *know*."

EVERY YEAR THE Fernheim Colony churches banded together to sponsor twenty-four-hour marriage retreats at Flor del Chaco, a recreational site, and we, keen to participate in local life, decided to attend. Two sisters-in-law agreed to babysit the boys.

Other than the respite of delicious meals I could eat without preparing them, the leisure of the event consisted mostly of sitting in rows in the chapel and listening to familiar topics—*Selbstannahme als Frau and Mutter,* self-acceptance as wife and mother, and that kind of thing. But then I met the colony archivist. Her husband, a physician, was speaker in one of the sessions and she had come along. She was older than I was, though not as old as I'd imagined, for I'd heard of this woman who did the colony's official archival work. She had a warm, intelligent face and a ready smile and we noticed one another, introduced ourselves, and sat down side by side to eat, and then we talked and talked—fluidly, for she'd studied in the United States and spoke an excellent English—not about accepting ourselves as wives and mothers but about the historical resources she managed. The Archives was located in the basement of the library and bookstore building just up our street at the corner of Trebol and Hindenburg. There was a full set of the colony newspaper, the *Mennoblatt,* she said, and quite a few settler recollections, and just last year she'd travelled to most of the Mennonite colleges in North America gathering materials relevant to the history of the colony.

"I brought five thousand pages back with me," she said. Including, for example, the letters to his home office in the States written by Californian G.G. Hiebert, the Mennonite Central Committee representative who met the immigrants on their arrival in the Chaco. The collection also contained a thesis—currently restricted—written by a Dr. Postma about the *Völkische Bewegung* or Nazi sympathy movement in Fernheim during the Second World War.

Before I knew it, I'd confided my writing project and my need for exactly these kinds of papers.

"Come and look," the archivist said. "Come any time." She was enthusiastic, and eager to assist. She would even see about permission to read the Postma paper.

Her encouragement felt bizarrely exciting. We set a time for me to view the collection and when I said I couldn't spare much time to research in the Archives rooms because I had two youngsters to tend, she amazed me even further by saying, "I could let you take some papers home."

3. Most certainly young

HELMUT SIGNED HIS contract: salary of 75,000 guaranies per month, about five hundred dollars at current exchange rates, out of which we would pay food, electricity, school fees, personal expenses, and personal transportation. The Mission would cover housing and medical insurance. The salary wasn't large but was comparable to that of other Mission workers. I had purchased enough Toughskin jeans and shorts and T-shirts for the boys in Canada to last two years, I thought, ditto for underwear for Helmut and myself. We'd lugged my sewing machine along. The enoughness of our situation gave me a feeling of security.

I also felt unencumbered. We'd rented in Saskatoon so had no house to dispose of, though we'd purchased a building lot for the future. We'd sold most of the larger items accumulated in seven years of marriage: freezer, table and chairs, beds and bedroom suite, sofa and matching chair. We staged a giant garage sale, and other than a trunk and some boxes full of personal items as well as bits of furniture on loan to others, had divested ourselves. We added the garage sale money to what we'd saved and realized enough to pay off the lot. We joked that we were landed gentry.

Simple living was the current mantra. Everyone we knew in Canada, it seemed, used the *More-With-Less Cookbook* by Doris Janzen Longacre, and I'd recently read, and reviewed for a Mennonite periodical, her *Living More With Less,* which expanded Longacre's simplicity theme beyond food to clothing, homes, transportation, celebrations, recreation, and more. The book offered five standards for living more with less: do justice, learn from the world community, nurture people, cherish the natural order, and nonconform freely.

My entire life so far had ebbed and flowed between accumulation and dispersal; we'd moved more than once, more than once started over. We didn't regret what we'd given up. Identity could be formed by getting rid of as much as by keeping, it seemed, and besides, we were young, there were years enough ahead of us to gather again.

WE ENROLLED THE older boy in kindergarten for the remaining few months of the school year.

"Why don't you ride your bike to kindergarten like the other boys do?" I asked him one morning while he got ready.

He had a yellow BMX bicycle. We brought it as luggage in its packing case. (We also brought one for the younger boy, though he didn't know it yet; he would get it when he turned four. He was still happy with a tricycle we'd purchased locally.)

The BMX bicycle had fat tires and no tire guards, like a mini-motorcycle with pedals. The latest and greatest for kids, in Canada at least.

"I don't want to," he said.

"Why not?"

"Because."

I persisted. "Why not?" He was an outgoing child with a quick, cheerful temperament, always singing or chattering. *A lovely sense of adaptability*, his kindergarten teacher in Saskatoon had written. He loved schoolwork, loved play. Both boys, by now, understood some German and Low German, the main languages of the Chaco Mennonites, and according to his teacher at the kindergarten here he was *ganz bei der Sache*, completely involved.

As sociable as he was, he was sensitive too. More than he let on to others. We'd been dealing with night fears, probably incited by the panther incident in *Little House on the Prairie* which I'd been reading to him. He sometimes worried about death. He refused to go out for kindergarten recess at first because two children made a funny face at him.

And now this reluctance about riding his bike, which he was otherwise so proud of. I pushed some more.

"They'll laugh at me," he finally said. "And stare."

Stare. Oh kiddo, I thought, tell me about it. How stared at I felt too. During the 1976 introductory visit especially, meeting Helmut's family for the first time. That memorable evening on Mama's verandah, the first or second day, most of the *Geschwister* gathered, an enormous frog leap-frogging across the bricks and it could have been an elephant for how it freaked me and then that huge black crusty thing—some insect—dropping on my sweater and more creatures buzzing around my face and neck and me desperately trying to be nonchalant about it all but petrified, sure I was under stealthy observation by everyone. (And grateful for Helmut's gallantry when he spotted a sizeable beetle skittering in my direction and, with his foot, casually pushed it away). Word must have spread round the entire colony that there was someone newly arrived, *Hein Dück sein jüngster*, Heinrich Dueck's youngest, and with a wife, that bride he picked up in the North. Oh I knew the sensation of being eyeballed alright, could definitely commiserate with the boy. Everyone seemed to know everyone here, or about them at least. Strangers in a relatively small and cohesive community were everyone's business. Those who belonged by some rights of long residency were naturally wary of newcomers, even sometimes regarded them with subconscious hostility. Would the One from Away be sufficiently subservient or complimentary or grateful, or did she think herself superior? And if she thought herself special in any way, it should be easy enough to find many ways in which she most certainly wasn't, shouldn't it? *Let's stare and find out.*

Or had I imagined scrutiny because of my own insecurities? Supposing I would be viewed as representative of something larger than myself, the entire notion of Canadian, for example? Impossible to measure up.

"No one likes to be stared at," I said. There was no point telling him not to let it bother him, when it also bothered me. No point plumbing the psychological dynamic of insider and outsider either, how both sides play at it, how if under subtle observation as tourist by locals, I was making sly judgments of my own, as tourists do; a case of tit for tat. He was still at the stage of concrete thinking.

But just like me he wanted to be accepted, wanted to be acceptable.

"My bike is different," he said. "I'm afraid they'll laugh at it."

"Well, you know what?" I said. "They *will* stare. I think they'll stare at your bike because they like it and wish they had tires like a motorcycle too." I thought that in this situation an attempt to impress, quite deliberately, was a reasonable strategy.

His expression was dubious but I could tell he was considering what I said.

"I think I can promise you almost one hundred percent they'll like it," I said. "Just try it once. Ride to school today. Let the kids look at your bike."

He was reluctant but I kept at it until he agreed. He mounted his yellow BMX, school bag with snack over his shoulders, and the younger boy and I walked beside him to the street and watched him pedal along the dirt sidewalk to his kindergarten half a block away.

He returned at noon triumphant. "You were right, Mom!" he cried, as if I was the smartest mother alive. The other children had clustered around him, admired the bike, begged to try it.

"And you let them have turns, I suppose."

"I let them! But the teacher made them stop because we had to come in. I'm taking my bike every day and everyone will get a chance."

SOME ADJUSTMENTS were easy enough. They were simply a matter of remembering that if you wanted farmer's sausage you had to buy it Wednesday morning early, same with vegetables (unless the trucks from Asunción hadn't arrived), that buns were only available Saturdays, and bread (delicious heavy wholewheat bread) must be purchased in the morning too, but not before ten. Brown sugar was never available, though white sugar was beige-coloured. You could pretend it was brown.

Even bugs and lizards became routine. A frog swimming in the toilet bowl was unnerving but would make for a good story later.

My biggest obstacle was language. The shame of a faltering tongue. I spoke a decent enough German, though my vocabulary was limited and half the time I guessed at the noun genders and cases, which affected the endings of words. I feared my sentences hurt the ears of the teachers in Helmut's family, though they graciously complimented me, said I spoke well.

My first language had been German, in fact; it was the language my parents grew up with. Though educated in English, they used German with me and my older brother in our early years, probably out of deference to their parents' generation. The language transition from German to English which happened in the immigrant Mennonite churches of Canada between 1940 and 1970 was often a bitter battle, with powerful voices arguing for the retention of German. When my parents realized their small children didn't understand what the people around them were saying, however, they switched to English in the home and from then on, I grew up English and my German disappeared. Later, in university and beyond, I resurrected the abandoned language in a German course and private study, and pronunciation at least was not an issue, no doubt because of my early hearing and speaking of it.

The Mennonites in the Chaco colonies knew German. They used it for school, church, Bible reading, prayers. And for people like me. The *lingua franca*, the vernacular in which they truly lived, however, was *Plautdietsch*, literally *flat German*, the Low German dialect. Low German was the insider language. I understood most of what I heard by now, and liked to listen to it, found it amusing somehow. Honestly, I would have liked to speak it. But I couldn't get it over my tongue. The consonants of *Plautdietsch* jammed together in the weirdest ways and I couldn't reproduce them in order.

I believed myself ungifted with language. French in high school had been excruciating.

And who would teach me? Helmut wouldn't have the time or inclination. It didn't seem to bother him that I couldn't speak Low German. Maybe he even liked it that I couldn't, a space of separateness such as marriages need.

No, I never considered it. Low German seemed a language you had to be born into, which I wasn't. It didn't allow for accents or mistakes or hybrids or wannabees. I had the impression that while errors or faltering in High German were kindly overlooked, I would be laughed at for trying and failing in the dialect. *Plautdietsch* opened to that kind of grinning bluntness. It represented what I couldn't become. This lack made me formal in the community instead of organic.

Or was my inability, my not even trying, actually a kind of snobbery? Before the transition to English in my Canadian immigrant community, there had been earlier transitions. Church leaders encouraged families to speak High German instead of Low German so children could follow church German. Both sets of my grandparents had taken this to heart. Although they might converse in Low German, they listened to their leaders and "upped" the standard to High German with their children. I grew up with the notion that the more educated and striving Canadian Mennonites spoke High German, while the rest spoke Low. Although "low" referred to the dialect's origins in the European Low Countries, not status, perhaps even the vertical relationship of the words subconsciously influenced me. In Fernheim Colony, *Plautdietsch* was ubiquitous in interpersonal speech and no marker of status but perhaps the stereotype lingered in me nevertheless.

But there was a reverse snobbery about Low German too, wasn't there? It was an earthy, even ribald, language with a unique capacity to subvert and tumble the "high and mighty." I envied its humour and lack of pretension, its swagger, but felt my Chaco personality not free enough to risk joining in. To try speaking Low German, it seemed to me, would be to mock myself.

The boys and I learned a few stock phrases—*Schlope gone*, go to sleep, and *Nü fuats*, right now and quickly—but in Low German conversations I listened, mostly understood, and when required, replied in my underbaked High German.

This marked me, set me at the edge of circles to which I wanted to fully belong.

WHEN I BEGAN working on this memoir in 2015—tapping memories, re-reading journals and letters, composing various drafts—I got a shock. I'd been thirty-two when we returned to the Chaco for the MEDA assignment, which was, I suddenly noted, the current age of our youngest child, and that child seemed—well, young! Wonderfully and very young. Which meant that Helmut and I had been very young too when we switched countries for a while. And once again I realized I was having this crazy misunderstanding about myself: surely in those years in Paraguay I felt myself much older than thirty-two seemed now, and now, in my mid-sixties, I thought myself far from as old as I'd considered sixty then.

I know that confusion about what constitutes old and young in the perception of oneself and others is a common human experience. We constantly reel backward or forward to keep an accurate hold. Retrospectively, I realized, I'd given our time in the Chaco a middle-aged tone. Which is nonsense and I saw it by comparison with my grown and mature but—I insist—young children. I was young, I was slender, my hair was dark. Ditto for Helmut. (How handsome he was!) Both of us were healthy, energetic, idealistic, striving, headstrong. Already wise, still foolish. We were Baby Boomer thirtyish, meaning we believed the world belonged to us. We had children to raise, homes to inhabit, experiences to experience, goals to achieve, and we assumed long unfettered lives stretching ahead to do it. We had sharp, ambitious edges. Yes, we were most certainly young. Gloriously young. We were everything I now, more than thirty years later, admired in my offspring of a similar age.

I can't say why my youth of those years was such a delightful revelation when I grasped it in relation to my children in their current ages. Perhaps it's simply the engagement with memoir which brings one repeatedly into a knock-about with time. Logically, one can't time travel, and yet one can and does: the mind wheels back and forth, freely, exerting its flit and perhaps risky twirls on the past. Memoir writing, author Lauren Slater says in a 2013 *Salon* piece, "is a wilful turning back of the clock, a logical impossibility, and yet you do it, because your mind exists out of time."

That I was young is the truth, and yet, in the memoir-writing-effort of existing out of time, my youthfulness at thirties-young seemed invention. And having coaxed this fiction/truth into text, I found myself suddenly standing next to my thirty-something children and in the flashes—swift and jaggedly stunning as lightning strokes—of knowing myself then and my children now, we seemed to meet as age-equals. As if we'd bumped into each other on some magnificent high bridge. The meeting amazed me, made me dizzy too. I was proud of these children, of who they were at the moment, and it pleased me more than I can express that the Me of the Chaco could, in this moment of meeting, be compared to them.

In her small book *Time*, Eva Hoffman notes that the Balinese don't tell you *what* time it is but what *kind* of time it is. In the meeting between my written younger self and the children's current young adult existence, I was Balinese for a moment, uttering not what time is it but what kind of time, the time wherein I knew how much I loved them as a mother but recognized them as mutual and affirming friends. Via memoir's impossible guile, I liked them and they seemed to like me. For a lit-up moment, we were peers.

4. Pushmi-pullyu

I generally wrote my parents twice a month. They tried to reply as often. I wanted them to follow the progress of the children. I wanted the children to have notice from them. My letters from Paraguay and theirs from Canada, like the rhythm of yarn on knitting needles, row after row, kept interlocking us.

I wrote by hand or by typewriter. (Besides the bikes, dishes, and cutlery, we lugged along two items I felt I couldn't be without: my sewing machine and a typewriter.) I wrote on regular paper or onion skin or the backs of Mission or school reports my parents might find interesting. I recounted what would help them picture our family's life, especially what their grandsons were saying and doing. "I hope you don't think I'm boasting," I wrote as I described the boys' accomplishments, although it was pride I felt and wanted them to feel as well. Wasn't applauding this steady parade of the children's cuteness and development what grandparents were for?

I told them that I met the kindergarten teacher at the Co-op, who said our older son was doing well, the other children sought him out to play with them; that the boys erected a small three-pronged monument with tile shards for a dead lizard, like the monument down the street, they informed me, meaning the one at the intersection of Hindenburg and Trebol which commemorated the fiftieth anniversary of Fernheim Colony and consisted of three narrow grey columns that reminded me of sawed-off hockey sticks, though they actually represented faith, work, and unity; that the younger boy was perfecting his climbing skills and could shinny up the metal *Schattendach* poles with his bare feet and hands.

I wrote about their fevers and earaches, and that the younger boy badly hurt himself while riding along with me to the store on the back of my bike because he leaned round me and caught his foot in the spokes. That the older boy was stung by a bee.

The ordinary things of life, often light-hearted in tone but confiding too.

"It's summer," I wrote November 10, 1982, "meaning watermelons, heat, and dirt. One never needs to consider even a moment whether to give the boys a bath before bedtime. Sometimes they get two a day and need it both times."

Being summer, there were more insects underfoot, including bugs busy mating. First Son called them "hitched-together" bugs. I read the boys the story of Dr. Dolittle meeting a two-headed animal called the pushmi-pullyu—*no matter which way you came towards him, he was always facing you.* They wanted to know if such creatures really existed. "It's a story," I said. "There aren't really animals with heads on opposite ends of their bodies." But the next day the three-year-old ran to me in a great stir, saying I'd lied. He tugged me to coupling insects as proof of pushmi-pullyus and would not be talked out of his assertion.

My father was a minister, austere in his outlook. Mom was extroverted but also reserved about sexuality. Proper about sex, they would say, meaning it was nothing to joke or blab on about. But letters were vivacious. I could say so much more on paper than in person. I could freely send my love—and I did. I used the language of affectionate personal and religious piety I grew up with, which felt easy and familiar to all of us. I didn't tell them everything of course, not by half, I wouldn't tell them if Helmut and I had an argument, for instance, though I might hint at discouragements, like the dollar to guarani relationship shifting badly just a few months after our salary had been fixed, affecting our buying power on imported items. But I related the pushmi-pullyu anecdote, let myself be amused though aware my parents might be less than amused, let myself express a casual honesty akin to my own child daring *liar* to me. Letters from the "foreign" outpost fulfilled the duties of travelogue for their recipients, and while information and delight were expected, so too were oddities of all kinds. A whiff of disconnection and discomfort, I imagined, was a subtle part of the charm. A letter was also a performance.

I always wrote about the weather. And the atmosphere, as it were. Mornings, the best part of the day, still wearing the peace and more bearable temperatures of the night, tender and silver with grace.

The wonderful turns that had us lifting heavier blankets out of the closet in anticipation of a cozy sleep as the temperature moderated downward. Cool days were jewels. We could leave the shutters open, allow day-air in through the screens.

Dusk. That was interesting too, the light not necessarily shading brown as I would have expected of dusk, but bronze. After windstorms, sunsets were stunning. We might encounter a sky so boldly orange everything in front of it was black and indistinguishable except as silhouette.

And evenings—so many evenings—when we could step outside and gaze into a welcoming dark, and then up and further into a black, immense basin crowded with stars. The moon perhaps, a hint of tangerine in its face. I didn't know the southern constellations but this didn't matter to me. The enormity and mystery were enough. Helmut said his father used to sit outside evenings and watch for Sputniks crossing overhead. He said that when he was a boy, he thought the darker patches of the moon were agricultural land for Russians. What else *would* they be? He'd heard so much about *how it used to be in Russia among the Mennonites:* the black soil, the advanced machinery for sowing and plowing and reaping and binding.

But am I speaking too much *here* about the weather? My inner critic fears that writing about Chaco weather, especially the extremes, will seem a ploy—an attempt at drama—and that railing about the *Nordsturm* and blistering temperatures won't provide context so much as cast me, the memoirist, as victim. Or more sentimentally, imply a heroine who endured. And will descriptions of lovely and refreshing times be sufficient counterweight?

The thing is, weather was an essential character of those years, perhaps the most tempestuous, but also influential, character of all. It had its fearsome reputation long before I arrived in Paraguay. The vast arid plain of grass and scrub forest (and near the river, swamp) in South America's heart, the Gran Chaco, has some of the continent's highest temperatures. It's been widely described as punishing and uninviting. Some who speak of it are blunter, calling it the Green Hell.

I was bound to the weather in Paraguay in a way I'd never been bound to weather in Canada. I grew up in a prairie town and after that lived in cities, and while vaguely aware how weather patterns determined crops, was completely detached from such concerns. My studies and work, as well as Helmut's work as a drywall contractor, happened indoors through every season. Drought or rain, storm or sunshine—these didn't affect much more than the colour of our lawn. And, pleasure or mild inconvenience, weather was always *outside*.

Now I lived in a place where weather was definitely news for letters, where the economy depended on crops and cattle which in turn depended on the weather, where the mood of the entire colony rose and fell with it, where inside and out were seamless, where I experienced weather insistently, endlessly, on my skin or under my feet. A conscious, consuming relationship.

It was more than city-girl-getting-country in her soul, and high time too. My new relationship with weather happened in Paraguay because hot climates foster a continuous and flowing engagement between outside and inside. Colony dwellings adapted to southern contingencies. (How I pitied the early settlers in their tents and small mud-and-straw homes.) But house in Paraguay was not distinct like house in Canada, where because of long winters, houses were constructed to produce and maintain their own climate. There, it seemed to me, inside and outside were deliberate states while in the Chaco I rarely thought about the passage from one zone to the other, rarely needed to consider it in terms of clothing or footwear. And we seemed to live in both zones. (Presently many colony buildings and homes have air conditioning, so it may be that this sense of things no longer applies.)

I skin-felt the cycles and their respective manifestations. What happened outside was always perceived. Sky, the phases of the moon, the effects of sun, how a storm builds, the various kinds of rain. I felt the entire overwhelming ethos of heat, the deceptively radiant sun and cumulus in a pretty blue sky, the wind and fine sand from the north—Bolivia or Peru—like an incinerator with its chimney set in our direction.

"You never get used to it," one long-time resident warned, as if suspecting I would try.

The extremes seemed hardest on women—Mennonite women especially, with their traditional twinned obligations of cleanliness and godliness. Children were oblivious, as children often are. Going outside to play was easy, immediate, blissfully thoughtless. Men wiped their brows and worried over the weather's effects on their finances but embraced the *gaucho* culture of Paraguay with its inevitable sun and dirt. And seemed the handsomer for their tanned and weathered skin.

But perhaps weather/climate is simply what any immigrant has to come to terms with first. The climate or weather particular to a region is a gate that has to be opened and entered. Immediate and unavoidable, it stands in for every adjustment to follow. Helmut experienced this when he immigrated to Canada in 1970. He arrived in June, when Canadian days are warm and long. "Does the sun never set here?" he'd asked in disbelief. Paraguay's relative closeness to the equator produced seasonal variations in daily light of only about an hour. Now he sat outside on a bright, late summer evening, and it was also humid and he was swatting mosquitoes. "Why didn't you tell me you have mosquitoes in Canada?" he grumbled. He'd imagined Canada differently, wanted to believe it a kind of Canaan, land of mild milk and honey. Then, come winter, he bought gloves for the cold, but not knowing better, bought flimsy ones and nearly froze his fingers. It took him years to learn the idiosyncrasies of cold and snow, how one lived with them.

I too, immigrating to the Chaco, had to acquire the vowels and consonants of this most conspicuous and sensate of languages: the weather. Which is why it showed up in my letters and journals, why it shows up frequently here.

I MADE A RESOLUTION though, that I wouldn't complain about the weather—especially the heat—in front of the locals. Helmut and I knew that disparaging comments from visitors or new arrivals simply invited resentment. Locals, of course, were allowed the most outrageous criticism of current conditions. Since they were mostly religious folk, they didn't use the word *infernal* when the weather was bad but they yammered and growled and came as close as possible. They did so because they felt the place belonged to them, climate included, they had settled and stayed, didn't turn tail as so many others, they had every right to complain about what was theirs. Opinions *I* offered would be seen as judgment by those who were thus invested; best I keep them to myself. Not even Helmut, born and raised in the Chaco, could complain with immunity. He once left, after all, and it would be said, "If you can't take it, go back to Canada."

I wondered, though: was there a magic number of years to get through before one *could* freely complain like Chaco dwellers did? Praise was always appropriate, but when would belonging be thorough enough to be a regular citizen with a common mix of appreciation and grousing? Did it require the formal commitment of a citizenship ceremony? My husband transitioned from landed immigrant to Canadian citizen at a ceremony in 1979. Perhaps after nine years he'd qualified there? It seemed that the burden put on immigrants to express admiration, refrain from judging, be grateful for the new country, could last a long time. In the meanwhile, I resolved to be careful, to not underestimate expectations real *Chaqueños* and *Chaqueñas* might have for those of us not deemed real enough.

5. Dog-paddling & documents

September. the new house was finally underway, the foundation in, one cistern for rainwater dug and the second begun. Together the two cisterns would give us some 60,000 litres capacity, plenty for our daily needs and the machine crew's needs and for watering trees or a garden.

The brick walls would be next, then the windows. Then the plumbing would have to be installed and the kitchen ordered, and . . . . The list seemed long.

It had been a tough year for the Indigenous people, reported the head of IBB (Indianer Beratungs Behörde), umbrella organization for the development side of the Mission, at its semi-annual meeting. Drought the previous spring, then rains during harvest. Crop prices were low. Only twenty percent lived off their own farming, he said, and there wasn't enough other work in the colonies for so many. He assured his audience that efforts to help *indígenas* with a settled existence from the Chaco soil would continue. "We know this is a slow process," he said, "but we are not giving up."

Since they welcomed the prospect of earning in non-farming ways and some were skilled in brick and tile work, Helmut employed Indigenous workers for the house construction as much as possible. He and the outgoing manager were busy, there was no end of trouble with the tractor, which meant repair work, and the bulldozer crew had to be kept doing contracts and supplied with provisions. (The repair of old machines would be the ongoing litany of his entire term.) When it rained, hours were expended on moving vehicles out of the mud. He did his best to keep the house construction going, while I waited for it to move along faster.

Be anxious for nothing but in everything by prayer let your requests be made known to God, I read in Philippians. The difference between nothing and everything was the difference between anxiety and prayer. I tried to practice the difference, kept busy with the usual daily tasks and projects of my own. I made a cheerful cover for the waterbed in a patchwork design of navy, white, and flowered blue squares and in a fit of energy one Saturday, baked a pumpkin pie, a lemon loaf, and buns with cottage cheese, which actually turned out fluffy instead of flat and hard like my previous attempts.

OCTOBER. A WEDNESDAY. I sat up straight and determined in the boardroom of the Mission office, half a block from our house, with three other women and Helmut but I might as well have been dog-paddling for my life in some muddy water hole, the way I was floundering. I'd been thrown into an intensive course in Spanish, eight hours a day and expected to last five or six weeks. Since we would soon live in Yalve Sanga, the centre village of the main *indígena* settlement, I'd been encouraged to take the course too. Each Chaco Indigenous group had its own language, but the common language of the Mission was Spanish. I would be able to communicate with the machine crew, other native Paraguayans, and *indígenas* of the Yalve Sanga community, and be able to help our older son, who would attend Spanish school there. Thus we'd reasoned, in deciding I should attend.

Of the five sitting at the boardroom table, all but I had studied Spanish before. They understood what the instructor said. German was the chief language of educational instruction when Helmut went to high school in Filadelfia, but he had gotten the fundamentals of Spanish. His goal was to enlarge his vocabulary and practice speaking. To me, he sounded fluent already. They all did. It wasn't a mud hole I was drowning in, but a stream, these voices of our teacher and the other students, a rushing babble like spume and water over rocks, pleasant enough if I could just listen and not have to think about repeating or understanding anything. The teacher spoke only Spanish; the course was immersion. I couldn't keep up.

Somehow, I survived to the end of the morning. Helmut and I rustled up lunch from leftovers and I flopped into bed for siesta, thinking *Mir sieht es schwierig aus*, to me it looks difficult, for German was beginning to infiltrate my English-stuffed mind, just when I needed to make room for Spanish. It wasn't just panic in my brain at not having a clue what was being said, but everything else I had to think of. Keeping up with the household. Finding childcare for both boys. First Son's kindergarten was finished for the year but teenage girls who might be hired were still in school. All I'd been able to arrange so far was one sister-in-law this week and another for the following.

Well, one day at a time. A tired mantra, but true. Maybe Helmut wondered how he would manage too, devoting weeks to Spanish, supervising the building of the house, and continuing his transitional training into the work. I could hardly give up after just one morning.

Back in class after siesta, I recognized several words. Words from the morning. I did my best to repeat and now and then my imitations sounded close enough. I was way behind already, but that's how it would be. The teacher had to gear the course to the others, couldn't waste their time going over and over *Buenas Dias* and *Buenas Noches* with a beginner. I would have to snag what I could.

WEDNESDAY AGAIN, same board room, same seat at the table, and glimpses through the glass of traffic along Trebol Avenue and the silver oaks that formed a green buffer in the middle of the road. A week of classes behind me. Helmut and the other students were speaking their parts. I signalled them to go on as if we were running a marathon and I'd finally resigned myself to walking the rest of the way. They sped away from me with their excitable sounds and chatter, out of sight.

I'd taken the previous day off, stayed home with the boys. It was October 12, a national holiday to commemorate the discovery of the Americas. (The European discovery, that is, the inhabitants they encountered not surprised or unduly excited about the existence of their own continent.) We three had set ourselves down at the end of our driveway to watch the annual Pepsi Trans Chaco Rally, a gruelling three-stage, 2259-kilometre rattle and roar through the Chaco, whose route included our very own street. Seventy-five cars had left Asunción, it was said, destination Mariscal Estigarribia north of the colonies and then back again, the route dusty or it might be muddy, and sometimes little more than a path through the bush. By the second stage, thirty-nine cars were still in the race, and it was these thirty-nine we watched pass in timed sequence, every five or ten minutes, noise and a kick of dust announcing its imminent arrival. The boys were thrilled with it all and pronounced on each vehicle—reasonably solid and steady, or battered and clattering—as it vroomed or agonized by: "He won't make it!" or "I think he'll win!" Like a dream, the car was gone and then they discussed what they remembered while they waited for the next. I loved listening to their conversation.

I'd decided to quit Spanish. The care of the boys, for one thing. Plus, as Helmut and I had discussed it again, reasoning it backward and out of our earlier decision, I wasn't directly assigned to a Mission program. He could cover the Spanish bits on my behalf. He'd realized he couldn't put in the full five or six weeks either, not with everything pressing on him. The course had helped a lot already, he said; he would gain further facility as he used Spanish in his work.

For me, there was also this: I was pregnant. And feeling lousy, as I always did the first trimester. Nausea and Spanish were an unpalatable mix.

I would finish today's class, bid teacher and classmates *Adios*, explain that I bought a book, *Spanisch in 30 Tagen, Spanish in 30 Days*, in order to proceed on my own. I felt relief. Like clouds rising in the blue sky when the soil needed rain.

Both boys were, unexpectedly, invited to a cousin's farm for the day. I'd planned to wash but immediately crossed laundry off my list. Not with a day to myself, a day to write. My head was crammed with scenes I'd been staging, sentences I'd been forming, revisions to paragraphs already drafted, details to incorporate. Soon after meeting the friendly archivist at the marriage retreat, I'd gone to the cool basement rooms below the library and bookstore building, where I found her as willing to help as she'd been at Flor del Chaco. I'd emerged with a packet of files, promising to be careful with them.

The archivist said she trusted me.

Since then, every hour not filled with housework or the children had been devoted to those papers. I knew the broad chronology of the colony's early years, but everything I read added detail, had novelistic possibility. The documents oozed specifics. What people thought, for one example, when they saw the *campos*—the sand-soil remains of ancient riverbeds covered in grass and occasional trees—where their village farms would be established. I read and listened for emotion. For how experiences were framed. Not surprisingly, the journey from Russia to Paraguay and the subsequent settlement were often composed in religious terms, in language like the prophet Jeremiah's *the people who survived the sword found grace in the wilderness.* Mennonite migration history was often compared to Israel's Old Testament experiences of exodus. This is how my characters would talk about it too.

But much more than pious *Gelassenheit*, yieldedness, slipped through these captured, archived texts. There was also despair. Strife.

I found it fascinating to pore through reports composed in this very place some fifty years earlier, here in Filadelfia, the centre of the colony, or in the villages where Helmut's *Geschwister* or cousins lived with their farmsteads—the *Hofs*—strung on both sides along the road, the elementary school building that doubled as Sunday meetinghouse in the middle. Like their villages in Russia. I closed my eyes and thought of sites in Fernheim where I walked or biked, thought of these very places disappearing into waving *campo* grass, then reappearing like time-lapse photography into what they were now. Fascinating, yes, and a tingle of voyeurism in me too, opening documents marked "Strictly Confidential," betraying the instructions of the author and assumption of recipients. The authors and recipients were dead, it wouldn't matter to them, but reading I found myself back in *their* moment of sending and receiving these lines and in *that* moment, I was a veritable snoop. It was like crouching beneath the open window of a room where a frank in-camera meeting was underway.

Here the report of Tobias K. Hershey, a North American Mennonite missionary in Argentina sent to investigate the conflict between Corporación Paraguaya (the company that arranged the Chaco land sale and transfer) and the new colony. Here the letters and reports of Gerhard G. Hiebert, a California fruit farmer who spent a year-and-a-half in Paraguay on behalf of the Mennonite Central Committee, assisting the Fernheimers settle. To the first-generation immigrants like Mama, Hiebert was a saint. There was even a village named after him—Hiebertsheim. But Tobias Hershey laid some of the problems with the Corporación at Hiebert's feet. Not simply the same story with more detail or slight variations then, but diverse and colliding stories about the same events.

Hershey's and Hiebert's papers were written in English, and reading them went quickly for me. In German, I read the partial—to 1931—recollections of a Johann Loewen of Friedensfeld, village No. 5. At the head of his story, he put Exodus 19:4: *I brought you unto myself [in bringing you out of Egypt]*.

I hadn't opened *Spanisch in 30 Tagen*. I probably never would. I had only so many hours available and wanted to give my spare ones to learning and then writing fictionally the language of the past, the story of Helmut's people in the Chaco. The novel's characters grew clearer in my mind, began to articulate themselves. I felt them becoming *my* people. I had the name—Anna—of my main woman, mother of the sister and brother I had envisioned first. More and more, the story was becoming hers. And her husband Jakob's.

That day I didn't think about my sons. I knew they would be having a grand time on the farm. I didn't think about my husband, off in Toyish or wherever the crew was working at the moment. (I tended to lose track.) I didn't think of the laundry, possibly smelly and gasping for air. I accomplished eight pages. Not as much as hoped for, but what I got done. I should have known by then that writing was always slower than I expected when I rolled the first sheet of paper into the typewriter. I never really learned it; throughout my life as a writer, I have continued to over-estimate how quickly I can get something written.

But time was peripheral as I sank into that day's scenes. I was several months ago released from Moscow, I was landing in the wild, warm Chaco, I was alternately exhilarated and dismayed, I was hot.

I wrote. Re-wrote. Eight pages.

YEARS LATER, I would be baffled by the fact that no one in Helmut's family told me about their father's diaries. He'd mentioned, yes, that Papa used to sit evenings at the table making notes but I had no idea this amounted to anything or that notebooks of the deceased father still existed. Were they stored in Mama's house then, or already in the sister's closet, where they remained some twenty-five years at least, until after that sister's death, when another sister took it upon herself to transcribe them? The diaries would have been as good as any other source I consulted for my novel about the early years of Fernheim Colony.

Were they off limits because Mama was still alive? Was the family itself, even the sister who stored them, unaware of their contents?

Or had I been so secretive about my novel intentions that no one thought to offer Papa's record of the early years?

Perhaps just as well. It would have been hard to separate my fictional characters from the person who was my husband's father, my children's grandfather. Distressing enough that some people wondered later if Anna was based on my mother-in-law. Not just wondered, but assumed it. (Really, how could anyone confuse my mild, reticent, pious mother-in-law with the spirited and willful Anna?)

Just as well, yes. I was gratified, however, when finally reading Papa's diaries in 2009, to see that my father-in-law's accounts corroborated the historical research I'd done elsewhere.

I'D ALWAYS VIEWED my Mennonite history through the lens of "north" and much of my initial obsession with Chaco Mennonites concerned what seemed—to me—a startling and unlikely intersection of northern sensibility with the landscape and culture of the southern hemisphere. My earliest forebears lived in the European Low Countries, claiming land-room from the North Sea, and then they moved to Prussia (today's Poland), which lay further north and pressed against the Baltic. When they migrated to Russia at the invitation of Catherine II, it was southward, but even that migration settled them in a latitude that seemed northerly to me—it's more or less across from the Canadian prairies after all.

As the Russian Mennonites sought more land and began to scatter to other parts of the Russian Empire (later the Soviet Union), they sometimes went to warmer climes like the Crimea but mostly—in the map of my imagination, at least—they followed straight lines eastward. Many who didn't emigrate in the 1920s were banished to Siberia and my impressions of Siberia were of ice and snow. Very north. And if the so-called golden age of the Mennonite sojourn in Ukraine was indicated in Peter Gerhard Rempel's photographs in his book *Forever Sunday, Forever Summer*, the trauma of the 1920s flights out of the country had a wintry hue, regardless of the season in which they actually occurred. Paraguayan Mennonites experienced their dramatic release from Moscow in the winter of 1929, or in equally dramatic crossings over the Amur River into China. An entire village escaped over the frozen Amur in the dead of December 1930. My forebears' stories were clouded with people, horses, train engines spewing northerly white breath into sub-zero air.

Then those Mennonites came to Paraguay and North met the torrid Chaco. It seemed almost absurd. Researching their settler materials, I detected the strong memory of their originating latitude and ongoing adaptation that rubbed and confused like heat rash or a blister. Although their presence no longer seems remarkable in the Chaco environment—there are now thousands of Mennonites in various countries of Central or South America—the contrast still seemed to bubble under the surface when I was there in the 1980s. At least it did for me. Hot evenings and the sounds of cicadas. Pale soil, brown instead of black. Spanish colours and temperament. "That they're *here!*" I would think to myself, North with its cold biting script sliding into the pages of the South, thawing the old story, writing a new one in hot Chaco ink. "Here! Somehow it seems unbelievable."

6. MERCY

IN SPITE OF morning sickness, I was thrilled about the pregnancy. Helmut was too. Happily, I wrote my parents the news, though I resisted making a joke about hitched-together bugs.

Locally, though, we would be cautious in announcing it, at least until I was showing enough for others to guess or know. I'd learned a lesson about undue jubilation on the introductory visit when pregnant with our first child. I'd wanted a baby so badly and wanted so badly for Mama to share our excitement that I begged Helmut to tell his mother soon after we arrived. (It seemed his job because he knew her best.) A conversation about the international travel vaccination required for Paraguay presented an opportunity: I'd been exempted, he said, because I was expecting.

There was no reaction.

"I don't think she got it," I said to him later. "Please tell her again in the morning." It seemed the most important thing about me at the time.

Over breakfast, he said it again, not sideways but straight out: we were in *Erwartung*, in waiting, for a baby.

"Yes," Mama said, "you told me yesterday."

And that was that.

"They're pretty quiet about anything connected with sex," he comforted me. "Not much is said until it's obvious, that's what I recall. Don't expect congratulations."

It wasn't obvious, that was true, I was hardly three months along. But that day at lunch, as we started in on delicious fried chicken, Mama slid the liver to my plate saying, "You need this," and I knew it was on account of being in *Erwartung*. The gesture touched me. And throughout the weeks we lived with her on that visit, she offered small acts of support like that, though otherwise expressing no emotion or comment. She made sure I ate properly, made sure I rested. "I don't need you in the kitchen," she might say, "go sit down."

I did as I was told and relaxed in a chair outside in the shade or in the sitting room. I'd brought along Grantly Dick-Read's *Childbirth Without Fear*. I was preparing myself long before it was strictly necessary, but I was excited and desired to learn everything about the topic. Women of my generation were intent on having more natural birth experiences than our mothers. Not for us the blockage of anesthesia or long hospital stays or birthing without our partners in the room.

Mama must have known what type of book I was reading, for sisters-in-law had seen it and inquired, but if she had thoughts on the subject, she didn't reveal those either. Nor did it occur to me to probe her experiences of birth. She'd birthed nine children with the help of a midwife and would have had plenty of *natural* experience to relay, if natural was what I wanted. I truly regret that in spite of her instinctive silence, I didn't probe with questions about her births. But she seemed so much older than I was, so much beyond me as the youngest daughter-in-law.

Now I was pregnant with my third, myself a woman with some experience with birth, and once again didn't think to draw on Mama's knowledge or wisdom.

THE MAN WHO'D been running the machine station returned to Switzerland with his family and Helmut was on his own. The two men had worked well together; he would miss having someone with whom to consult. The upside of the departure was that material objects belonging to the MEDA outfit now devolved to us—an ironing board, a family-sized fridge, as well as the MEDA freezer for crew provisions, which meant space for provisions of our own. The extended family occasionally butchered a cow on Mama's ranch and shared the meat. *Asado*—barbecue over wood ashes—was an extremely popular meal in the Chaco, though I preferred to receive the hamburger and stewing cuts. I'd grown up on ground beef, baloney, chicken, and wieners, and my teeth ached after gnawing on *asado* as if they'd never been toughened for real meat.

The new house in Yalve Sanga progressed, though not without the sacrifice of three snakes, one a metre-long deadly half-moon curled in the bricks of our future bedroom. Fortunately, having just swallowed a rat, it could barely stir itself. Snakes, my husband explained, were the reason the field around the house would have to be plowed, not remain a sea of grass as I'd suggested.

Speaking of sea, waves of homesickness washed over me as I remembered that my Canadian family was celebrating Thanksgiving in the mellow orange and gold of autumn while I was in the midst of spring and facing into the extreme heat of summer. More weeks passed with another round of fever and earache for our eldest. Helmut hurt his back and slept for a solid day-and-a-half to recover. On the road again, he popped into a seldom-used outhouse and was stung on the butt by bees. An entire week registered 40-plus degrees. The exchange rate was unfavourable, fuel prices the highest in South America.

December then, and Christmas neared without the familiar stimuli of pine scent and snow. I was sated with busy-ness, not exactly discontented but not exactly joyful either. I finished the patchwork bed cover and tried to keep pace with the weeds in the huge yard of the Filadelfia house, finally hiring some nieces and a nephew to whack and rototill some of it, though it rained after they were done and a new crop of weeds promptly sprouted on the heels of their work. I was often tired, my hemoglobin too low in spite of iron pills, and I suffered frequently from headaches in the heat, but I made pickles and froze cherries and the boys' eagerness about the upcoming holiday season was at me like a prod. Together we made a Christmas wreath of greens and candles, which excited them far beyond its measure.

I supposed I knew everything there was to know about the original story of Christmas—what it meant, what it ought to mean. It was an event for children after all, what else was there to ponder? Until after a restless night, when I woke convicted. A strong, old-fashioned word, convicted, even stronger than its roots in *convince*. But it's the only word that fits. Charges like fingers pointed at all that was worried and withering and Scrooge-like in my spirit. Though cheerfully unencumbered with the clutter of things and a keen proponent of simple living, I nevertheless often grew anxious that there wouldn't be enough. I preferred my simplicity outlined against a hefty backdrop of security. Fear made me scrimp on generosity, not only in things, but in relationships too.

It wasn't the first time I had to confront this aspect of myself, nor would it be the last. When I spent hours baking, for example, I liked nothing better than to tuck the cookies and cakes safely into a freezer where they would stay for *eventualities*, instead of freely offering them up to the children and their friends or guests who had—they insisted—simply stopped for a coffee or *tereré*, so fine, except that one of our sons might put me on the spot and remind me of the cookies; there *were* cookies, weren't there, and wouldn't it be nice to bring some out? It wasn't even about the ingredients, but rather the time given up to make them, which as soon as the cookies were eaten, would have to be expended again. I wanted to do too much, to read and write on top of everything else. I felt perennially short of hours.

That morning the finger inward was pointed and specific, and—I knew—altogether justified. The specifics ranged from parsimony in my contribution for a potluck party to my over-concern about the boys being "good" in public. The conviction was uncomfortable, like viewing my reflection in a convex mirror, grotesque and out of proportion. But it was bracing too, a surging hunger for another shape, something better.

Lord, have mercy. In acknowledgement, in prayer, my inner self burst open, the tightness loosened and released. I was free to range and move again. It's almost paradoxical how this works. Space expanded for the vulnerability of the Incarnation event. Gratitude like a swell. Something new in anticipation of Christmas after all.

I was comforted by a hymn stanza by William Cowper:

> Ye fearful saints, fresh courage take;
> The clouds ye so much dread
> Are big with mercy, and shall break
> In blessings on your head.

The word for mercy or compassion in Hebrew has its roots in womb. I loved the intertwining of mercy and womb. What I felt for our unborn child—protectiveness and brooding over and empathy for—was the tenderness also given my crabbed spirit, poured into its necessary growth. In such a scenario, womb turned into a verb and the *Kyrie Eleison*, the Lord-have-mercy prayer became *Womb me please, for I am still unborn.*

7. CHANGING PLACES

ON A SUNDAY AFTERNOON, the head bulldozer driver—an Enlhet man—and his wife and his daughter appeared at our door. They'd been to Asunción, returned by bus, and needed a ride home to Yalve Sanga. Helmut scouted around town to see if anyone had driven in from there for the day. No one. There would be people going in the morning, he said, himself included.

The man was adamant: he and his family would not stay in Filadelfia for the night.

Helmut said he would take them home. The boys were keen to go along and I was keen as well because it was Sunday afternoon. Family time. Besides, I liked road trips with my husband. Always had, whether short or long. I liked how driving put us in the same place, facing the same direction. I liked the possibilities for talking, or not-talking but thinking instead, side by side. I liked that I could bring a book along and read, though I rarely did so on the bumpy roads of the Chaco. I liked that both he and I would see whatever could be seen, even if we were different when it came to looking. I gathered impressions, which might bubble into land- or idea-scapes in my head. He observed with impressive acuity what was there, an antelope bounding into the bush, the zigzag trail of a snake, the exact make of a passing vehicle. On his work trips, he generally kept a shotgun in the truck. Once he sighted a large lizard and shot it and gave it to an Indigenous man for whom it would be a delectable treat. Another time he shot a rabbit. Since he was near his brother's village, he stopped and traded the rabbit for watermelons. He knew that I—his dear wife—wouldn't have a clue how to get a rabbit out of its skin and onto the table.

We all climbed into the truck and set off for Yalve Sanga. Our family sat in the cab, the Indigenous family sat outside in the box. It was an old truck, prone to flats, and sure enough, a flat tire interrupted us on the way. The record for flats so far was four in one day. The men had plenty of experience repairing the tires and soon had it fixed. The drive resumed.

At the Enlhet village, people gathered to greet the bulldozer driver and his wife and daughter. Our boys said they were thirsty. We had forgotten the water jug. Someone fetched the youngsters a cup of water. It was pond water, nearly black. The older boy glanced at it and passed it to his brother. The younger boy wouldn't drink it either. Watching this, the Enlhet laughed amongst themselves.

Helmut always drank *terere* with his *indigena* friends and workers, unlike some Mission colleagues who refuse to share the metal *bombilla* interracially. In spite of that, neither he nor I pushed the boys to drink the water. We felt we simply couldn't.

The laughter embarrassed me though. I couldn't interpret it. Had we insulted the Enlhet, or were they merely amused at these finicky white children?

The differences between us seemed as wide as the Grand Canyon. I stood beside the truck, smiling and smiling, and the Enlhet laughed while the boys remained thirsty and shortly we would ride away in the battered old truck and all we had in common, it seemed, was the ground we were standing on.

Come to think of it though, the Chaco ground was a considerable something we had in common. These formerly nomadic peoples, who crisscrossed the region for generations, wanted to settle down on it. The Mennonites, long rooted in another place, then fleeing in desperation, had come to this place and were settling down on it too. And for a while, so were my husband and sons and I.

You readers may be distressed about the Enlhet family sitting outside in the back of the truck. Looking back, I am too.

It was common, but not safe, and perhaps it's been banned by now. I remember an outing to Mariscal Estigarribia with two other families, six adults, ten children, one truck. Most of the group travelled in the back, under the roof of the sun. It was warm and windy and not that comfortable. It had its risks. The main thing was to keep everyone, especially the children, seated. They must not, under any circumstances, stand up.

But also the way the journey with the Enlhet family looked, and was. Racially. I can't defend it. All I know is that we could never have persuaded them to any arrangement other than the one we had: the *Patron*, boss, and his family in the front, and they together behind us.

In 2007, long after my Chaco years, I was on an airplane and paging half-bored through the inflight magazine *enRoute*, when I came across an article called "The Mobile Age, Part 1: Modernism" by Vancouver writer Timothy Taylor. It re-set my thinking about migration.

It made me consider, for example, that I too have been something of a migrant, though I'd never thought of myself that way before.

Taylor's broad topic was mobility: the compulsions behind moving from place to place, the shaping power of changing or not changing places. The nomadic impulse could be traced far back into human history, he said, as if moving is simply what humans do. Moving got particularly urgent with the rise of industrialization. A range of push and pull factors as well as advances in transportation provoked millions to move within countries, or, more drastically, change countries or continents altogether.

At play within the human impulse to move, Taylor said, was another human impulse or disposition: the yearning to settle. He plotted degrees of mobility against the degree to which mobility is voluntary to produce four "archetypes" of mobility: refugee, nomad, prisoner, settler. The refugee is involuntarily mobile, the nomad is voluntarily mobile, the prisoner— whether literally imprisoned or bound to a location by other forces—is involuntarily immobile, and the settler is voluntarily immobile. Taylor posited that the yearnings of one archetype to become another defined the "modern" era of mobility.

The irony wasn't lost on Taylor that his words would be read by someone like me, flying from one city to another, thereby also contributing "to a complicated web of cultural forces," altering the places I visited by what I left behind and being altered myself by what I brought back, including, he suggested, "the very idea of what home itself should be."

I wasn't sure if it was allowed, but I carried that inflight magazine off the plane so I could read the Taylor essay again. His ideas swirled through my mind. It was heady stuff, this: laying my autobiography and genealogy into his charts and words. I could easily peg in the movements of my grandparents (Russia to Canada) and Helmut's parents and grandparents (Russia to Paraguay) as the "involuntary mobility" refugee archetype. They yearned into the settler category. In the case of my paternal grandparents, settling didn't quite take hold until they strove for some years from Manitoba to Saskatchewan to two communities in Alberta and finally British Columbia.

But thinking further, into the generations beyond the 1920s and 30s, I realized I'd been making a big mistake: I had relegated migration—those dramatic tales of dislocation and re-location that made up our family lore—to the distinct and separate past called *history*. Migration with its archetypal sequences of refugee and settler defined Mennonite history, it was the great big looping theme of it, beginning with the Anabaptist movement of the sixteenth century and its attendant persecutions and flights. Subconsciously, however, I'd concluded that with the end of those "mass" movements of my people, migration stopped. Home lost, home found, end of sentence. A kind of happily ever after, except for the melancholy of the first generations of exiles who still remembered what they'd left.

Now I saw a thick thatch of mobility or immobility scenarios sprouting from my family tree beyond the 1920s, when I figured they'd ended. The urge to wander and the urge to root had survived beyond forced wanderings or rootings: dozens of fascinating mobility studies lurked in the corners of my life and the lives of relatives. Each engaged with place, each combined the Taylor schemata in unique and riveting ways. Many were individual rather than communal in nature. Had I forgotten the most obvious, that my own husband migrated, just one of hundreds who abandoned the Chaco?

I thought, for instance, of Helmut's family, in counterpoint to him, and how tightly most of them had clung to the Chaco. His parents, who met in the refugee halls of Germany and married in Paraguay, worked hard to put down roots. One of their ten—a niece who became adopted daughter—moved to Uruguay to nurse and married there. Several children or their partners moved to the capital Asunción or to Uruguay or Argentina to study, but this was always considered temporary; they were away because they were planning to come back to be useful in the colony. Most of the children's children stayed as well. Were they voluntary settlers or was there the pressure of family ties, the pressure of assumption? Why *would* they leave? Their souls seemed to have drilled into the soil a kilometre deep. Many were economically well off by now. Is this what held them?

Those who stay in a place find "home" easy to define, they don't need to think about it much. It's those who leave who find the word complicated. Helmut and an older brother felt themselves "prisoners" of colony restrictions and religious expectations, as well as the struggle to establish themselves financially. It was they who yearned nomadically and broke away from what seemed a monochrome future to try their fate elsewhere. But the lure of the Chaco is surprisingly strong for those born and raised in the Chaco and the brother eventually returned to Paraguay with his family, happy to be "home" again. Helmut stayed in Canada. But if he'd had the money those first years, he told me, he might have gone back too. He would see an airplane flying overhead and long to be on it. By the time he could afford to leave, however, he no longer wanted to. Plus, he had married me, a Canadian.

He and I imagined ourselves solid settler sort of people, but now I saw that the nomadic impulse in us was never entirely suppressed. We moved if we had to, which meant leaving Winnipeg and re-locating to Saskatoon when construction work ground to a halt. We moved if we wanted to, spending half a year in Europe early in our marriage. We visited Paraguay. We lived in Paraguay.

And I thought of my parents and how the nomadic particularly twisted in them. I blame our branch of Mennonites, the Mennonite Brethren, which developed a strong missionary program. Under the influence of preachers and missionaries, they felt called to such Christian service. Was this voluntary mobility, or was it, because of their religious commitments, actually closer to involuntary? Once a Yes had been said to the leading of God, what further choice did they have? *I'll go where You want me to go*, they sang.

My parents hoped to go to Africa. They prepared themselves for that. For reasons I'm not entirely clear about, they were not given an assignment to Africa but asked to consider missionary work in Mexico instead. They travelled there on a temporary visa, with three children (I was three), and stayed for several months. Born in Russia, however, they couldn't get permanent visas. Had the circumstances been just slightly different, I would have grown up in Africa, or in Mexico.

They ended up living in Canada, and I grew up in Alberta and Manitoba. My older brother insists our father never quite recovered from the disappointment of not being assigned by the mission board to Africa. But if now stuck in Canada, they weren't entirely settled down either. They were still mobile in response to the calls of church ministry, pastoring in congregations in Alberta, in Manitoba, and in their retirement years, alongside a church in Vienna.

Because of this, I grew up far from grandparents and aunts and uncles and cousins. I believed this normal and unremarkable. My siblings and I felt freed to roam where we "must" as well, following callings or jobs. We were never expected to cluster around our parents. I lived in the three prairie provinces, in Ontario, in Paraguay. The longest "home" was Winnipeg, Manitoba, but that 40-some year sojourn too would come to an end when we followed our children west, to British Columbia. Move and stay, move and stay, in various combinations, the tension between these impulses was both difficult and fulfilling.

Thinking of these moves I wonder if friends or onlookers ever questioned our core dependability. We must have seemed flighty, mildly unstable.

Nevertheless, every change of place had its own indisputable logic.

Interesting, though: we returned to Paraguay eager to help nomadic Indigenous people develop a settled life. We stood together on hard packed earth beside the truck the day we dropped the Enlhet family off at their Yalve Sanga village, unmindful of our own mobility and sporadic unsettledness, unmindful of how migrational all of us were, Mennonite and Indigenous, white and brown, inhabiting brief stops and crossings, sharing common ground for a while, touching the shape of one another before our feet shifted on the ground.

8. ANGUISH

I CLAPPED MY hands outside the director's house at Escuela Mariscal José Felix Estigarribia in Yalve Sanga. Here, one clapped instead of knocked, clapped at a respectful remove from the door, at the gate if there was a gate. The school director's wife, a pretty dark-haired woman, stepped out. Her greeting was polite but neutral.

Could I speak to the director? The wife said to wait.

Waiting, I scanned the buildings and grounds. They seemed to be waiting too, stretched out languidly under the sun as if asleep though presenting a formal demeanour, being the school with the long name to honour the hero-general of the Chaco War after all and children not yet tumbling about the playground or lining up at its cream-coloured doors to the classrooms or dining hall. The school itself was an L-shaped structure in red brick with four or five classrooms and a verandah. Silver oak and *paraiso* trees stood guard. There were dormitories—the boys' to my right, the girls' behind me—and a dining hall which doubled as an auditorium, and red brick houses for the teachers and kitchen and maintenance personnel. A swing hung ready for someone to swing, an unpainted teeter-totter posed at a diagonal. The sandy earth was freshly tilled between neat lines of succulents and an oleander bush sparkled with yellow blooms. The soccer field seemed immense. Staff, except for the director and his family, must be away, for nothing stirred but the faint chirr of the heat. And that distant radiant sky again, so bright blue and white.

Kindergarten for our first son was over for the year and November to February were summer holidays. He'd turned six in November. Since he would be months into Grade One in Canada by now, we'd assumed he would attend in Yalve Sanga when we moved there—hopefully soon—and when the school year opened late February. Thus, returning to Canada later, he would be more or less at the right grade level. This school instructed to Grade Six and was mainly a boarding school for Paraguayan children from outlying communities and *estancias*—Paraguayan in this context meaning those who weren't Mennonite or, as we said then, Indian. The local Enlhet and Nivaclé had their village schools.

The boy had liked kindergarten. He was eager to learn, to do things. He'd been flying through as many of the English workbook pages I brought along as I allowed him, as well as some Grade Three and Four level material I purchased from an expat teacher returning to Canada. But I'd discovered a philosophy of education at odds with what I was used to. In Canada, kindergarten was considered preparation for Grade One: reading and arithmetic readiness skills were introduced. Here our son did crafts, sang, listened to stories. Learning to sit still and behave—to be a good boy, I groused to Helmut—seemed the most important activity of all. I'd been told teachers were annoyed if children came to school already knowing what they were about to be taught. But did they—the anonymous and ubiquitous *they* I was complaining about—have any idea how hard it was to hold back a child who wanted to read? By himself? Even his three-and-a-half-year-old brother was chafing to begin. "That lucky duck!" he grumbled when the older boy went to kindergarten and he grumbled it still when his brother did school pages beyond his own comprehension.

I wanted to fit in, to go with the flow of how it was locally done, which is why it seemed imperative to get First Son going on his school education while there was still some Grade One material he hadn't accomplished. We began to make the arrangements and then, unwittingly, had found ourselves in a muddy mess.

The boy wouldn't be allowed to attend, we were told. He was six and the starting age for school was seven. We put in a request to the school director and to his supervisor in charge of the entire educational program of the Mission that our son be considered an exception. We explained that when we got back to Canada, where children start at six, we wanted him at his age level school-wise. Because his birthday was late in the year and the school terms didn't correspond (starting in September in Canada, in February in Paraguay) he would, in effect, be two years behind if he didn't start now. The exception seemed obvious to us, easy enough to grant.

Not so. The overseer told Helmut that they—that anonymous *they* again—didn't want to admit him. More specifically, he further informed him, the *they* was the director, who'd declared, "That boy won't enter this school." First Son's classmates would range from seven to twelve, he said, and our boy would not be as mature.

"Are you prepared," my husband pushed back, "to have a child in Grade One next year who can do arithmetic, reading, and writing at a Grade Two level? Yes, he'll be doing it in Spanish instead of German or English, but still, he'll be far ahead."

The overseer took another tack. He said the Yalve Sanga school was much inferior to a Mennonite elementary school.

"If it's good enough for the Paraguayan kids," Helmut said, "why isn't it good enough for ours?"

The overseer seemed flustered by that.

Perhaps it was true, perhaps Escuela Mariscal José Felix Estigarribia didn't match colony education in German, but the point was, what option did we have? We would be living in Yalve Sanga, it was the only school there. We felt we'd been walking cheerfully, carelessly, along only to brush against one of those thorn bushes common in the Chaco with a thousand tiny invisible thorns which had now snagged us tight.

We soon discovered there were any number of pre-existing tensions around education for the children of Mission workers in Yalve Sanga, tensions far bigger than our one case. There were children coming up, one just a year behind our boy, who would need schooling too. Worker families had suggested a German teacher be hired to provide instruction at the Mission, an idea to which the overseer apparently responded, "*Blödsinn!*" Nonsense! Rumours swirled. The school director was unpopular because he didn't want to serve the staff children, the parents were frustrated by his attitude, the overseer was unable to assert his authority over the director. We absorbed some of these tensions, but for us it was all about our son, and our dilemma seemed obvious—how wasn't it clear to the people in charge?

Without our knowledge, Helmut's teacher sister got involved, pleading our case to the overseer herself. She must have persuaded him or worn him down, for he said he would take it to the executive committee, he didn't want to make the decision on his own. The committee then voted, also without our knowledge, and agreed to allow the boy in the school.

The director then agreed as well—what else could he do after a vote of the executive committee?—but reluctantly. "Only," he said, "if the parents take full responsibility." The message was conveyed to us.

I felt it time to speak to the man myself, find out what he meant by *full responsibility*. We'd heard so many gloomy reports about the school by now, reports that surged and then shrank and turned inside out as I waited in front of the director's house that day, surveying the sleepy green and brown peace of the place. I imagined our boy walking here, along that path, up the steps to the verandah, into one of those doors. I could see him doing that, couldn't I? Couldn't I? It helped that Helmut was sure we needed to persist, to stay the course; it helped that other Mission workers were cheering us on. I myself was sure one minute and doubted the next.

The director appeared, looking rumpled and as siesta-sleepy as the campus. Had I caught him in bed?

He didn't ask me into the house, didn't ask me to sit down outside. We faced each other on the path to the house in the day's suffocating yellow warmth.

I may have been sweating. My very correct aunt in Canada had once informed me that horses sweat and people perspire, but I was pregnant and the Chaco heat shunned semantical niceties. I'd been sweating a great deal for months.

I said I'd come to talk about my boy.

He said he knew what I'd come about.

I rehearsed the matter for him again. I felt I was keeping it low-key, reasonable. I was speaking German and I tried to use the right words.

"He'll be the only white boy in a sea of brown," the director said. He didn't look at me. From the beginning, he'd scarcely looked at me. I did my share of glancing off sideways as well, at the chairs on the *Schattendach*, at the house corner, at the pale ground at my feet. Both of us were nervous.

"He realizes that," I said toward his skittery non-gaze. "I think that will be okay."

"You have no idea how different they are," he said. "Some of the beginners have never even held a pencil."

Our son wouldn't know a word of Spanish, another child wouldn't know how to hold a pencil. There would be a lot for all of them to learn.

"He can come," he sighed, as if I ought to know he'd already agreed. "He can come if you take full responsibility."

He continued, his voice hard, "If it was me, I wouldn't experiment with my child like this."

His sentence was anguish to me. Did he think the precious boy a guinea pig we were trying outlandish ideas on? I gulped and told him some folks in Yalve Sanga were encouraging us to proceed. I told him I'd heard the teachers were kind and good, that the boy would surely be okay. I'd met his teacher. The woman's round blond face, her eager affability swam up to me.

He sighed again. "I only hope it won't damage him more than help."
I trembled. First *experiment,* then *damage.* He was defeating me.

"There won't be any special *Schutz* for him," he went on. "No special
protection."

"Well," I said, suddenly indignant rather than afraid and making my
German as precise as possible, "we're not asking for special protection, for
a bodyguard or something, but surely when we've paid for his schooling, a
fee we're paying the same as everyone else, when we pay and thus entrust
him to your keeping in exchange for so many hours a day, surely we can
expect some kind of care and oversight on your part. The same protection
you surely give *every* student entrusted into your care."

He looked at me and I sensed a tiny shift. I was relieved I'd stated my
point clearly enough for him to acknowledge. We were trying to do the
right thing by our child, I reiterated, that was all.

"He can come," he said. "But I just—"

"We'll review it," I said. "Let's talk again three weeks in. *Kommt Zeit,
kommt Rat,* time will show us what to do." Helmut and I had already
decided that if it wasn't working out for our son, we would withdraw him.

He nodded again. We said goodbyes. They were brief but cordial.

Still, I walked away feeling thwarted. If he only knew how it tore
me half to pieces to surrender my six-year-old to a new, strange school.
Kindergarten was nothing in comparison. It would be hard enough letting
him go into this new stage of his life, but even harder here, the *youngest,
the only white child in a sea of brown.* Whom no one but we would dare
experiment with.

REGRET, WITH ITS etymological suggestion of *weep over again,* is too
strong perhaps for what I feel—looking back—about our decision to send
our firstborn to the Yalve Sanga school, but it's close enough. This is the
situation that distressed me most when I began looking back into our years
in Paraguay. It was as if I was still caught in the dilemma, still puzzling
over the best solution, still surprised it turned into such a big deal. I heard
the director's words again and knew they didn't come true, which didn't
mean that the boy wasn't the youngest, and *the only,* and in that respect
even something of an experiment. It doesn't mean either that the next two
school years were some relentlessly feel-good tale, like movies that pit a
David-figure against a Goliath and have him emerge the winner. He did
well but like many children's experiences of school, it wasn't perfect either.

I've wondered why I didn't simply school him at home. Homeschooling wasn't as common then as now but it had arisen in our deliberations. In hindsight, I realize we had an exaggerated sense of what school provides children in their first years of attendance. Academically he would have had no trouble adjusting to school in Canada. He was a bright kid, and in truth already more or less done with Grade One. But we thought going to school was a rung on the developmental ladder every child had to step on, in the proper order, at the right time.

I also felt he needed the structure, the routine, though it may have been me who needed the structure of him going to school. I was pregnant and low in strength and struggled to manage the architecture of our days. It was hard to channel the boys' relentless energy. And though I loved to read to the boys and to transmit knowledge informally, I wasn't a natural teacher.

The reasons we laid out for the overseer and director were real. We knew we would be asked to extend our two-year term, and the adequate education of our children would play a huge role in that decision. And we'd picked up the concerns of other Yalve Sanga families with children reaching school age and hoped we could make a difference for them.

Fine, so it all worked out. But why agonize now, in the return of memoir, about those school years so long gone and irreversible?

On one occasion when these memories pierced my consciousness, I confessed to our oldest son—long an adult with children of his own—that I was sorry we sent him into that Yalve Sanga school environment, into the resistance of that director. He said, as considerate grown sons are apt to do, "Oh Mom, that was fine! Stop worrying. It was good. It was all good."

Had he forgotten the tears and fears? It seemed he had. What I'd remembered, he'd forgotten. He hadn't known how fierce we'd been on his behalf, hadn't known either that he was the ambassador of our ideals and tenacious opinions. We'd vowed to be positive about the school and contribute what we could to its welfare, even help break walls that had risen between the school and the Yalve Sanga community. Through him.

I'd told the director in our conversation outside his house that we weren't trying to prove anything. But of course we were trying to prove something. This is what parents do.

I've noticed something else. Writing this while churning with regret, perplexed that we memoirists take on the past as if we can change it even though we can't, wondering why it's hard to let it go—well, in the exercise of that, there was a change. Recalling it, posing the questions about our decision—all of that helped. It was as if I'd walked away from the director's house lighter and older, no longer carrying the regret but delivered of it. After writing the scene, I mean. The children, too, delivered from every kind of adjustment and grief. For a while at least, I was soothed. I saw our oldest son, a small white kid with his darker-skinned classmates, and remembered how they enjoyed him, though a few teased him for some long-lost reasons of their own. I recalled how he made friends. How he shone as a tiny light, not because of his skin colour but on account of the smile of his personality and his learning capacity. The memories hardened like a bridge and I crossed over it.

On that side I even found sympathy for the director of Escuela Mariscal José Felix Estigarribia. I imagined another meeting, or maybe the same one again, except this time I invited myself to be seated on the *Schattendach*. We'd later heard he was under some scrutiny, censure perhaps, not because of his inadequacy as an administrator but because he smoked. On the sly. What we heard was true, but the imagined part is this: he may have had some troubles himself as a schoolboy and felt himself unprotected. I was amused about the displeasure of his superiors over his smoking because it seemed so typical of religious communities, how easily we latch on to superficial signs of behaviour for disapproval rather than something more core in the character that might make a person miserable or unsuited for their position. In this scenario I invited him to go ahead and have a cigarette while we discussed the matter of Grade One for the six-year-old boy. A cigarette might have relaxed him, and the scent of it coiling into my nostrils would have mellowed me too.

LATER SOMETHING else showed up in the process of writing this memoir, to which I've also assigned the label *healing*. I spent two days at a Mennonite archival centre in Winnipeg, paging through old issues of the *Mennoblatt* from the years we lived in Paraguay. I wanted to refresh my memories of the colony context of those years. Suddenly I spotted our son's name in an article about the Mariscal Estigarribia school. I'd seen it at the time— even pasted it into our son's scrapbook, he informed me later—but had completely forgotten it.

The report, published July 1, 1983, was called *"Bunt durcheinander gewürfelt,"* Colourfully mixed together. Written by the director. It was delightfully cheerful. He described how on February 25 and 26 of that year some 110 students were registered at the school and how orderly those first days were as everyone assessed their classmates and their teachers, got used to the place, heard new accents, began to test the limits.

And what a variegated bunch, he wrote, in origin, language, skin colour, and age.

> Why, 31-year-old Juan in the sixth class could be the father of six-year-old _____ [our boy's name] in the first; was not the father though. The one was brown and spoke mainly Lengua [Enlhet] or Guarani, the other was white and spoke mainly English or German.

There he was, named and established in the mix. It was a surprise like joy to see him in the middle of these paragraphs, especially because the director sounded fond and patient and even proud about the 1983 year at Escuela Mariscal Estigarribia and his oldest and youngest students and everyone in between. Our son also appeared as a number in the breakdown of the first two grades which shared a classroom and the young blond teacher: 5 Argentinian, 2 Chulupi [Nivaclé], 2 Guarani, 17 Paraguayan, 1 Mennonite.

This sighting gave me a last dab of salve for my anguish over putting him in that school.

9. Home

"We're home," I announced with a sigh. I'd begun to lose hope of this moment, but now, on this Friday afternoon, February 25, 1983, at the end of the summer school holidays, it had finally arrived for us and our truck load of possessions. The roof of the house glinted and gleamed as we approached, the silvery-blue metal too industrial-looking for a red-brown dwelling laid upon roughly turned brown earth, but it's how the newer homes were built, the metal sheets the most cost-efficient material and the large low-pitch construction the most effective for collecting rainwater. It shone and stretched and covered the house like a shield, like a space-age surveillance aircraft tied down by verandah posts on a bare field, but incongruence aside, it was all utterly welcoming.

The younger boy must have detected the relief in my voice. "Mommie," he asked, "will we live in this house for the rest of our lives?"

"Not forever," I laughed. "But a long time." Long at least in the measure of his child-size comprehension, long enough to feel like long. He and his brother clamored out of the truck, dashed indoors to find the room they would share. They had gotten in the way of the men loading furniture in Filadelfia just once, in their eagerness to get their small suitcases with toys loaded too, but otherwise they'd been behaving with near perfection. And now they could call at their bliss through the screens, run inside and out, race round and round the verandah. They might as well let Yalve Sanga know we'd arrived.

I've lived in houses I've loved, and houses I've struggled to love. I loved this one immediately—perhaps because it was new, perhaps because we'd incorporated our ideas and ideals—a relatively small house that nevertheless seemed roomy and was efficient.

It wasn't quite finished yet: the fireplace had to be bricked, tile baseboards placed, walls caulked one more time, doors and window frames painted, curtains hung. It seemed naked without curtains. But it was fine. All so fine. This was good bones and skin, and it would soon be dressed. I had brought curtain fabric from Canada in cream and soft teal with a thinly rubberized underside to aid against heat as well as a light fixture frame to wrap in the same fabric for an informal chandelier over the table. The house would be relatively plain otherwise, nothing fancy, furnished with a stiff wine-red faux leather two-seater sofa and some chairs passed along from others, a table and chairs, our beds. But there would be a fireplace for winter cold and a bookshelf beside it and those curtains, and the house was new, and roomy, and I liked it enormously.

It sat on the outer rim of the Yalve Sanga community, on a large field previously covered in buffalo grass. Several algarroba trees, young and airy, their fern-like fronds almost coquettish in the breeze, marked one side of the field. When the Mennonites first arrived in the Chaco, everyone looked for a *Schattenspendenden Baum*, a shade-dispensing tree, to set down beside, but we had only these few, too removed from the house to be useful. The wide verandah would be our shade instead. There was roadway on two sides and crop land to the south, the Enlhet Co-op and pasture to the east, an experimental field to the west. On the north were other residences.

Wide open, the site breathed. Just like the Canadian plains.

Two building spots had been proposed for the new house: this particular field and another lot backing into bush. We'd said that we were okay with either. But I'd hoped, I confess, for this one with its frank accessibility, with its evocative link to an earlier sense of myself. I grew up in central Alberta where low rolling hills rippled from the Rockies toward the vast prairie like an ocean wave coming to rest on a beach. I can't recall consciously studying my environment as a girl, neither do I understand the sequence by which children process their first places, but I absorbed most vitally the two immense, infinite planes of ground and sky. The first home of my childhood that I can recall was tucked into a mild valley near a railway station and grain elevator and the church where my father was minister. The terrain was generally treeless, and always, it seemed, I could see all of it, the horizon in the distance, and just as far, the azure vault of sun and clouds and sky. It seems a miracle to me how one can move so smoothly out of a dark womb into the knowledge of the Above-us and Beneath-us, and love its appearance without question the way an infant loves its mother, thinks her beautiful, the specifics of that first knowledge becoming one's sense of original creation and the version of what's most pleasing to the eye. The child is born and she looks and sees and notions of attraction are born in her too.

My husband grew up in the flat Chaco and his childhood home was at the then-edge of Filadelfia. This location pleased us both. We would plant trees of course; Helmut intended a citrus orchard. We would plant a castor bean hedge along the west side of the house, which grew from seeds into a full-fledged barrier almost as quickly as the magical vine in the tale of Jack and the Beanstalk. But none of these plantings would inhibit the vast air and openness to light, the access to sunrise and sunset.

Helmut began to set up the beds and I tossed supper together in my astonishing U-shaped kitchen—fridge and gas stove on the ends of the U, counters and sink and cupboards ranging across in the middle. We ate and he carried on with the beds and the boys played and I set water to heat for my first round of dishes in the sink. I would have to heat water for dishes and laundry in this house as I did in the other, except on days when the water in the elevated outside tank got hot in the sun, but heating water was of no consequence whatsoever. Not compared to the thrill of water swooshing down the drain when I finished the dishes. After seven months of carrying used kitchen water outside in a pail, it seemed the most marvellous sound in the world. Which some women never hear their entire lives, I knew, but happiness is relative, isn't it? That day, because of dishwater disappearing down the drain, my heart was a helium balloon.

On Sunday I scrounged for writing paper and managed to find some. I hadn't written my parents for a while, what with the move, and before that, whole days spent going back and forth to Yalve Sanga to varnish doors and frames, to paint the insides of the kitchen cupboard with a liquid solution against cockroaches, a preemptive manoeuvre—and the only one necessary, I hoped—in the perpetual battle with insects here. I was tolerant of spiders but cockroaches with their arrogant long feelers and ants with their infallible sense of finding and getting into food were, for me, strictly and screamingly *verboten*.

I wrote how busy we'd been, preparing on one end, packing on the other. How heavy rains had set things back. The younger son told me to be sure to say that we'd moved. Dear boy, I thought, what else was there to talk about? It was the main event, the only one. But just because moving was the main event didn't mean it filled a letter. A letter had to earn the price of a stamp. I could say I had come down with the flu, that I was teary-eyed and exhausted and clumsy with pregnancy too, though by the time the letter was read I was sure to be better. Helmut had just recovered from the same but now it was my turn, and both boys were listless and feverish too. All they'd done today was eat and sleep.

Ah, a flock—or a swarm, was it? a congregation? ah, yes, a pandemonium—of bright green parrots settled into a tree in the nearby field, all of them jabbering at once. Did their racket mean anything? *Cow, cow, cow.* No cows here, I wanted to shout back at them, but dear God, I was much too happy to have landed here at last and much too tired, too sick, to shout. Perhaps the parrots heard the English syllables floating toward them from under the gleaming grey roof, perhaps they were simply trying, in their mischievous parroty way, to say Hello. They were a racket and a nuisance but they gave me the gift of a closing paragraph for the letter.

HOME: A WORD widely and variously applied. People leave, seek, miss, reach it. Though probably never reach it entirely. We'd used *home* seven months for the rental in Filadelfia. We used it when we talked with expat friends: *back home*, we would say, meaning places like Canada or the United States but also the everything of culture and traditions there. Home could be mobile. I felt *at home* in certain people's company or when Helmut and the children and I were spatially close, say in the truck or lined up close in a church pew. Which made me think it was really a category of *with whom* rather than location, though it seemed true when I was alone as well, when I could forget the rest of the family for a while, simply be the *me, myself, and I* of my own being, the human trinity at home with its ontological existence. As I write these pages, home floats within a trinity of time as well: the then-present of pleasure and belonging and responsibility which has become the past of nostalgia and memory, the then-future which is the now still containing everything that shaped and formed me there.

In 1983, in the now of then, *home* travelled to Yalve Sanga with us, flexible in meaning but wishing only to harden into our younger boy's "forever." A place of relief like a hammock. In spite of temporary illness and the work that had to be done to finish it, settle, get ready for the baby, I lowered my soul into this home's deep curve. The months spent in Filadelfia between our arrival back to the Chaco and arrival at our assignment destination disappeared behind us.

Yalve Sanga, meaning *pool of the armadillo* in the Enlhet language, is a roughly triangular tract of land almost smack in the middle of the Chaco's three Mennonite colonies. The TransChaco Highway runs alongside and through part of it. Half was Enlhet settlement, half Nivaclé. At that time, although I don't have the exact figures, there were perhaps a thousand people in each group.

There were some eight or so *indígena* settlements in the area, but Yalve Sanga was the oldest and most populated. While the name Yalve Sanga referred to the entire settlement, the small community that formed the administrative centre of the Mission and settlements, as well as the Indigenous church association, also bore that name. The centre wasn't large.

The villages of the Enlhet and Nivaclé surrounding the centre were laid out much as Mennonite villages were, houses on either side of a single street. The villages had Indigenous names but biblical names as well, like Nazareth, Caesarea, Joppa, Bethania, and Tiberia. When my parents wrote that they were planning a visit to Israel, I suggested they could come to the Chaco for their "holy land tour" instead.

There was no village called Jerusalem, however. Perhaps the Mission centre could have qualified, a complicated place both loved and wept over. The school compound, of which I've already spoken, lay somewhat unto itself to the west. There was also a Bible school building with one-room student houses, a small hospital and clinic, a central office building for agricultural and administrative concerns, and various staff residences. To me, Yalve Sanga the centre had the feel of a community sprung up unexpectedly and now adjusting this way and that as needed, like a roving band of wanderers who'd parked their caravans at an oasis—this *tajamar*, waterhole—discovered in the midst of thorns and bushland. Compared to Filadelfia with its wide streets and hanging dust, its busy enterprise, its striving for straight lines and as much attractiveness of yard as could be managed against the odds, Yalve Sanga seemed careless—pretty enough, to be sure, but disheveled. Windblown. It clustered itself around several roads at straight angles but there were shortcut paths to everywhere as if roads were redundant when the place was entirely walkable from end to end.

The centre bustled at times but was just as likely to be relaxed, cheerfully nonchalant, resigned to its existence in the Chaco rather than resistant to it as Mennonite towns and villages seemed to be. Was it because no staff owned their houses? Felt, therefore, no obligation to make a good impression? We tried to maintain our properties, as good missioners should, but perhaps we absorbed the inevitable temporality of our presence, or perhaps subconsciously deemed it wise to blend into the similarly untidy and relaxed environment of our Indigenous neighbours.

To imagine caravans may imply a homogenous community, but it was not. Besides Indigenous staff of the two groups, there were Mennonites from the surrounding three colonies working in the various programs—mechanics, agriculturalists, doctors, nurses, cooks, teachers, advisors of various kinds, social workers, and more. There were also staff from Europe, the U.S.A., and Canada. A whole handful of agencies—local, government, international—had money or people invested in projects which related and intertwined in ways I never bothered to figure out. Besides us, there were some ten couples or families and maybe fifteen to twenty singles living on site. Others drove into the settlement every day for their work, just as Helmut had the past months. Indigenous staffers lived in the surrounding villages, though a few resided in the centre too. The people who worked and lived in Yalve Sanga shifted frequently, almost continuously it seemed, those whose terms ended being farewelled at a Sunday afternoon coffee and others initiated at the next.

Weekends the place could seem almost deserted, on the non-boarding-school side at least, as staff returned to their families or visited in the Mennonite colonies. There was no regular church though an informal get-together or service was occasionally planned. We usually attended church in Filadelfia once a month. But there was always someone around if it was other people we wanted for a morning or afternoon round of *terere* and gossip, and always there was this lovely hodgepodge and green randomness surrounding us, the gallant young algarroba trees along the edge of the property doing their best and the stately eucalyptus at the far end of the field doing even better, fruit trees and orchids and potted plants, houses new or sagging. Diversity, congeniality, gossip, yes, and arguments. As many opinions about the Mission as there were mission workers. Always there was home, this home into which we sank one day after the other with what mostly felt like fondness and peace.

SOON AFTER WE moved, Helmut and the bulldozer crew did a job a great distance from Yalve Sanga. He didn't like to take on work that far away, but the machine station was supposed to be self-sustaining so he accepted contracts where they came. I couldn't visualize where they were going, I didn't keep a map in my head, though we hung a calendar version of the Mennonite colonies map on the wall; I could have pinpointed the destination if I'd asked but I didn't orient myself to the details of his work any more than he oriented himself to the details of mine. Even remembering where things were stored in their cupboards seemed beyond his capacity much of the time, as was mine at placing which Indigenous settlement or *estancia* the machines were working in now. I rarely drove in the Chaco, that was part of it, not having a vehicle at my disposal, and simply a passenger to the larger scheme of Chaco roads.

He would stay the week with the men. They bunked in the yellow *Buda*, trailer, and cooked and ate outside. During a slow period, the crew had re-painted the wooden trailer and it rolled along now in the entourage of truck and machines looking as sunny as a crate of lemons.

Back in Yalve Sanga, our older son started school. The first morning, he cried. He said he hated getting up in the dark. (School started at 7:15, the sun rose about seven in the current season.) The light from the kitchen—a comforting glow evenings when he drifted into sleep—seemed shrill and too white mornings, he wanted to blink it away. But he got up and then the first day of school was done with and after that he usually went willingly enough. All in all, it was going better than we'd hoped. He ate his breakfast of bread and jam, cheese and milk (the beloved and expensive Corn Flakes a treat for occasional Sundays), and then I watched him walking small but confidently away from me, scholarly in the school uniform of dark pants and white jacket shirt, until I couldn't see him anymore, and every day he went *mit Gebet begleitet*—accompanied with prayer. He stayed in school until ten, then came home for play, lunch, and siesta, and in the afternoon returned to the school for an hour and a half or so to do homework. This, for the beginners, was nothing more than busy work to give structure to the day since most of the students were boarders. As the director so persistently insisted, our son could not be an exception and had to show up for "homework" too. He didn't mind; he seemed quite content, in fact, to colour and work with clay, or to fill practice pages of *1*'s, *a*'s, and *o*'s in cursive.

Three weeks in, we did the promised check-in with the school director and Grade One teacher. My conversation with the director was short; we didn't re-hash our views. He agreed that things seemed to be going well. I couldn't tell if he was surprised by this. I was careful to seem neither surprised nor unsurprised. Then I invited his teacher for an afternoon coffee. She seemed too young, too placid, to manage a classroom of children, but our son liked her and she liked him and this mattered most. We traded warmth and friendliness and sipped at our coffee—always instant here— and nibbled at sweets, and perhaps each of us acted for the sake of the other. Each of us was at the beginning of our respective positions, testing the inevitable mutual wariness of teachers and parents. Scholastically, the Miss reported, he was doing well. He was trying hard to learn the Spanish language. Socially, language barriers isolated him somewhat but he wasn't doing too badly.

I cautiously asked about reports he brought home of rough-and-tumble interactions and the teacher said there was a bully who'd been a problem at the school before. Our son, she said, handled himself well. This is what a mother wants to hear, but I also knew more, knew better than the teacher that the child would hide his fear. When I told Helmut about the bully later, he seemed as unconcerned as the teacher. Tussles and nastiness are par for the world, he figured, they would occur in any schoolyard the boy would land. I suppose he was thinking of the adult world of the Mission too. At any rate he was sure his eldest would be fine.

Meanwhile, our younger son adjusted to being without his brother during the school hours. The boys were compatible in their love of Lego and games of pretend, completely alike in their capacity to scrap and just as suddenly be the best of friends. Both of them loved to go along with their father if allowed. "Three big Daddies, marching off!" the youngest declared, as the boys strutted after him down the driveway one day after siesta.

Now, however, I could more easily observe the differences of personality. When the older boy played alone, he usually sang or produced sound of some sort. He *brummed* while riding his bike. He serenaded himself while sitting on the toilet. "I'm a boy with songs!" he told me one day, as if I hadn't noticed. The younger might talk to himself but I didn't hear him sing. He amused himself for hours at various little games and explorations, moving about as if by stealth, as if one idea led to the next. The privilege of going along with his father now fell most often to him and nothing of it seemed to discomfort him, not the heat, dirt, long rides, or waiting for the work to be done and the trip home for supper. He hung about as workmen built a brick path to our house and dug the foundation for a supply garage and a hole for the outhouse. I watched from the kitchen window as he hopped onto the wheelbarrow each time one of them returned from dumping his load. He didn't tire of jumping on for his ride, it seemed, and I was grateful that the men let him do it, over and over. The Indigenous men were patient and kind with our boys. I noticed they had a forbearing spirit with their own children too.

10. With whom

THE BOYS SQUEEZED against me on the short red sofa, one on either side, pressed as close and determined to me as Velcro. I opened *The Lion, the Witch and the Wardrobe*, read the title and author. C.S. Lewis. I'd given in, said okay, we would start. I'd purchased the book from an expat's leaving sale and both boys had been paging about in it, fascinated by the illustrations: children tumbling out of a cupboard, beavers eating at a table, a strange creature with a goat's bottom and man's top, who was Tumnus the faun though they don't know that yet. This half-and-half creature walked with a girl through a forest filled with snow, holding an umbrella over them both.

They begged and begged me to read it to them and I'd been resisting. I thought they were too young for it. The book seemed important, and necessary for them too, but the timing had to be right. The older boy would ask the meaning of every single word he didn't understand and there were sure to be many such words. He thought I was a dictionary on legs.

Worn down by their pleas, I finally said yes, and now I was expectant and eager too.

"Once there were four children," I began, "whose names were Peter, Susan, Edmund and Lucy. This story is about something that happened to them when they were sent away from London during the war because of the air-raids. They were sent to the house of an old Professor who lived in the heart of the country, ten miles from the nearest railway station and two miles from the nearest post office . . . "

The boys were rapt. Not even four sentences in—clear, purposeful sentences with an excellent read-aloud sway to them—and I could practically feel them listening, as if everything around them had been carved back to reveal in sharp relief their keen receptivity. They held themselves motionless so not a word from my mouth would escape their notice. They held themselves on to me and the strong rails of the story and we were on our way, from this red sofa to England, to Narnia.

And evening after evening we went there, through this book, and the rest of the Narnia series, and many other books as well, roaming the countryside and characters, until each story was done.

ON A WEDNESDAY evening at the end of March, we boarded the night bus for Asunción and hoped we'd be able to sleep, the boys nearly beside themselves with excitement. We were on vacation. Vacating the Chaco, that is, vacating our regular, ordinary, daily lives *to be empty, free, or at leisure.* We'd often travelled with the children, but always to visit grandparents or other relatives, or come to Paraguay. This was our first family holiday just for us.

Helmut and I settled one boy each against ourselves, surrendering to be curl and pillow and sleep-wrap for child-limbs while trying to doze off too. It was no thorough sleep for me but envelopment in a skewed narrative of dreams, the rhythmic movement of the bus, intrusions of yellow light and crisp voices into the warm dark on our occasional stops. We reached the MennoHeim in Asunción at four in the morning. The night watchman opened the gate for us and we staggered in and took a room. Helmut chased a cockroach off one cot and more cockroaches scurried into the drain when I flicked on the bathroom light but I was too tired to care.

At seven, we were awake again. We dressed, then ate breakfast, then headed downtown. Then, and then, and then: the itinerary of holidays, one new and potentially interesting experience after the other. The boys were thrilled with the harbour and the old town's bustle and buildings grander than the Chaco's, they walked block after block without complaining, though it's true, they nibbled at their restaurant lunch and then announced their hunger afterward, barely outside the restaurant, and one of them wanted a popsicle, didn't his parents know, why had they ordered him an ice-cream cone, and thus the family holiday was well underway in every respect, from enthusiasm to eventual weariness and whining.

We had to get some paperwork looked after as well. The officials we met treated Helmut as Paraguayan, even though he'd emigrated thirteen years ago and become a citizen of Canada. They issued him a *cedula*, a legal residency card, but would not issue one to me. Explanations and entreaties about us being in the country as a married couple with joint purpose and two-and-a-half children had no effect. The men at their desks collected money to stamp an extension on my visa and told me I would have to leave the country every three months to renew it. There was nothing to do but accept this for now, impractical, even impossible, as such a regimen would be. We could only hope someone at the Mission office would help straighten it out.

On Friday, we rolled out of the city in another full bus, through the lush countryside and rust red earth of eastern Paraguay, through towns and villages with houses in pastel pink or blue or green and glimpses of churches, the roadway frequently fronted by sellers of clay pots, lace, crafts, kitsch, foodstuffs and fruit, enticements of colour, through forests exuberant with trees and vines climbing and hanging on like affectionate monkeys, toward Iguazu Falls across the border into Brazil. I'd travelled this route when Helmut introduced me to Paraguay seven years earlier, and then again on a tour we took during our four-month visit, but I wasn't tired of it. No wonder, I thought, this region's early reputation as a New World Eden, no wonder it attracted adventurers, conquistadors, runners-away in search of paradise or riches, though the rumoured silver and gold was never there but in Peru, and in the meanwhile the iron-red ground soaked up generations of suffering and blood, though it was hard to believe as I peered out the bus windows at the *tranquilo* happiness and startling fecundity with which it seemed blessed.

I was also struck again with the beauty of the Paraguayan people. The majority of Paraguay's inhabitants are *mestizos*, mixed European and Amerindian, with perhaps five percent "other," including Indigenous tribal groups and a relatively sizeable German population, among them the Mennonites in their various manifestations. A stone bas-relief on the outside of Asunción's cathedral, donated by a former Spanish ambassador, portrayed the arrival of Spanish conquistador Domingo Martinez de Irala, the sixteenth-century governor of the territory and "father of Paraguay," in mutual embrace with a Guarani chieftain surrounded by lithesome, fruit-bedecked Guarani women. The historical facts weren't quite as pretty as the scene in stone, for if the Guarani welcomed the Spanish as allies against other warring tribes and offered their women as a token of that alliance, they soon found themselves in servitude, the conquerors taking large numbers of concubines (Irala claimed seventy) and everyone forced into agricultural labour for the rulers' ends. "Genetic colonisation," writer John Gimlette calls it, with the result that when the conquistadors' days were over, the country was in the hands of "its half-breeds, the new Paraguayans."

Paraguayans are proud of their unique racial construction and fiercely patriotic. Paraguay is also unique in South America for being the only country where an Indigenous language—Guarani—is considered an official language. Spanish survived as the more official language perhaps, but Guarani is widely spoken as the language of the heart and home, except of course by the "other" people. The speaking of Guarani, like Low German among Chaco Mennonites, isn't linked to class. Apparently even president Alfredo Stroessner liked nothing better than to hold forth in it.

The perceptions gathered from the week-long tour Helmut and I had taken a year earlier doubled up on me now as we holidayed forth. I felt again the distinct differences in the two regions of the country: the verdant green of these hills and plains east of the Paraguay River and, on the other side, in the Chaco, a green that was small-leaved and huddled close, each stalk cooperating tightly for an impression of silence. I remembered Helmut's uncle, who'd grown up in Russia and settled in the Chaco, saying—after several days on the tour in Eastern Paraguay—"I still haven't seen anywhere here I'd like to build a house." Someone chimed agreement, and I thought about how places eventually work their way into the marrow of the soul, how they become the home one prefers above all others. Though really? I thought. Nowhere here?

The highway unwound past towns where the Jesuit missions of the seventeenth and eighteenth centuries lay in ruins but this not being a tour bus there was no stopping this time, just the memory of what I'd learned about the astonishing empire the Black Robes forged, both protective of "their Indians," and paternalistic, all of which would double forward for me again some four years later with the release of *The Mission*, a favourite movie because of its spectacular scenery, story, and music, and the dilemmas it explored but didn't solve. The legacy of colonization, the legacy of the Church. The serpents of power and greed in Paradise. And its unforgettable scene of slave trader Rodrigo Mendoza, lugging the symbols of his former life around him in a net while seeking redemption and finally reaching it at the hands of the people he'd enslaved and harmed. His tears and then the laughter of the Guarani, the priests, and Mendoza himself—it was the best representation of forgiveness I'd ever seen.

We reached the border. I hate borders, hate how arbitrary they are, how official they have to be, how they make me fear, even believe I've done something wrong when I haven't. The churlish suspicion of borders just by being borders. How in spite of the same soil, same sky on one side as the other, lines on a map can produce entirely different histories and sensibilities. "What if borders at their most basic are just desires written onto lands and lives," asks Kate Harris in *Lands of Lost Borders*, "trying to foist permanence on the fact of flux?"

Twice we disembarked the bus, once at the Paraguayan border, once at the Brazilian. I was nervous both times but tried not to show it. We had to give up 2,500 guaranies, about $12, because an official in a booth said my visa, which we'd just renewed in Asunción, had expired. We didn't argue. One didn't argue when there were soldiers who seemed impossibly young standing by with guns, one didn't say the official in the booth wasn't reading the paper the way it was written, or the way it was meant to be read.

But then we were through and it wasn't the end of the world but only another country, and we found a hotel in the town Foz do Iguazu, and the hotel was pastel-pretty and clean and comfortable and the price was reasonable and palm trees waved in the courtyard and altogether we felt touristy and special and could easily recall we were on vacation. After shopping—shoes and clothes were cheap in Brazil—and a nap and supper, we wandered the streets of Foz and when we chanced on an amusement park with merry-go-rounds and other kiddie rides and a snack shop that swirled up milkshakes like we were used to from Canada, the boys decided it had been a perfect day.

The next morning, after stuffing ourselves at the huge Brazilian breakfast buffet, we bussed to our holiday's ultimate destination: Iguazu Falls. I recalled how eager I'd been to show Helmut the Niagara Falls on our honeymoon trip from Manitoba to Ontario. "Is this it?" he'd asked, sounding unimpressed. I was upset. How could he ask such a question, in such a tone, about this Canadian treasure? He'd done his best then to restore the delicate harmony of our brand-new marriage and it was the only discordant note of the entire trip, but the disappointment registered. Later, however, when we flew to Paraguay to meet his family and he'd taken me to see *his* falls, I had to say, "Oh, now I get it." Iguazu isn't one set of falls, but a whole necklace of them, each view along the walkway more wondrous than the last. And here it was again, a tableau of thunder-spilling water, black rocks shining in the mist, greenhouse-green foliage.

But this time we were keenly aware of this as something our sons were seeing too. I watched them as much as I watched the falls. I watched their eyes taking everything in. The first narrow falls like a pour of milk from a pitcher, a cry of praise. The larger falls homage too, but a roar of terror instead of worship, the sheer unexpected drop of it over the precipice shattering the river's hope for equanimity.

The boys liked the falls, but liked the butterflies as much, Iguazu Falls being one of the world's best places to see butterflies. They flittered everywhere, their flights seeming random and unconcerned, like play, and the boys pounced after them, exclaiming about this design, that colour—lime green, vermilion, turquoise, blue on black, and more. Winged creatures dressed in a splendor that belied the brevity of their existence, beside the endlessly falling falls, the endlessly rising spray.

Back at the tropical hotel, the oldest boy complained about earache. I had a small pharmacy of ear and eye drops and Tylenol in our bags, and did what I could for him, sympathetic to his moans because I suffered terrible earaches as a child. His brother calmly coloured a Santa Claus in his colouring book and seemed fine but was coughing and I feared he would be next.

Sure enough. The older boy was his usual cheerful self the next morning but the younger one moped, feeling ill. Good thing he could sleep on the bus. We wouldn't visit the massive Itaipu Dam, largest hydroelectric dam in the world, which Helmut and I had viewed under construction the previous year. It wouldn't mean much to them at this point, no need to cram their heads full of interesting facts about how much concrete, iron, and steel it took, how much rock and soil were moved, how many people were required to build it (about 40,000) and how many died in the process (149). Nor did we mention the Guaria Falls, which disappeared on account of the dam, and certainly not the news that haunted me when I heard it, the dozens of people who tumbled into Guaria's depths—falling like the falls—as they crowded forward for a final look and the suspension bridge they were on collapsed. Earaches were calamity enough for one holiday.

I STARTED THIS journey back to my 1980s Chaco because the 2015 Mennonite/s Writing VII conference in Fresno, California chose "Movement, Transformation, Place" as its theme and I proposed a paper titled "Visitor, outsider, pilgrim: What in the world was I doing in the Chaco?" I planned a personal essay that would interrogate the positions I'd found myself in at various times while there: a tourist/visitor trying to see, a resident outsider trying to belong, perhaps a pilgrim with a quest. I would also consider how that place affected my writing.

The proposal was accepted but circumstances of Helmut's health led me to withdraw from the conference. But since I'd begun thinking about movement, transformation, place, and since I'd been reading my Chaco journals and letters in preparation, I decided to work on the piece anyways, which eventually evolved into this longer recollection and reflection.

I supposed the narrative would include my husband and children. They would have to be there, on the periphery I supposed, of my probes into "what in the world was I doing in the Chaco." Periphery was fine. But it wasn't long before I realized that these other humans had affected my sense of place at every turn, that my roles as wife and mother were key to its themes of belonging and identity. They influenced, in ways both limiting and enlarging, my entire engagement with the Chaco.

This creates dilemmas. I've rarely included my children in my writing. Back in the days when I wrote articles, I wrote a few on the day-to-day of the young parent's life, the constant demands and stresses, in which my children were the jumping-off point. I embarked on the topic because of them but wrote to work out answers for myself. If I used anecdotes about them, I asked their permission. But mostly the mentions were general. I felt strongly that their lives belonged to themselves and were sacrosanct as far as implicating them in my work. Blogs didn't exist when they were young, but I'm sure I could not have been a Mommie-blogger.

I'm not sure why I felt—and feel—this so rigidly. Is it fear of embarrassing them, fear of them hating me for it? Poor Christopher Robin, miserable about the uses to which his name and childhood and teddy bear were put by his father, A.A. Milne. Surely his father had no intention of making him miserable; perhaps he even considered the stories an act of love. Bad enough for my children that I'm a writer, putting my own life into the public, though thankfully not famous as Milne was. I expected they would eventually recognize that writers inevitably create personas, or are created in some way by readers, but why make the children characters if I didn't have to?

Or do I fear they may step up with counter stories of their own, about me?

Writing memoir, these matters are real and urgent for me. I see that it's impossible to write from my life without touching upon those in my intimate circle. Writers reach different conclusions about the extent to which the lives of family members may be "exploited" for narrative purposes, and I don't want to judge those who decide differently than I do, especially now that I've pushed over some of my own barriers by writing here about my children when young.

All this to say that here they are, my children, as inevitable and necessary as the weather, in this memoir about a place—here to an extent I didn't expect when I started. I began, after all, by remembering as an "I" and only in the story-forming process did the "they" wrapped in my skirts become obvious. The relationship with Helmut, though longer and closer, seems different somehow, I haven't worried as much about mentioning him, he was a parallel fact I could run alongside without worry, and what we shared he could corroborate. And he had his own Chaco work and stories.

But I find myself wondering, as an aside, if he'd written a memoir of these years, how and where would I figure into the narrative? And how and where would the children appear? Entry after entry in my father-in-law's diaries concerned his work; the children seldom showed up. I think of my father who, in his last decade, set down the story of his life. He claimed to be writing his memories for his children—who else?—but I think he was writing it for himself as a reminder and pleasure in having existed. Like many who embark on such a project, he expended a great deal of effort on his childhood and youth, which he seemed to remember best. When I typed his entire set of notes to duplicate for the family, I noticed that he scarcely mentioned his eight children. Not their births. Not his interactions with us. When I asked him about this, trying for a teasing tone, he replied with the faint indignation I still associate with him, "I was writing my story, not yours."

Touché.

But still. Not to mention us even in summary fashion? Is it a man thing, then, of its time, the work-infested diary of my father-in-law, the nearly childless record of my busy father?

And mine a matter of maternity? Perhaps. Living in that place—the Chaco—the children were the biggest part of my consuming daily work, they were the biggest item on my docket. At that stage, the word *home* was spoken as a circle with other people inside it. These people were my particular *with whom*. So, the children have to be here. They'll read this before it's published, they may comment. I've kept them apprised of their names through the drafts, from pseudo-names to real names to no names. Perhaps un-naming them in this final revision steps back as far as possible to shield them while speaking for myself, accepting vulnerability for myself while guarding theirs.

But, a few words in public to my offspring just the same:

You're the ones behind the references to children in these pages. But that was then, and now is now, and you're still your own hallowed, remarkable selves and so much more than the mentions my memories might convey. These are fragments of you. I've kept them relatively few. Your whole selves—that would be impossible. But we were together and one answer to the question of what in the world I was doing in Paraguay is this: I was doing the same thing there that I'd done before and would do after. I was being your mother. I wanted children and you fulfilled my best wishes for them. You—I see this more clearly now—made me belong. The brightest colours Paraguay offers in my memory were coloured by you.

11. Silence

THE YOUNGER BOY claimed he would be a bulldozer-man and work with "Daddy's Indians" when he grew up. The older boy's latest aspiration was scientist. We'd borrowed a set of Childcraft for a while and he spent hours with the books. The discoveries he made there about nature and how things worked were what he believed scientists did.

But when a Sunday school teacher asked the class what they wanted to be someday, he said, "*Taller-mensch.*" *Taller* is the Spanish word for garage and repair shop, used locally instead of the German equivalent, and *mensch* means person. Thus, a mechanic.

He related this to us after church. "I didn't know the German word for scientist," he said, "so I changed my mind."

"Well," I comforted him, "you can change your mind many times before you're all grown up and ready to be something."

A sweet and minor reversal, this change of goals, but it was another reminder of the power of language to restrain and shape, another reminder that language was core to my still-becoming. Who was I really? Here. When I had so little opportunity to be fully known via speech. In Filadelfia, I'd had a friend from Manitoba, English-speaking of course, with whom I'd felt instantly comfortable, but she had returned to Canada with her husband and five daughters for a three-month furlough. Helmut's family, especially the women, were as wonderful as ever; one had been a huge help in the move and all were unfailingly kind to the boys. They knew and loved me as their youngest brother's wife, they'd seen me now in many family scenarios, and it was comforting to adhere to them, to be loved by virtue of a bond decided by my husband and me. Belonging to clan or family is a force, it wraps like a cocoon. It can be a prod to conformity, also true, and can be too exclusive at times, but mostly I was relieved that we had a belonging not afforded many other expats.

But this was a German-speaking clan and within myself, I reiterated the old frustration: in German, thinking and talking seemed separate functions for me. Speaking was a clunking, squeaking, grinding procedure that wore me out in the midst of it. I felt I was saying things I didn't quite mean, or took shortcuts to the passably true, just like our son revising his ambition into words he could say to his teacher and classmates. Not lies exactly, but truths abridged, edited, and perhaps more than I knew, representing a midstream change of mind, fishing for words and hooking a tangle of reeds. Sometimes I put myself in the minds of Chaco sisters-in-law and acquaintances and realized how much work it must be to listen to and converse with me. I wearied on their behalf, feared it wouldn't be worth their effort, wanted to give them the freedom of another conversation just around the corner in which they could fly, be linguistically skyborne. I extrapolated my disquietude from incidents where I'd been on the other side of such conversations, talking with someone in English, say, who wasn't wholly proficient in English. Ordinarily, I realized, most of us don't care enough to stumble through mistakes and limited vocabularies to know someone deeply. It's too much like tugging a blanket through a peephole.

Ordinarily, a great deal of conversation is superficial. But how much more so when the speakers' mother tongues are not the same.

"No one knows what a great sense of humour I have," I lamented to Helmut after a family gathering. Since I understood most of what I heard, I had several times thought of a dandy bit of repartee I couldn't get to my tongue properly or fast enough. I liked to participate that way. I really did. I enjoy exchanging ideas, stories, points of view. Making a wee joke or two.

Then again, maybe it was good for me to let it flow around me, to listen. Isn't it essential for writers to be listeners above all, constantly and at any number of levels? In the etymology of *listening* are intriguing suggestions of glory and wonder: *to hear oneself called.* Attention, and connection. I was still trying to sneak in research and writing now and then, and listening yielded stories, details, local worldview. Snatches that summoned me to incorporate or ponder them.

And I certainly knew enough German to ask good questions.

Nevertheless, regarding wit: my family of origin often used humour as a shortcut for affection. Affection in Helmut's family was more overt. His was a family of hand-shakers (the men) and huggers (the women). It had been good for me to learn this, to become more of a hugger. Quite apart from the differences in family culture, though, wit wasn't exactly at the top of anyone's list for womanly virtues in Mennonite Paraguay. I admired the women of the Chaco, so competent they all seemed to be with food, with animals, with growing and harvesting things. They stirred up gallons of guava jam without Certo and lined their verandahs with exotic plants in pots that they remembered to water. They sewed and baked and cooked and faithfully observed the rituals of their faith. The roll call of their capabilities could go on and on. Some drove motorcycle. (When Helmut tried to teach me to drive his small Honda motorbike, I ran over the boys' Fischer-Price riding-horse and refused to take another lesson.)

The women of Helmut's family were no dour bunch—more than one sister had an infectiously noisy laugh—but they weren't big readers and wit wasn't high on the list either. It didn't have to be. Or, I should probably say, it may have been there, but I was missing the punchline nuances of another tongue.

I was lonely for wit. For the perception implied, and for the twist of it, the way it sees from other angles. For irony and paradox. Even quickness of speech would do. I didn't mind living relatively isolated in Yalve Sanga, I hadn't changed my mind about that, I was an introvert, but I was learning that the possibilities of loneliness are wide, and even when not experiencing loneliness as a continuous condition, a sliver-like absence could be a recurring prick of pain. Some assumption about life, some specific quality. A taste or smell available only elsewhere. A certain song. A friend, not just any kind of friend, but the kind you might telephone for no reason but to say Hello. The option of wit.

We didn't have a telephone. Not that I would call anyone anyway just to chat. Connecting to Filadelfia by phone was an ordeal of shouting and static and we had never attempted a long-distance call to Canada. It would be taken as bad news, as emergency. If a local call was absolutely necessary to arrange something or convey information, Helmut undertook it in the necessary shout from the radio-phone at the Mission office. (And even decades later he hadn't shaken the habit of raising his voice on the phone.)

I was lonely now for a friend with whom rapid, even short, but serious conversation might be possible, including banter, someone with whom there might be a larger overlap of knowledge and interests than I was finding otherwise. English-speaking. The kind of keeping company in talking that fluency allowed instead of sliding shifts of the mind under the provocation of insufficient vocabulary. There were people in Yalve Sanga who spoke English, some as their first language, some as a strong second. I was getting acquainted with some of them. I was hopeful.

I FOUND HER. MY NEW friend had been a teacher in the U.S. She was married to a newly installed doctor at the Yalve Sanga clinic, mother of two daughters slightly younger than our boys, and would be involved in various programs with women and children. They were sponsored by Mennonite Central Committee and lived in one of the oldest residences in the place, a house comprised of two separate buildings set in an L-shape: a kitchen and eating space with a dirt floor in one building, the bedrooms in the other. They filled their ancient lodgings with optimism and MCC-chic decorating. They were intelligent, diligent, hospitable. They kept themselves alive on meals-in-a-pot and other intentional simplicities. I remembered Doris Janzen Longacre, author of the *More-with-Less Cookbook,* declaring in her simple living manifesto that towels need not match; the doctor and the teacher were a couple whose towels definitely didn't have to match. They were committed to peace, and to social justice.

They were the first Swiss Mennonites I would get to know. While deeply Christian, they weren't pietistic or evangelical-speaking in the way I'd grown up—the way many Fernheim Mennonites were too, a distinction

I couldn't articulate well but one that seemed to offer a critique of the Mission ethos we were living in. Their relationships with Indigenous people had an accepting ease in them which deeply attracted me.

My new friend was artistic and had also worked as a writer and editor. Soon we were having the conversations I'd been longing for. Short conversations, to be sure, patched together between the interruptions of children and other demands on our time, as mothers' conversations often are. (Once I ran over for a quick hello, forgetting I'd put the water hose into the washer to fill it, only to return to a sea in the house.) Probably no friendship would have been enough for my acute neediness at that time, but this one nourished my heart. We lived just a dash over a field and a road apart and often got together as families, for meals, and if possible, early Tuesday evenings for a house church of sorts, to which other English speakers in Yalve Sanga were welcome as well: a bit of singing, a story for the children, Scripture, sharing, prayer.

The boys adored her and her husband, put Aunt and Uncle in front of their names as if they belonged the way family did. One late afternoon when my friend dropped in to borrow something, our younger son joined us in the kitchen. After waiting politely for a break in the conversation, he asked Aunt if she and Uncle and the girls could come for pigeon *asado* supper. Helmut was outside plucking the twenty-one pigeons he'd shot that afternoon. Wild pigeons were a nuisance for crops and descended into the harvest fields by the thousands, which sent people out in large numbers too, to hunt them, as the birds tasted delicious when fried. Being small, it took a lot of them to make a meal, however.

Second Son looked up with his question, we looked down at him. Blue eyes, curls, the cute baby teeth. My friend and I looked at each other. I nodded my willingness. I assumed Helmut had sent him in to suggest it. Aunt said yes, they would come. Which made him happy, made him hurry outside to tell his father. In the midst of our feast later of fresh buns, fried pigeon, and stewed pumpkin, a true fruits-of-the-Chaco meal, it came out that Helmut never mentioned it, it was solely the boy's idea. Everyone had a good laugh and thanked him heartily for the invitation and he beamed over what he accomplished, all of us together around the table.

APRIL, AND I WAS reading Richard Foster's *Celebration of Discipline.* Reading it slowly. The month had been pleasant so far, the evenings cool and relatively insect-free—possible then to read or write by electric light without all manner of moths and other flying creatures getting inside and dive-bombing around the lights and my head. We slept under wool-filled comforters we'd purchased locally, slept with the gift of being soundly wrapped, slept without perspiring.

I was particularly able to read on those evenings when Helmut overnighted with his crew, once the boys were in bed. *My house being now all stilled*, as St. John of the Cross had put it.

I took notes as I read. I'd borrowed the book from my friend so didn't want to mark it up. But it wasn't just that. I seldom took notes on books outside formal study but this one seemed crucial for me, would need to be absorbed. Notes made absorption possible. Richard Foster, a Quaker professor at Friends University in Wichita, described twelve classical practices for spiritual growth: meditation, prayer, fasting, study, simplicity, solitude, submission, service, confession, worship, guidance, celebration. Published in 1978, the book had spread swiftly through the American religious scene so I was certainly aware of it but hadn't read it yet.

My parents had attended an Institute for Ministers and Laymen at the Mennonite Brethren college in Winnipeg some years earlier, at which Foster was speaker. "He was unique," Mom had said. Slight of build, plain of dress, but a wonderfully pastoral way about him, she continued, and what struck her were his remarks about fasting: fasting from others, for example, and from media. And his emphasis on silence and listening. People, he had said, were frightened of quiet.

The denominational periodical reported that there was some audience resistance to Foster's talk of using imagination in meditation and prayer. The Mennonite Brethren branch of Mennonites—the branch in which I was raised—began as a renewal movement in Russia characterized by pietism and an emphasis on missions. Once in North America, MBs leaned heavily into the broader evangelical Protestant—even fundamentalist— stream. *Word* was paramount. The set-down, written Word, preached every Sunday, and in between. The authoritative Word, easily becoming literal, schematic. So Foster's invitation to the Institute ministers and lay folks to consider sources of understanding besides the "thus said" of their experience with the Bible, to encounter something living, more personal and slippery, must have been scary as well as wonderfully pastoral.

And now Foster's invitation to imagination was being extended to me via *Celebration of Discipline*. Foster drew on traditions much longer than my Mennonite Brethren's hundred-plus years, longer and wider than the Anabaptist tree from which it grew. Those with historical memories of martyrdom by the Catholic church weren't easily attracted to practices associated with the older church. I'd heard disparagements about Catholic involvement with the local Indigenous people, Paraguay being mainly Catholic after all; somehow working together seemed unthinkable.

I was ready—perhaps bolstered by the influence of our new friends—to stretch away from these attitudes. Reading Foster on topics like prayer, study, church attendance, and service, I traced familiar ground. But imagination! And mystery that was closer—*here.* Jesus apprehended *here.* I was surprised to realize that my imagination—involved, even when not recognized as such—had always drawn my gaze upward, to God afar, God *up there.*

How strange, as I reflect on it now, that I was hungry for a fuller speaking on the one hand, yet also hungry for more of the contemplative or mystical, for solitude and silence in my spiritual practice. For giving up words in their tedious servitude to Word. I began to pray with my imagination—could see, for example, God as hands around our six-year-old walking to school, climbing through the gate on his shortcut, sitting in his desk, having an ear pulled by the bully perhaps, lifting his child soprano lustily in singing hour, wandering cheerfully home.

I was hungry for growth on many levels. For transformation. For letting go. I was trying to manage the household, and my family too, and this gentle Quaker was asking me to heave aside the critical frame I'd been hammering around myself and others. "[W]e must come to the place in our lives where we lay down the everlasting burden of needing to manage others," I copied into my notebook. He spoke a *must*, but there was truly only benefit in putting such a burden down.

"Joy is the keynote of all the disciplines," I copied. Nothing hairshirt about that, not a public hairshirt at least. I was ready for joy, ready to be less anxious. To hear Love as I listened instead of the play on fear and boundaries I'd heard too much of in the past. I'd had a relatively generous childhood, yet walls had been built, qualms and unworthiness like piled bricks.

I was familiar with doubt but this wasn't about moving from the core of my faith. Mystery seemed entirely congruent with uncertainty. With journey. With learning and rest. Enroll as an apprentice, Foster said, enroll without shame "in the school of contemplative prayer." In my upbringing, prayer was wordy too, it was all about talking. You knelt, talked your words and your lists, said Amen and got to your feet. Done. My Mennonites eschewed liturgies of Catholics or what they called the mainliners, considered them rote and thus careless, but how easily the so-called extemporaneous forms became a rote march too, marching into cliché and shallow vocabulary, into a special voice and pious intonation. Helmut and I sometimes chuckled together about a man we knew who had a whole other tone on tap for his preaching and prayer.

I'm telling here of beginnings. When I read again my novel that grew out of this period in Paraguay—*Under the Still Standing Sun*—decades after it was published, I found myself less comfortable with its particular language of piety than I must have been when it was written and published. I visualized a Mennonite audience and I used the prevailing religious language of my protagonist's environment. It was hers, it was theirs, but largely mine as well. But I also remember that mystery and some necessary spiritual reticence was slowly building its house in those years of its writing. Foster's voice seemed steady and calm. He reached back to the spiritual masters, reached back into that which was older and deeper, as if he'd found its pulse. Old things that were new to me. In the lovely month of April, in the quieter quiet of Yalve Sanga, I read and took notes and mulled upon the familiar and the new, upon reminders and appeals, and the sentences tugged with intelligent fervor at the personality I was or longed to be. I was not ungrateful for my upbringing; every tradition offered its gifts.

And every tradition had weaknesses, did damage.

Perhaps my inability to speak fluently in the Chaco was a gift as well. My blundering and often inarticulate German and nearly non-existent Spanish pushed me to the margins, grieved and continually foiled my wish to fit. It reiterated, I think, some even stronger fear that I'd always been an outsider, awkward, not making friends smoothly or easily, too studious and serious and precocious, too melancholy. But could there be some blessing in the mute confusion of my immigrant person struggling for words? In being compelled to say less?

Silence makes people feel helpless, Foster said. I wrote this down. This, he explained, is because we're used to employing words to manage others. And to manage what others think of us. To manage how or whether they'll know us. Silence, he said, "is intimately related to trust."

I'd been given a friend to fill some of my profound need to exchange wisdom and wit. I was also being instructed that it was time to be blessedly still, that it was time to uncover the offerings of silence and listening.

12. Birth

I QUOTED MORAG in Margaret Laurence's *The Diviners* to my friend, because I found Laurence's observation true: "The terrible vulnerability of parents . . . your life bound up so centrally with this other one." She knew exactly what I meant. Her daughter fell at four and knocked out a tooth and "I grieved," she said. "It was this terrible grief, over her altered appearance for the next two or three years until she would have normally lost it."

We were drinking tea in her kitchen. Our children played outside.

I told her how our son had recently arrived to his classroom late, everyone else but the teacher already there, and when he came in the others laughed. He said he'd cried. I tried to comfort him, tell him that, as he knew, the teacher often left the classroom but expected them to behave when she was gone, and the students, hearing footsteps, thought it was her and hushed for her entry, then laughed for relief when he came through the door instead.

I felt quite sure of this explanation but he seemed unable to believe me. "It's so hard to undo a child's first impression," I told my friend, "to reason it another way."

She nodded, murmured affirmation.

I'd ached with the boy, empathetic, but had also been impatient and jumpy lately, unsure of myself as a parent. I'd gathered that some in Yalve Sanga thought our sons too wild, energetic, mischievous, too domineering perhaps, taking advantage of the dynamic of being among the oldest of the staff children. Most of the time I didn't agree with such assessments, because as far as I was concerned their wildness was of the best kind, climbing trees and staging mock battles with sticks and implements of warfare like brooms and washer lids for shields. I thought that playing Mennonites and Philistines at war is exactly what boys who live among Mennonites and hear Bible stories would play. I figured that of course they would climb machines and scramble into various structures. I thought they were terrific. Honestly, I thought they were remarkable. Sure, they whooped around Yalve Sanga, got into mischief, climbed on machines they shouldn't climb on, teased the local girls when they shouldn't, rode their bikes into the muddy *tajamar* when they shouldn't. (Helmut punished that one—clogging their bike chains with that gunk!) I knew their faults but their personalities too, their multi-faceted and complicated natures. (If I'd ever imagined children as blank slates, I had long learned better.)

At other times, I confess, I cared enormously about such judgments. It was almost too much to analyze, to mull over, and the blame I took upon myself for my mothering made me short with them, which I would then regret. My friend and I sipped at our tea, we agreed and agreed. We understood the other's vulnerability. I'd heard her raise her voice at her children too. Sometimes friendship was simply a confessional.

We moved on, talked about how weird it was to be in our thirties, how much older thirties felt than twenties, how jarring to have a past when we felt we'd only had future until now. I said I wished it were possible to live two different lives. This one, here and now, pregnant and with the boys, but maybe a life of teaching literature or something academic too. We bit off thoughts like nibbles at biscuits. It was nearly time, though, to separate the children, take the boys home, think about supper. I would have to chew the exchange further while cooking, mull regret that so much fell into the ditch in every choice one made, that the days that composed years unfolded but once. My friend and I were infected by the women's liberation movement and wished to have it all but already knew we never would. Just one life was possible at a time. And it was May. And what I was, was *hoch schwanger*—highly pregnant—and what I would have next, no choice about it at all, was a baby.

WE ENDURED rain much of that month, not hard or heavy downpours but day after day of *Nieselwetter*. Drizzle. A pervasive condition of sogginess. Mustiness crept into the winter quilts, green mold formed on our suitcases, shoes, heavy jackets. Our books and papers went limp. The salt in the shaker clotted. Laundry took forever to dry. At the machine station, the bulldozer stood still and the tractor's only work was extracting vehicles mired in the muck. The fields were saturated, the roads soft and often impassable. Transport in and out of the colony had more or less stopped. When we managed to get into Filadelfia to shop one day, we found the stores completely out of sugar, flour, and fresh vegetables.

The weeks passed and the season of moisture was finally done and it was a relief like falling into bed when overly tired. Which is what I'd just done one night, when I was suddenly afraid. Helmut flopped in beside me and the waves under me surged. "Whoa, and easy does it," I said. I already felt like a whale. (Had I been this large my last two pregnancies?)

He chuckled and assured me our next waterbed would have baffles.

I told him not to even think about it, I would never want another waterbed.

It wasn't an argument, just a tired old tease, and the ripples calmed, and I said, into the dark, "Oh, if I could only stop time."

A grunt, sympathetic. He reached for my hand.

"I'm so completely finished," I said. "But I'm not ready either."

"You said you were ready. The room—"

Yes, yes, *that* was ready, the crib on loan, cute baby-room curtains made and hung, twenty-plus diapers and receiving blankets sewed and piled, the women of his family surprising me with a shower, which added six diapers, night shirts, sleepers, crib sheets, soap, baby oil, mini-towels, a blanket, a bathtub, and a stuffed animal to the upcoming infant's kit.

I wasn't ready for the birth, I said.

He muttered that he understood.

I didn't think he did but I let it pass. I said I was afraid.

He promised I would be alright.

What else *would* he say? I probably would be. But if I could just stop time, prepare for whatever was about to happen. I thought of how women died in childbirth, women and more women and more women still, throughout history, and now I was close to the event myself and I couldn't help it, I had to face the fact that I might die.

He murmured assurances again but they sounded slurry by now and his hand's grip slackened, his breath slowed, turned throaty and snore-like. How easily this man of mine could fall asleep.

I was sure to be fine. It was my great-grandmother, even grandmother, who might have had reason to be terrified. Apparently my grandparents didn't have sex—*relations*, as my frank but very correct aunt put it—for an entire year while appealing for and then undergoing their emigration journey from Russia. They feared she wouldn't survive a pregnancy because hunger had taken its toll on her body during the hard times of the civil war and food shortages, not to mention the strain of travel. I considered my grandparents' restraint, especially Grandfather's, commendable. Noble. Comparatively, I was reasonably free of stress, we weren't going anywhere any time soon, we had plenty to eat. Maternal deaths from childbirth, infant mortality rates too, had plummeted in most countries over the century. The hospital in Filadelfia, where the birth would take place, might not have an incubator but it was generally well equipped. There were trained doctors, midwives, nurses within reach. Right here in Yalve Sanga, in fact, if we couldn't get to Filadelfia. They would be able to staunch hemorrhaging or combat infection. An emergency caesarean would be possible if it came to that. And I'd had no complications in my previous births.

But it was true, what I'd said to my husband. I'd simply wanted to drop into bed after a strenuous day to sleep and foreboding crept under the covers to keep me awake. For the third time I was close to the childbirth brink where time careens without compassion toward the dreaded, horrendous pain and, every positive statistic aside, the possibility of death. If only I could halt the rush, the inevitability, compose myself, deal with this panic. Nine months of growing this child, almost as many anticipating its arrival with pleasure, and now I felt I couldn't go on, face this unavoidable thing.

Sleep had by-passed me and taken Helmut far away. I was alone, spent, my mind swirling with the effort to will away dread, to grasp and believe positive probabilities. To grab time. Time with a beating mind of its own that would not stop. Trying to submit to it, to what it would bring. But I was a blubbering beggar: *Please, please, I want to live.*

WAKING THE NEXT morning—it was the last day of May—I felt rested and energetic, as if I'd never been troubled by fear that I wouldn't live to a ripe old age. I waddled through my tasks like a cheerful Mother Goose: getting the older boy off to school, setting the younger down with crayons and colouring books, washing dishes, tidying, sweeping. The usual. When I opened the fridge to start lunch, I saw how badly it needed defrosting. That ugly ice. I ought to get it out of the way before the baby arrived. There would be no time afterward for such extras. I unplugged the fridge and between the chopping, peeling, frying, boiling required for cooking— we ate our larger meal at noon—hauled its contents onto the counter. I noticed my stomach was upset. Maybe a touch of diarrhea.

We ate and sent the boys to their room for siesta. A spasm like a dishcloth being twisted wrenched through my middle. It wrung out, then let go. I was fine again. But the pause seemed ominous, like something winding up for another twist and squeeze.

I carried on clearing the table and then I felt it again, a spasm like the one before.

It occurred to me that I might be in labour.

"I think I'm starting," I told Helmut. "I think we'll have to go."

But I wasn't sure. I sat down, clutching my middle, staring at him, at the dishes, at the mess on the counter. The painful sensation had passed. Already it seemed unimportant. I'd remembered and forgotten I was pregnant in the same few moments. It was a big deal to drive thirty-five kilometres into Filadelfia and back again if this was a false alarm. Because of the hours lost to the drive, because we paid mileage on personal trips. Money was always a consideration.

Another contraction. They weren't close. But they weren't tentative either. The cramping and clenching seem desperate: full-on.

What had possessed me to empty the fridge? A gift of pre-birth vitality probably, which I should have been saving instead of wasting. But honestly, it hadn't dawned on me that today might be the day.

Should we go or not?

I'm almost embarrassed to say what I did next. I cast a lot. I scribbled Yes (to going) on a small piece of paper and No on another, closed my eyes, mixed them up, and drew. Someone would tell me later God didn't speak like that but I remembered the verse in Proverbs: *The lot is cast but God determines the outcome.* The hospital was a good forty-five minutes away and my last delivery had been short. Besides, if this was a form of magical thinking, I was in good company. An entire branch of Mennonites chose their ministers by lot; a slip of paper would be placed in one of the Bibles or hymnbooks on a table, and the ministerial candidate who picked that book was the chosen one. Incidentally, Orie O. Miller, head of Mennonite Central Committee, after whom a Filadelfia street was named because of his key role in Fernheim Colony's founding, was three times a ministerial candidate in his congregation without the lot ever falling on him.

The paper I drew said Yes. I told Helmut we needed to leave. I grabbed a bag of personal items. We woke the boys and shoved the perishables back in the fridge. The rest of the kitchen chaos was what it was. We set off for Filadelfia in the rickety yellow Datsun.

The road, hardened after weeks of rain, was a mass of ridges and pits. The truck shook and bounced. We shook along with it.

Midway to Filadelfia I had to admit, "I haven't felt anything since we set out."

False alarm then, the boys sitting wide-eyed between us on account of this strange journey, their siesta interrupted.

"Well, we've come this far," Helmut said. We rumbled on.

In Filadelfia, he drove to the hospital and stopped to let me out. As if the child within knew where we were, the contractions had resumed just minutes earlier and were urgent. I gave the boys quick kisses.

"Have a good time!" the younger one called after me.

I entered hours then that have blurred in memory. I do remember I was assigned a midwife, that the midwife escorted me to some other wing of the hospital. Or was it another building altogether? Was there a brick path, a flowering hedge running alongside? I undressed, put on a gown. The room seemed small, closed in, but safe, like a cave. I heaved myself onto a bed in the middle of an agonizing, crushing wave of pain.

Now the midwife was sentinel, standing close to where the wrenching occurred. She was slim and dark-haired and seemed young, but authoritative too, kindly and unafraid. She said she would stay as long as it took for the baby's arrival. I think I asked her how many births she'd attended and later I thought she'd said ninety-nine, though this seemed a lot for someone young and I was no longer certain if I'd heard correctly. Ninety-nine was the number of sheep who were safe in the fold when the shepherd in Jesus' parable went out searching for the hundredth, who was lost.

But never mind, I felt myself in good hands, lost sheep or not, and she was wind, persistent and powerful wind against the moaning of my inability to breathe while my body shattered to pieces. "Like this," she would say, loud enough for gasping me to hear and obey. She led, I followed. She led again, I staggered after. She led me to oxygen at slow tempo or fast. No medication was given here for birthing, not even a relaxant. But she didn't matter to me. I was aware only of myself, I was the centre of the world. The world was my body and this unstoppable compulsion which had overtaken it like unexpected terror. Falling upon me and about to split me open. It was my own body pulling me into a vortex so deep I knew I would drown unless I could persevere at whatever was required or commanded. My own self cruelly sucked me in, my own self fought to climb up and out again, to bolt and survive. Over the top, they said in the trenches of that awful war. To live or die. It was beyond my control, yet everything seemed to depend on me. I recalled some ancient promise that eventually it would end but I no longer believed it.

I wasn't thinking of the child either. I knew the child was ready, had to be born, but the creature, if creature it be, seemed as helpless as I was against the punishing onslaught of myself. It was I who called, I who answered. If a bomb had exploded outside my room—fine, bombs away! If the secret of the universe were whispered into my ear, I would slap it away. I was a solitary planet turning on her axis. On the verge of spattering into space.

Helmut appeared around 2:30, after dropping the boys off at his sister's and running some quick work-related errands. "Good thing we came," he said, "this doesn't seem a false alarm," and I said grimly, "No, it isn't." I predicted the baby would be born before five. He muttered encouragements and compliments which I heard but found superfluous and the intensity rolled on, and then the urge to push could not be stopped and the woman with the strong wind waiting at the point of the pushing gave me permission, said "Go ahead and push," and I felt a swoosh, the release of something like a stone through the pathway of my pain—the head then—and moments later I pushed again and felt a further lumpy release.

I heard a cry. An infant's cry.

Helmut exclaimed it was a girl. The infant cried and now I was crying too, for relief to be done, for joy to be done, and for—did he just say it was a girl? I meant it when people asked, when I declared it wouldn't matter, boy or girl, I was very pleased with my boys, and now I was crying for the awe sweeping over me that I was alive after an episode that felt like death, and on top of that we had a daughter! And now I knew how much I had wanted her.

13. Overlap

THE BABY WAS washed and wrapped and I was moved into a regular hospital room to recover. Helmut brought the boys to the hospital for a quick look before they returned to Yalve Sanga. He said they "went nuts" when he told them they had a sister but now, standing beside the high white bed and looking up at me and the tiny bundle—apparently this sister of theirs—they were solemn. The younger boy seemed bewildered too. Clearly what was lowered to his level for a closer view wasn't quite what he'd expected. No limbs visible, just a face with black hair and closed eyes and scrunched up features poking out of a white flannel wrap. Then the face opened a toothless mouth and began to wail. The boys' solemnity deepened.

I was elated to see the boys, hug them, feel their sturdy solemn bodies in my arms. Once they'd been babies this small, and look at them now. We had *three* children, though I wasn't used to that yet. I found their awe and uncertainty about the howling bundle endearing. Later Helmut told me what our older son announced on the drive back to Yalve Sanga, as if he'd worried it through and reached a conclusion. "I'll have to close my ears when the baby is crying," he'd said. "I have my work to do."

I STAYED IN THE hospital five days. It seemed long, but that was the rule. The facility was old and small but fastidiously clean. Antiseptic whiffed out of its pores. Mornings, I was woken at five to take a shower. The food was *mennonitische*: basic meat and potatoes or manioca meals at lunch and *Prips* (a coffee-like drink made from kafir) and roasted buns for afternoon snack.

Our daughter was healthy, nearly nine pounds at birth, and she latched on and fed well except that, as newborns will, she would fall asleep without filling up. The nursing staff, slavish to some pattern of sleeping and feeding they'd established for their own benefit, bottle-fed her between. I didn't bother protesting. We would be done here soon enough and we would figure it out.

What a difference in my confidence to have two babies behind me already! I remembered how a churlish nurse scolded me one night after our first son's birth when his weight after breastfeeding wasn't discernibly greater than before, and I whimpered back that I'd done everything I was told to do to keep him awake and eating—uncover him, pinch his heel— but it was all wet feathers against the woman's rigid disapproval. I shrank against my pillow and shed some tears, the baby borne off to the nursery by the amazon nurse, but the next day my sister-in-law's father, a physician who happened to be at the hospital, stopped by to congratulate me and, as he sat for a few minutes on the edge of the bed, I found myself telling him of my discouragement about feeding. He patted my hand and said to never mind nurses, it would all work out when we got home. And it had. I had no anxieties now about feeding my child. I had mastered it twice, knew the milk would come in, already recognized the feeling of its "let down."

Apart from the strictness about schedule, the nursing care was generous. The staff must have been aware I wasn't local and heaped on tender friendliness as if they'd discerned bearing a child on foreign soil must include a current of heartache under joy, my own mother not available as most other women's mothers were. Their attention made me feel *geborgen*, secure, as if swaddled. Or maybe it was just the limelight any woman owns for a while after giving birth. Whatever the reason, for a few days I basked in it.

My room smelled beautifully of roses. I received fourteen visitors— friends and in-laws—in two hours the first afternoon and six magnificent bouquets picked from home gardens, any one of which could rival the best of a hot-house florist shop. They were dark red, pink, orange, white, and shades between.

"You're the talk of the town," one visitor said. It reflected the excitement our extended family and the Yalve Sanga community felt together with us, I think, coming to Paraguay on a development assignment and then double-blessing the endeavour by having a baby. Had it also amazed them that Canadian City Girl knew how to have a baby when there was so much else she didn't know? Accomplished the feat here, of all places? Did anyone imagine things were so modern up in Canada that we just unbuttoned a vaginal flap and slid the infant out? Silliness, perhaps, but I felt I'd proved something essential about myself and was immensely pleased at my achievement. Plus having a girl after two boys! And not only that, but a baby with a full head of dark hair (never mind that it would soon be blond), and dark is what Mama favoured since most of her own children still had hair as black as night.

WHEN NOT FEEDING the newborn and enjoying private get-acquainted sessions—infant head filling the cup of my palm, infant ears begging for a fingertip's tracery—or being served meals or receiving visitors or showering pre-dawn, I read. Reading was life to me but there was usually too little time for it. Now I could read guilt-free, nothing required of me but to recuperate. I had borrowed books from a local expat with a good library. I had read for hours while in hospital after the boys' births too. It was the sweetest overlap of the diverse parts of myself, this pocket of time to be blissfully invalid, not from dire illness but simply from birth, the work and waiting resolved but the relevant maternal responsibilities still in abeyance.

I felt myself odd on account of this need, this determination, which reading in this setting seemed to represent. I kept it to myself almost covertly, much as I did my writing. If caught reading instead of mooning about my newborn I could chuckle it away as a filler, a kind of entertainment, but I knew it was much more than that. Books were midwives that helped my mind and spirit breathe. They both produced and countered the natural melancholia of my personality, but kept me manageably proportional. Our second son had been barely two months old when I signed up for two courses at the University of Winnipeg, "The English Novel to 1830" and "Mennonite Authors," and it was ecstasy I felt getting on the bus for my weekly three-hour classes, the children safe with a babysitter, the air always especially crisp it seemed when I ran out the door to the bus, and for those hours no one asking about baby toys or baby gas or baby diapers or baby anything. For those hours, I was babyless, and sometimes I felt smaller because of it, but most of the time I felt balanced and solid on my feet, the children known to me like a treasure but too valuable and hidden for public consumption. I read the course-assigned books between supper preps and evening baths and nursing the baby, Rudy Wiebe's *Blue Mountains of China* and Samuel Richardson's *Clarissa* and Daniel Dafoe's *Moll Flanders* and Arnold Dyck's *Lost in the Steppe* and many more.

Why is it hard to say aloud that my husband, my children, weren't enough? That they were everything to me, but not actually everything? It seems a paradox, but surely like the capacity to love a second child without dividing love for the first, then adding a third without diminishing love for the other two, the soul easily opens that wide. And it's true that *everything* can mean *everything* but be simultaneously separated and distinct and even incomplete on its own. That is, not enough. It was the maternal script of either/or foisted on women that was inaccurate, untrue.

I no longer believe that script, and obviously I didn't believe it then either, but I wasn't without my fears in getting the balance right. I feared, for example, that my children might feel slighted to discover, someday, how desperately I required these other outlets, these intellectual pursuits. That in fact I'd had a rather rich life apart from them. I never regretted the choices Helmut and I made about how we would divvy up family roles, which looked—from the outside—entirely traditional, for they fit our circumstances and temperaments, but I'd also been adamant about complicating our lives by determining to write. By serving my mind. It had seemed urgent to get my BA degree (and years later an MA), not because education might make a better mother of me but just because.

I read in my bed in the Filadelfia maternity ward for the same reason.

I HAD HOPED TO manage the household by myself but Helmut insisted we hire help for the first two weeks I was home. I was glad he did. I was weaker than expected and still bleeding a fair bit. The helper we hired was a young woman from Menno Colony, nineteen and astonishingly efficient. She took care of everything, even baking bread, while I rested and tended the baby, who slept in short segments throughout the day and soon lasted up to six hours at a stretch at night but not without an entire evening of prior fussiness.

Now there were three laundry days per week: a main washday for family clothes and bedding and two more for diapers and baby things. We had an electric wringer washer but the hot water had to be heated on the stove and carried to the machine. Each item of clothing was pressed through the wringer into rinse water after it agitated for its ten or twenty minutes or whatever time elapsed before I got to it, then was pressed through the wringer again after the rinse, shaken open and hung on lines on the *Schattendach*. Then, when dry, taken down to be folded or ironed. I liked the procedures and gestures of laundry, the lifting and wringing and shaking and bending and pinning, the cool caress of a clean damp diaper billowing open like a sail against my face as I pinned it to the line. "All those white flags of surrender," a single nurse laughed about those lines full of diapers.

It was just that laundry took so much time, so often.

After the helper finished the two-week stint at our house, I asked the Nivaclé woman who'd been assisting me with dishes and floors two hours twice a week to add a third day for a while. I'd agonized about hiring *indígena* help, as development workers in other countries often do. The pay wasn't much compared to our Mission wages and I feared such arrangements merely accentuated the disparities between the cultures. The Mennonite women I consulted, however, long used to employing *indígenas*, told me the benefits were mutual, told me to abide by current local pay levels, told me I *must*—for the sake of my strength and health.

And it made a huge difference, indeed, having that large field of floor tile regularly swept of grit and washed.

My Nivaclé employee was tall, attractive, deliberate, steady. She usually brought along her daughter, about five years old, a child whose brown eyes sparkled with curiosity. Beyond my few Spanish phrases, we communicated with signs. It wasn't difficult to let her know what had to be done, and once the routine was established nothing further had to be said. Halfway through the morning I set *tereré* and a snack on the verandah, and she took a break.

But I could never lose my consciousness of the Nivaclé woman working almost soundlessly around me. I wished I could speak with her, learn more about her life and thoughts. I'd done broad reading about Paraguay and its history, then narrowed myself further to reading about the Chaco and its history; I knew a little about the Indigenous people of the region. But not, in fact, that much. Strangely, I realize in retrospect, the Mission never gave us any cultural orientation to the people with whom Helmut worked. My own life, as well as research for the novel I was writing, was focused on the Mennonites of the Chaco. I descended through the layers of Paraguay like opening a Russian nesting doll and then concentrating on just one, perhaps the smallest, doll inside.

There would not be much about the neighbouring Indigenous peoples in my novel of Anna in Fernheim Colony. Anna would arrive as a teen full of romantic notions and idealized attachment to the Chaco she'd not yet seen. She would discover how bitterly the austere environment acted against her, what it cost to immigrate and re-settle, and discover too, as her relationships and chronology unfolded in that place that all the while it was seducing her within, becoming home. Her response came full circle, ended again as a kind of love. And the Indigenous people? When they showed up in Anna's story, they would be what they had been for many Mennonites in the early years, a foil for her fears and those of her mother before her, fears that if they didn't maintain traditional standards of cleanliness and culture they would soon be "poor Indians." In the story, they would be on the periphery as labourers, as they were for me, or as those with superior skills when people went missing in the bush, when they were finally called in—sometimes too late—to assist. They could see the snap of a twig Europeans missed, the faint print in the sand. Mutterings about them by Anna and Jakob and their children would be various shades of prejudicial, though historically accurate as far as Mennonite attitudes were concerned. These attitudes were a continuum, of course; at the better end were sincere efforts by many in both groups to live together well.

But who can really say who misunderstood whom and who adapted the most, tried the hardest, as far as Indigenous and Mennonite were concerned? Anthropologists criticized the missionaries of the region and vice versa. I knew that both sides had impossible expectations of the other, that both groups behaved as who they were. My head could spin thinking of it all. But my character Anna thought of it less than I did.

HELMUT WAS NEARLY a year into his assignment and we were beginning to discuss whether we should extend our term after his two-year contract was done. The sponsoring German group said they wanted a year's notice either way.

The machine station was busy. Helmut was pleased with the crew. The men had proven intuitive with large machinery and were good at their work. Their jobs were considered desirable, which made them proud of their achievements and responsibility.

I asked which way he leaned.

"I like the work," he said. "The men. And you can't accomplish much in just two years."

"And you have their full confidence." The sponsors, I meant. Our contact person had said so in a letter.

The hardest part, he said, was the working-together dynamics in the Mission, especially issues of leadership. Lack of communication. Saying one thing to Indigenous representatives, another to the program staff. There were so many personalities here, so many competing wishes and demands. Some people were easy to get along with, others grated like sandpaper. I knew my husband could be dogged too. Sometimes Mission situations caused disagreements between us, each of us mulish on our own perspectives.

"I like it here too," I said. "I'd be open to continue. Though it all depends on the school situation. If the schooling here won't work. . . ." I was adamant I wouldn't let our son live away from us during the week—boarding out, that is, to attend school in Filadelfia. Not at his age.

I said that otherwise the isolation and my inabilities language-wise were actually gifts. No one asked me to help with anything outside the home—no committees or clubs or women's groups or Sunday school or what have you, the kinds of things I was regularly asked for in Canada. I was blessedly off the hook for anything external and realized I rather liked it.

"We've got time to decide," he said. "They won't be rigid about the one year's notice business anyway."

Which way did I really lean? Schooling was one thing but sometimes it simply depended on the weather. When the *Nordsturm* galed from the Andes of Bolivia and Peru—what had the younger boy said the other day when he got up from his nap, that he dreamt an airplane was starting up outside, but found it was just the wind?—it bent me one way. Then a stretch of calm, not too hot, just pleasantly warm days, or the moon throbbing with benediction, or clouds lining up in pretty clumps like fish scales made of pearl, I could easily lean the other. It depended and it depended and it depended.

HELMUT'S FAMILY gathered at the ranch one day. I think it was during the short winter school break in July. A steer was butchered, ribs roasted for dinner, the rest of the meat divided. We made circles of our chairs and visited. I scarcely saw the boys, so thoroughly were they drawn into the company of their older cousins. The baby slept, waking only briefly to charm her relatives. She was beginning to smile and respond. That morning when Helmut picked her up and carried her into the room where the boys slept, she squealed for joy to see her brothers.

The ranch was Papa's creation. My late father-in-law purchased the *legua* (roughly 1800 hectares) of campo and bush for its *palosanto* trees, which he harvested to extract their oil, and as a source of income for his later years. When the *palosanto*-cooking enterprise ended, he built up a cattle herd. This place he loved was also where he died, of a stroke at age sixty-seven, in January 1974, before Helmut and I married. He'd dismounted, crossed the reins neatly over his horse's back, lay down as if to rest.

On the day of the gathering, more than nine years had passed since then and Mama, the family matriarch, was in good spirits, her children still marvelling how positive her move to the seniors home—which she'd resisted at first—had been. We ate and talked and laughed, here in this place where Papa's life had ended and there was nothing unduly sorrowful that day, it seemed, about the fact of his death. Everyone was used to his absence by now.

For me, the last daughter-in-law of the family and the only one who never saw, heard, or interacted with him, his absence was of someone who had never been present. I wanted to know him but could only cobble together a sense of him from photos and second-hand stories, told about him if I asked.

The news of his father's fatal stroke had reached Helmut—the youngest son—in Winnipeg by shortwave radio. There was no possibility of him attending the funeral. The colony had no facility for holding a corpse, only ice brought into the *Totenkammer*, death chamber, for twenty-four hours at most against the unkind heat, just long enough to notify those who were away and summon ministers for hastily prepared sermons of admonition or comfort. The service and burial took place at five the next afternoon.

During my introductory trip to Paraguay in 1976, Helmut and Mama and I went to the spot on the ranch where Papa died. The day was cool, the spot the same as any other on the campo that day, pale, silent, oblivious to us, except that it was marked by an upturned red *quebracho* stem, the iron-like wood of the Chaco, which the other sons had set there as memorial. We had not intended this stop but were in the vicinity as guests of an uncle and aunt, Mama along with us, when we noticed one of Helmut's brothers passing on his motorcycle, presumably on his way to the ranch. We decided to follow him. Mama hadn't been to the ranch even once since her husband's death. This seemed astonishing to me, but what did I, young daughter-in-law, know of the intricacies of mourning?

But now she had to go. We caught up with the brother, the one who had found Papa dead, and he led us to the place. Then he strode off to be alone, as if shocked anew at what he'd discovered under the tree. Mama sobbed. Helmut propped her up and cried as well.

I also stepped away from the scene, watching them stand before the *quebracho* memorial, my husband in his plaid jacket and his mother in a grey dress and brown sweater, the plaid arm stretched over the brown back for comfort, their heads down. I snapped a photograph. The sky was grey, the photo would look drab. There was no question who should be in the picture and who out. I'd cried as well but felt it intrusive to do so in their company of two, in their sacred insider moment. Helmut had returned from his far country, and his father's death had only seemed real to him when he entered the home kitchen on that visit and realized Papa wasn't there, his loss clasping his mother's like a hook and eye. My ties to the place were tenuous, they had barely begun.

14. Pilgrimage

I remember that on the bus trip from Asunción to Filadelfia, when we returned to the Chaco in August 1982 for the MEDA assignment, I read— in snatches—the Songs of Ascents, those fifteen psalms near the back of the biblical Psalter. Short psalms associated with travel, apparently sung by Jewish worshippers going up to Jerusalem for the pilgrim feasts of the religious calendar. I must have chosen them for their brief, epigrammatic nature, the possibility of single phrases repeating in me like refrain, like the doleful or hopeful Kumbayas of long-ago youth-group firesides. Reading them, surely, for an inner shoring-up, some resolution of what lay behind and equilibrium for what lay ahead, *the sun will not harm you by day, nor the moon by night.* Perhaps I resonated with their upward motion too, going "up" to the Mennonite colonies in a northwesterly direction, though *up* was entirely metaphorical, the Chaco as flat as the Canadian plains.

It was a long trip and would have been warm. I dipped into the Songs between keeping the boys happy and fed, *your sons like olive shoots around your table*, between the looking hard at everything I mentioned earlier, at a landscape changing from the lavish greenery of eastern Paraguay to the mid-winter pallor of the central Chaco. Small dwellings slung beside the road, little more than the shelter of roofs, they seemed, and people—women and children in colourful clothing—popping up to my gaze like twinkling lights or flowers, and maybe a horse tied to a post, a scrawny dog, a hammock or two, thin lines of smoke lifting from hearth fires. Briefly glimpsed scenes of *home* to feed the reverie of travel: curiosity, yearning, regret, *why am I here?*

As I return to that road decades later in this backward view, watching myself pull from a bag again and again the tiny Testament and Psalms—a gift from my father to each of his children the Christmas before—to read *As the eyes of a maid look to the hand of her mistress, so our eyes look to [You] . . . have mercy on us, O Lord, have mercy on us*, what I notice isn't simply a habit structured into me from childhood, but a question. Was this re-location from Canada to Paraguay a kind of pilgrimage, in fact? To which the Songs were a clue? I'd been a tourist of sorts, trying to see, I'd sat down as visitor for four months before this return. Was I aligning myself as seeker now, as pilgrim?

But if pilgrim, pilgrimage to what? The very essence of pilgrimage, after all, is Elsewhere, the desires present in the place of Coming From re-assigned to a goal Somewhere Ahead.

Partially, I think, it was my historical past that I was after in Paraguay, a search for the Russian home—the customs and structures and language of community life—of my grandparents and great-grandparents which, oddly enough, seemed more accessible to me in the Mennonite Chaco, still visceral in this starkly non-Russian place. My people more unassimilated here, still bearing original signs of Departure and Arrival. A past un-diluted by my thoroughly Canadian—British-based, that is—education. A place to trace the homesickness of my Mennonite people as they moved from one place to another. The place of myth, this Russia, to be sure, but territory I was bound to by virtue of my birth to people who had also come from there.

I also sought, between learning to mother and learning to write, a deeper kinship with my husband's first homeland and family.

But if pilgrimage, perhaps it wasn't just about arrival. I know something of the late anthropologist Victor Turner's work on pilgrimage, though not enough to toss symbols and signifiers and signs about with any ease. Nevertheless, ever since I learned the word *liminal*, I've been fond of it. The state of transition, of in-between. Potentiality, Turner said. I stir liminal and pilgrimage together and think, in retrospect, of those two-plus Chaco years in the early eighties as a kind of wandering, not quite anywhere except "on the way." Living on a threshold, as it were, a circularity between places, dancing on the edge of both the *previous* and the *now*. I wonder if immigrants ever escape liminality.

There's irony in the notion of wandering. Once the bus unloaded us, I was more or less stuck in a house with small children. Unlike mythical journeys men take, which may be depicted as solo dragon-fighting expeditions or beautiful-princess-rescue-operations, I was rarely alone and my movements were confined and repetitive. My journey was housebound and could thus be assumed to be easier and smaller, though I didn't believe that for a moment—no woman does if she's honest: smaller and unimportant is the assumption of a hegemonic patriarchal culture. I'd claimed the phrase *in the house of my pilgrimage* the moment I encountered it in another psalm-song (119:54) and would later write a poem about a year spent in an apartment with three children to express what I meant.

> There are not many steps
> forth, forth, and back
> in this house of my pilgrimage:
> it's a small place.
> The floors are beige,
> the walls flat white,
> they muffle the shadows,
> blur day and night.
>
> From the kitchen to the bedrooms,
> sofa to the hall,
> daily and endlessly I travel
> this plain where I cook,
> draw water, enfold children.
> These rooms, my camp;
> this carpet, my path.
> I look to horizons
> in carefully framed and treasured pictures.
>
> Here I utter my complaints,
> eat God's patience as a brown spotted quail,
> sing in a windowless kitchen
> the songs of ascents.

IF PILGRIMAGE, THERE would be holy spots, wouldn't there? Every community, writes architect Christopher Alexander and his team in *Pattern Language*, needs sites that are sacred where the rituals of life and meaning can be enacted. If so, what on the ground of the Chaco was holy ground to me? Or, to use the language of Celtic spirituality, where were the "thin places" in which earth grew near to heaven or heaven to earth, the divine experienced with immediacy, intimacy?

I thought and thought.

How surprising to me, as I reflect on it, that in the Mennonite settlements whose entire existence was predicated upon religious considerations, where every centre had its spacious brick churches and nearly every village its school turned into a sanctuary on Sunday mornings, I associate none of its buildings—or objects—with holy encounters. They were fine—if plain—and solid, obliging places, so I mean nothing negative, plus Sunday worship can serve as a regular re-orientation without needing to be memorable or dramatic, but the fact is, they don't recollect to me as "holy" in any way.

Well, except for one, probably because I put it in a poem: a Pentecost Sunday service in the one-room school building of village Hohenau. A thin place of fancy and amusement, and holy for all that, in the humour of what it celebrated versus what it was that day. Pentecost in the Book of Acts was a gushing event of everyone-speaking-at-once and wind and fire-tongues to mark the Spirit's "pouring out" and I suppose that's what the preacher was droning on about but its commemoration in Hohenau that morning was drowsy with familiarity and boredom, the congregants trapped in rows for the sermon, waiting for escape. In the somnolence, one could dream, however. Could pine for Spirit.

> In Paraguay, Pentecost falls in winter
> so we need a fire in the morning
> before the wings of the sun
> have brooded us warm. By the time
> the service begins it is pleasant
> enough: the meetingplace windows
> are unshuttered.
> There's no wind; the sky holds nothing
> but a haze in the east which suggests
> someone is burning
> his pasture.

I have a cold; I slip away
in the middle of the sermon.
I listen outside and wait;
he has turned four or five pages,
he must be nearly
done.

The village lies quiet and green.
Red bricks gather heat; on holy days
swept verandahs sleep and I wait
on a bench in the shade and dream
as they finish. I wait
for *palosanto* smoke to warn
up the wide white street,
for the rush and the whirr of wind to lift
the bouquet from the pulpit and sow
the roses in sand. I'm ready
in case the minister's books blow
as leaves over my lap. Pigs
on these farms, rooting, may spring
fences and flee and we won't
follow; we'll forget what we intended
with their heavy
flesh.

The benediction opens the hour
for *maté*. I join those
emerging at the door; we stretch
held-modest limbs, remove jackets
and shawls and walk
on a hard earth path to somebody's house
to drink the ritual tea
and cheerfully plan
tomorrow.

The other bits of *holy* I recall escaped the sacred buildings too. Discussing my daughter with God on the day of her birth, for example, my hand cradling the black-haired head like a halo. And a quiet evening in Yalve Sanga,

> the peace of the nascent moon dropping,
> fluttering to rest
> on village roofs:
>
> long silver wings gleaming
> on tin to echo tender light . . .
>
> every wish weaned and settled
> in the generous dark.

And an adventurous, child-like bike ride my friend and I attempted on an unknown path through unknown territory outside Yalve Sanga. Or a less happy episode in the small clinic hospital in Yalve Sanga, waiting in a dim room for the doctor, the younger boy feverish on my lap, my thoughts feverish too, for he was sick again and what was the matter this time, me weary and he lurching from one round of swollen glands and blocked nasal passages to the next, steaming him with eucalyptus leaves in water, I'd tried that already, and please not just another vial or bottle plucked as a trial off the understocked laboratory shelves, Madam Doctor seeming unable or reluctant to tackle the boy's almost continuous sub-health. Calmed then in the dusky quiet by a sense of Jesus. Hearing *I am here* until convinced of it.

I was prone to doubt. I had questions the same as the four-year-old in my arms, who asked "how do we know that God is?" We don't, I had to say, not for sure, though my spirit reached over and over when needy, or when grateful, to the Thou called God and I was nurtured by the incarnation, the *becoming* of journey, the truth and narrative of weak become strong, the rock discarded being chosen as the cornerstone. Grace. My doubt was not a wild swing away from faith as much as an ache, a rub along the side of it. And faith was thought, sense, voice without sound, like steady waves to shore: *I am here.*

15. Someday

"THE COUNTER IS UGLY with dishes, but I need to leave them," I confided to my notebook. "To hold this day."

"There are so many things [about life here] I want to save," I carried on. "It will soon be past and is significant. Perhaps I write stuff down for the sake of fixing it [in place] . . . Someday I will grab it all together and make it mean even more than today. This is an exciting thought."

Someday. Nearly four decades later, which is how long it has taken me. I journaled in spurts. I must have believed that scattered jottings, like seeds, would grow everything thickly, greenly back. They help, of course, and I have letters as well, which thankfully my parents saved, but memory, I'm discovering, is unexpectedly sluggish, the past not easily grabbed.

I wish, now, I'd taken closer, more regular, notes. At this remove, the ones I have seem sketchy or banal. They were loose or scattered in a number of exercise books so I gathered and re-wrote them later—re-wrote them in a steady and consistent handwriting, blue ink for narrative and black for quotes from books—but their organized neatness only further subverted the raggedy nature of the actual experience.

I'm also realizing that what I retrieve out of long-ago sentences and the flotsam of my mind doesn't necessarily produce the *mean even more* I imagined. The original was real, dense, animated, too crowded to catch in the limited time I had for myself. The notes that I believed would be prompts into scenes loaded with action simply shuffle together, the few of them, and pose as if for a still life painting.

But even a still life can say a lot, can tell a story. And perhaps, in fact, keeping a journal isn't as much for the future as for the present. Like the rare hour of sitting on the *Schattendach*, pen in hand, the boys gone to play with friends so that one hour freed of their shouts and chatter and hundreds of ideas, of the obligation to respond, and the girl asleep. Noticing the sky and clouds, the anticipation of rain. Grey blue, like pewter, and in the west, gaps where the sun reached through to touch the trees, giving them a bright just-born appearance. Wind rippling the palm one street over. And then the rain, pinging at first, but gathering intensity, the pewter curtain yanked away, a deluge of streaking white instead. Rain in waves. Whoosh, reprieve, whoosh again. A horse-drawn buggy with two Enlhet men passing, no faster than usual. The driver wore a large black leather hat but the other man's head was uncovered and he was soaked, his back glaring through his thin wet shirt. It rained heavily, and then, after some time, the rain grew finer, the clouds mere fog-like clusters now that their heavy black bottoms had been dumped, floating away. As I stood up, leaned against the red brick of the house still warm with midday heat, I realized that when I caught a scene like this in my notebook, I felt good about the day, I felt I'd *done* something. I'd panned for time like gold and found it. An illusion, time in a pan, I knew that too, but it measured as concrete, even permanent, as counterpoint to other days when I was mainly conscious of life passing me by in one routine task after another.

Although the journaling was irregular, I did manage, especially in the spring months of 1983—September and October—to work on the novel. Helmut's sister loaned us a small table so I had a permanent spot for my typewriter. I aimed to complete a draft of the first and second sections, 1930 to 1937; my Yalve Sanga friend had offered to read them. I wrote and re-wrote and the writing gave me joy. I'd changed approach and structure several times already but I felt it was finding itself, a focus on Anna, arriving in Paraguay at sixteen, and following her—and husband Jakob—through their pioneering lives. The characters were fictional but I wanted to be accurate to the setting and history of Fernheim Colony. I was especially interested in the love-hate relationship Mennonites had with the Chaco, their notions of suffering and divine sovereignty, and how they used the stories of their past.

I think I was hoping, in this roundabout way, to write myself into the Chaco. To impress myself as a worthy resident upon its shape and psyche, impenetrable though it might be, and then show it off, as good guests do, to eventual English readers in the North, offering the narrative of Anna's relation with the place—first naïve, then suffered into experience—as my compliment to the Chaco's persuasive power.

But maybe I was simply writing the Chaco into myself. Coming to terms with my life the only way I knew. This seems more selfish, less noble. But also true. Maybe writers write because they can't otherwise cope with things. Since I was beginning to claim writing as calling, as vocation, as that which I ought to do, but discovering it also as necessity, as that which I couldn't be without, the Chaco was my closest opportunity for both, the one that was at hand.

I read Madeleine L'Engle's *A Circle of Quiet*, reflections on finding proportion and meaning in a life, which like mine, was a wife's and mother's but also a writer's. *Yes, yes, oh yes*, I thought as I read. Line after line expressed what I felt. If something deep within even the most tentative and minor of artists didn't think their work good, they would stop forever.

And, of a book waking one at night, insisting to be written. I was strangely heartened by L'Engle's decade of rejection too, though she was eventually resoundingly rewarded with a Newbery award for *A Wrinkle in Time.* I pocketed such stories like water and trail mix in case my writerly fate would take me into the desert as well.

L'Engle told of a lecture by Mary Ellen Chase in which she'd drawled that all literature could be divided into "majah, minah, mediocah" and while no writer wanted to be minor or mediocre, perhaps that wasn't much of a choice either. The point is, one did as best one could. I was learning that if the desire was strong, the effort would be made. The only solution for the sputtering flame was to feed it by writing—writing and writing and writing. To improve skills and understanding. I burned with every new idea, every draft or re-write. This time, I thought, I'll have it, I'll read the sentences back to myself and know I've arrived.

As with Richard Foster, who mentored me into new spiritual practices, I made notes of the book. L'Engle said that as vocabulary grows, so does the power to think, so I kept my dictionary close and noted words like *ontology, hubris, icon, soporific, esoteric,* and *pristine.* She quoted Somerset Maugham and I copied: "The common idea that success spoils people . . . is erroneous; on the contrary, it makes them, for the most part, humble, tolerant, and kind. Failure makes people bitter and cruel."

Oh to be successful then!

And then there was the day I heard through the screen the pedal-turn of a bike, steps in a hurry, and it was my friend, holding the sheaf of my draft beginning sections. I steeled myself for her first words. Perhaps she'd been planning them carefully too, knowing of my terrible insecurities about writing and having worked as a writer and editor herself, but she'd promised to be honest. What tumbled out of her mouth was even more than I could have wished for: "Oh, you must finish it. I want to read the rest." She went on to say she got going and couldn't stop, that she sometimes forgot whose book she was reading.

Had she any idea the tingle such affirmation, such encouragement, provoked? How my body unexpectedly goose-bumped? I was hardly prepared to believe such sentences but I heard them, oh yes, and I repeated them to myself when she left, I memorized them. Praise be and praise be. My dear friend had delivered more help to keep me going than she would probably ever know.

AFTER THE ECSTATIC and rejuvenated claims of "I am writer" that followed this affirmation, I got a rejection letter in the mail about a little article I'd written on an aspect of parenting. I'd sent it to a Mennonite family magazine in the U.S. I thought it was good and fully expected the editor to love it.

He complimented some aspects of the piece, but was turning it down, he said, because the various thoughts weren't integrated well enough. I skimmed it and saw what he meant; yes, I'd leapt all over the place.

Now I hated it. *I'm no good as a writer*, I groveled. *Embarrassed too.* Why had I told my friend I'd written the article and targeted this editor, whom she knew personally? The pain actually felt physical in the region of my heart.

It's not that I'd never had writing rejected before. Nearly every writer experiences it, but I was still learning to understand and moderate the alternating euphoria and despair of the writing life. Writing, one was alone; seeking publication, the competition was legion, some rejection inevitable. This rejection was minor, and I'd been given the reason for it, which was a good thing, yet it hauled up every rejection, real or imagined, I'd ever experienced. I'd never had any luck as a kid sending jokes off to the *Reader's Digest.* There was that children's novel, which I gave up on after a few tries and stuck in a drawer. I remembered the published piece edited—though my word was *mangled*—almost beyond recognition. Envy of established and more accomplished writers surfaced behind these memories.

I trudged to my friend with my disappointment. She was hanging wash so I spoke to her back and her answers as they came fell into those soft damp clothes and sounded comforting. They were sentiments both of us had exchanged before, that one has to accept the gift given and not look at the gifts of others. That one has to keep on. Keep on trying.

I went home, set the failed article aside, but removed the cover from the typewriter and clacked away for a while on the novel.

As VOCATION settled and firmed, a certain necessary stubbornness settled too. I remember finding myself in conversation about Chaco history with a minister and his wife under the shade of a tall prickly bush, all of us waiting for lunch after a retreat event. As I usually did, I asked questions. Listening, as always, for anecdotes, details, attitudes. The more human bits they spilled, the better. I hinted that my interest connected to some writing I had underway. The man caught the hint, and perhaps a whiff of danger if perchance I got something wrong or was critical, and unfurled a string of lessons for me, as if a sermon he'd given before. The main mood of the Chaco settlers, he emphasized, was gratitude. The escape from Russia was too wondrous for anything else but divine intervention. In his case, for example, the night watchman's cart overturned when his family fled their village for Moscow, which caused Soviet soldiers coming to apprehend the family to change their course and miss the fleeing family.

Since I'd reached the years in the novel when a portion of Fernheim enthusiastically embraced the Nazi rise in Germany, to the point that some were willing to surrender a theology of non-resistance, which then divided churches, families, the colony—all situations I couldn't get people to talk about—I asked about Fernheim Colony's relationship to Germany. The close relationship developed, he told me patiently, after they left Russia, because Germany alone was willing to take them as refugees, even if only on an interim basis, and had been generous in their *Ausruestung*, equipping, and was generous still, supplying textbooks and other educational help.

I knew all this, but hoped he would reveal more about the splits within the colony this close relationship had produced.

"You can't imagine how primitive we lived," he said instead. "How simple our lives were. How we hated the dirt."

"Especially the teenage girls," his wife chimed in. "What they went through."

But the children, he said, those who were children, such as he was when they arrived, soon loved the Chaco. The landscape, flora and fauna. Even the weather.

I said I'd noticed this, that those who were young or born here loved it.

People milled around us, perhaps also wishing to speak with the couple, but now he had a story to tell me about the Christmas his father bargained something of theirs to obtain a "real" Indigenous bow and arrows for his son. He'd hardly dared dream of it, and now it was in his hands, a powerful symbol of where he belonged.

I said I thought it a beautiful story.

But the minister had additional points to make. He was a minister after all and couldn't easily give up, it seemed, his appreciative and interested audience of one as well as the compulsion to set me straight. Just in case, I supposed, I might imagine anything otherwise. "The history, nature, food, and language of the Mennonites here have formed together into a *Denkensart* [way of thinking]," he said pointedly, "that's different from the way North American Mennonites think."

I nodded, humbly enough I hoped.

He wanted me to know that progress had been visible. To settle in a new, strange land is to experience a continuous series of firsts or markers, he said. The first high school. The first teachers' training school. The first … the first … Steps and satisfaction one could see.

He'd given a familiar summary and I could nod along throughout it, and I liked his story of the bow and arrows (which was the kernel for a short story of mine later published in an *Augsburg Christmas Annual*) but I was definitely sensing I didn't pass muster as a possible teller of this past. It wasn't just the remark about North American versus Chaco *Denkensart* but phrases like "it just can't be understood," or "it can't be imagined," or "and another point that's difficult for you to see," which punctuated his commentary.

This both wobbled and hardened my resolve. Was it really impossible to imagine how it was? The very act of writing fiction asserts that imagination is capable of entering experiences other than one's own. Within myself I argued—though unlikely to win the argument with him—that I shared his Russian-Mennonite and home-seeking roots, that *Denkensart* could be accessed via research, living here, listening, experience, and yes, imagination. I also believed there were advantages to being an outsider. On the edge of things. Unbeholden to those inside. At an angle to see and hear differently, but also what was true.

How I REALLY knew I came from Away: I dropped everything for as long as it took to read the mail. For nearly two months, we'd had a grand total of two letters, one from my dad, one from an aunt. Rumour had it that mail from the North was stuck somewhere, in the capital perhaps. Ignored, or worse, being opened and emptied.

But one day, a bonanza of it. A letter with photos from my parents, a letter and parcel with Kool-Aid packets and shampoo samples and chocolate bars and other small delights from my sister and sister-in-law, another parcel from a friend which contained a frilly pink dress for the baby. Nine *Maclean's* magazines. We'd subscribed to the Canadian periodical to keep up with the news, and now we would be current to February, which was six months past. But never mind, though we'd already heard the broad strokes in other ways, the details would be new. The recession back home, Clifford Olson in jail, another electoral triumph for Peter Lougheed in Alberta. Ararat, Haig, Reagan, Begin, Thatcher. Deaths from Tylenol.

Prime Minister Trudeau pirouetting behind Queen Elizabeth's back and the National Citizens Coalition wanting him out for disrespect. Glenn Gould dead, ballerina Evelyn Hart at her prime. We knew Joe Clark had been replaced as head of Canada's Conservatives, but here he was, the question still open, on two successive covers at the beginning of the year: "Joe Clark on trial" and "After Joe, What?" Weird and fascinating, reading from away, from behind.

16. Reaching

REACHING SEEMED THE main characteristic of the developing infant, reaching arms to me, to her father and brothers, to the world. We held her standing on our laps and she stiffened to be taller in space. When I fastened her into a back carrier and rode with her on my bike to visit someone on the other side of Yalve Sanga she shrieked with excitement and stretched upward behind me as if to pluck at what she saw.

The boys were growing, learning, reaching too. School reports wouldn't be out until year's end, but the teacher handed the papers to her students for a look and our son had 10s, the highest possible mark. Twice he came home glowing to have won sweets in a math competition because he finished first with all answers correct. He also complained that his pencils, erasers, and sharpeners were being stolen and he was afraid to ask for them back.

"I sat and pretended to write," he told me after one homework-afternoon. "My pencil was broken and I had no sharpener."

Yet he seemed irrepressible, going cheerfully to school, singing on his way home. When an Indigenous man appeared at the yard and Helmut wasn't home, our son would listen and translate and answer for me, as the children of immigrants do. He was proud that he knew so much more Spanish than I did. By now both boys also spoke a fair German and Low German. The ease with which they picked up new languages made my plank tongue hurt with envy.

If his things sometimes went missing, our son had also made school friends and had allies. He was excited to be picked as the littlest goat, the goat who jumps into the clock to hide in the story of the wolf and seven goats, the play his class would perform for the closing program. He was beyond excited, actually. He had seven or eight lines to memorize.

Play practice happened evenings. It would be dark, but his teacher promised to make sure he got home safely. When I asked who had walked him home, he said, "The wolf and the hunter."

We celebrated Second Son's fourth birthday. Helmut and I eagerly watched his face as he opened the box with his new bike. He was as happy as we'd hoped. Now he had a BMX bike like his brother's! He had learned to ride a two-wheeler at three. The only thing he needed help with was the start, because his feet didn't reach the ground. But he had shot up and Helmut had been helping him mount and launch on his own, using his brother's bike, and he'd learned to do it, just in time. He'd talked often about a bike of his own but we'd downplayed the idea, acting as if he would have to wait until he was "a really big boy" and back in Canada. But now he had it, his own BMX two-wheeler.

We gave him something on the other end of the toy spectrum too: a teddy bear. He loved to cuddle and had a weakness for stuffed animals. His poor blue elephant was frayed and about to burst its stuffing.

When he opened his teddy, he was indignant. "I don't want a doll!"

"But it's not a doll," I cajoled. "It's a bear. Look how soft it is. And your elephant is falling apart." I drew him close, ruffled his hair.

He scrutinized the brown bear, considered what I'd said. Soon he was carrying it with him everywhere he went.

THE EUROPEAN MENNONITE agencies that sponsored projects in the Chaco sent representatives periodically to check on their investment. One, reputed to be the richest man in Hamburg, had come in April. He had a good grasp of the programs, was business-like, asked many questions. I was glad he realized it was the wider *wirtschafliche Lage,* economic situation, that accounted for the machines standing idle at the time of his visit.

Our direct contact, the German "boss" with whom Helmut had been corresponding for a year, planned to come in September. We had no specifics, however. Then one Saturday, I was informed he would arrive shortly to stay at our house. Helmut had taken the freezer into Filadelfia for repair and I had hardly any meat left, and next to no flour. What an inconvenient time for Paraguay to be out of flour! I scrounged enough from other Yalve Sanga households to quickly make a cake and a small recipe of sweet buns. There was cabbage and cauliflower in the garden and a sackful of grapefruit as well as papaya. I made *borscht*—cabbage soup— for supper and our guest graciously declared it *ausgezeichnet,* outstanding.

Sunday, I managed a meat loaf.

He was a shyer man than expected. He spoke slowly, quietly. He too asked many questions. The first day, he seemed weary. Jet lag, as well as a certain discouragement about the local Mission programs, I thought. The next day he appeared fresher, though in conversations I witnessed him having with others, I felt he was being fed a bleak view. Helmut and I tried to encourage him as best we could. We understood that those from abroad who give thousands of dollars annually also want distinct progress and results. But it felt unfair. They—local Mennonites as well as the helping groups—were asking, actually insisting, it seemed, that Indigenous peoples change their whole way of being. Their culture. How much had the Mennonites changed? Didn't we hang on to exactly the attitudes to work, family, and money we learned as children? For generations?

I wished I could comfort our German boss, speak to him as slowly and quietly as he spoke. But what exactly would I say? Just that I wished he not be discouraged? I was glad the weather was pleasant at least. Helmut and I had purchased a radio and joked that since we could now hear the weather reports we knew whether to be hot or not. Per radio, we knew Sunday's high was a perfect 20 degrees.

I was also relieved the truck stalled while our visitor rode along in it. And that he wondered if there wasn't string or wire or something to hold the truck doors more tightly shut. Whenever Helmut drove home from anywhere, he and his clothes were covered with a layer of fine dust that puffed in through holes in the floor. And when we drove into Filadelfia as a family for church, we wore old clothes and changed into clean ones there. The truck was close to *kaputi*, broken—a word that embraced all languages in the Chaco. But, we'd told ourselves, at least it was a motor and wheels and a roof over our heads.

It wasn't that our German supporters hadn't been sympathetic to Helmut's assertions that the station needed a different truck. But always it came down to finances. Now that the boss saw the old truck for himself, he suggested a new one would probably be in the works. He also told us that if we were willing to return for a further two years, we would be given a family furlough to Canada at this term's end. He said their organization wished to transfer the machine station to local hands; it was too difficult to administer from a distance. In that case, the local Mission office would have to renew the contract.

It was a lot to think about and consider. But if the boss seemed discouraged, Helmut found the meeting invigorating. He was enthused again. We were still uncertain about our future but he leaned in the direction of another term and I was okay to lean along.

THEN I WAS CAST down with disappointment. My good friend and her doctor husband would be leaving Yalve Sanga in a month and it was not their choice.

They were devastated, as were many others. How could it be, to lose these people already? We knew no details, but conflict between the two doctors—different personalities, vision, methodology—had been muttered about. Had he asked too many questions, offered too many ideas about relating differently to the Indigenous people they'd come to serve? Did the other physician, who required the absolute loyalty of her staff, feel threatened? We were friends with both parties, and supposed it complex as conflict usually is, but felt the termination unfair.

"We want foreign money here," Madam Doctor had once declared with her characteristic frankness, "but not foreign ideas."

But had anyone tried harder to fit than this couple? Now their lives, so brimming with hope and intention when they came, had been checked. A blow for them, and for us who would miss them.

WHAT STAYED WAS the day to day of weather and season—41 degrees and the mulberries were ripe—and the day to day of parenting. The boys set off on a "treasure hunt," by which they meant going for a walk to look for stuff. They returned in a buzz of eager noise. Stepping outside to find out what the commotion was about, I saw a small, decrepit washtub, one side of its rusted tin bottom torn and jutting, the other side piled with wood coal—the charred remains of burnt logs—which, they declared, made great black chalk. Already the two artists, one seven, one four, were kneeling and drawing houses, trees, and squiggles.

The sight of the crude dark sketches and that hideous old tub with its dirty "chalk" congealed and I comprehended only one thing, that most depressing of things: mess. The black drawings would wash off, but with how much effort? My mouth opened almost automatically to protest. And just in time, thank God, like a movie flashback, an episode from my childhood arrived to silence me. The tub was bigger but the same oval shape, me and a friend dragging it home, panting. A tub full of marvels like books, wallpaper, trinkets we found in the "nuisance grounds" where people dumped garbage. I'd been teased for that craziness over junk but nothing had been said to detract from the adventure. Now I swallowed the scold that nearly reached my mouth and bent for a closer look at their pictures.

Almost invariably, the gift of memory pointed me in the direction of mercy rather than criticism. How good it felt when I remembered in time that kids are kids, life is life. Oh how good indeed, when I got it right. Like the day the children and I strolled to the Yalve Sanga *tajamar*. It hadn't rained in a while and the pond wasn't deep. We ate a snack, the boys threw sticks, the girl gazed about and produced her characteristic happy noises.

Three *indígena* boys about the size of our sons showed up. They stripped and jumped in for a swim.

My two watched. "That looks like fun," the older one said wistfully. The younger agreed. They glanced at me.

"You want to swim?"

"Not naked," they said, nearly in unison.

"Go in with your shorts on then."

It was all the permission they needed. They flung off their shirts and were in. The water was dirty but what did they care? What did *I* care today? No chlorine, no rules against running on the deck or splashing, no admission fees. I could care horribly one day, and be fully carefree the next, see only freedom and advantages.

The other boys accepted mine amicably into the pond and soon all five were springing and leaping and dashing in and out and trying to paddle and generally having a wonderful time. They played for an hour or so and all the while the baby was cheerful and I was a contented mother sitting in the longish grass and fondly observing my tanned-brown sons at play in the cool muddy water and the little still-untanned one beside me in a puddle of green. And when the boys felt I'd been particularly favourable, like today, or when excited about something, they could be out-of-this world effusive with affection. "Mommie, I love you!" they would say, thrusting their arms out for a hug, and in the reciprocation of our fondness, every other domestic consideration dissolved.

THE BULLDOZER needed repair but was finally intact again and sent off to a job in Toyish. For a few days all was well, then the axle broke. Back to Yalve Sanga with it then. Helmut and the crew and a mechanic got busy making a new steel axle at the station. It was one thing after another. It was frustrating, but my husband rarely stayed down for long. The truck cab, he said, was his prayer chamber. He could set out for the work site in one frame of mind and arrive with a better one. I was often amazed, in fact, how cheerful he was, this travelling manager, buyer of parts and fixer of doddering machines, also known as husband and Daddy, whom the boys were constantly pestering now to "fight" with them when he came home from work. It was hilarious watching the little guys, all bravado, grimaces, bounce, and fists. They dived at him like kamikaze pilots. He laughed and easily fended them off. Even lying down, disadvantaged, they were no match for him.

"But it won't be so easy in fifteen years," I warned him, laughing too.

ANOTHER BROKEN part and he was off to Asunción and then Brazil again. I wanted to hold him back, let the problem pause, as if the bulldozer or tractor might fix itself if he just let it gel overnight, but he left hastily because he wanted to catch the night bus out of Filadelfia. I was clingy, I didn't want him to go, didn't send him off with a blessing, which of course I regretted the minute it was too late to reverse.

And while he was gone, our friends pulled out of Yalve Sanga, their small green pickup loaded high. Mennonite Central Committee would re-locate them to Argentina for the remainder of their term. Were they shaking off the dust of the place as they bumped down the road, turned onto the TransChaco Highway, direction Asunción? Two years before they'd driven in with wonderful ideals, vision, enthusiasm, prepared to make a long-term commitment. Buying supplies as if to stay. Volleyball nets and a wooden hand washer. Months of Spanish study, then German. Recently they were tackling the Enlhet language.

My eyes were wet. It seemed unbearable, people I loved driving away from me.

My husband returned of course, with what he needed for the machines. Then we attended the Mission Workers *Rüstzeit*, retreat, though I was in and out with the baby during the sessions and didn't get much out of them. I was dispirited but gained, near the end, a measure of forgiveness for the whoevers and whatevers of our friends' termination. A sense of lightness then, the assurance that God hadn't left Yalve Sanga with them after all. Well, left with them, yes, but stayed as well. It seemed obvious, set down later in my journal, but at first appearance the thought felt profound. And the sunset was gorgeous, really something to watch while driving home, the sun sliding out of sight like a shining globule of blood.

Back home, we discovered the compressor in the freezer had burned out in our absence.

But somehow in the middle of the day to day, the good and bad, in conversations driving to and from the *Rüstzeit*, we'd made a decision. We would add three months to our contract, stay until November 1984, a little better than a year away, but not return for another two-year term. Not leaning now but upright with having decided.

17. Diapers and a firefly

We lost two diapers to wind at the MennoHeim in Asunción.

The MennoHeim, short for Mennoniten Heim (Mennonite House), was founded in 1943 by Mennonite Central Committee, the agency that facilitated the settlement of Fernheim Colony and, after the Second World War, Neuland Colony. It was a walled compound with sleeping rooms of various kinds—communal rooms for families or groups, slightly more upscale rooms for individuals or couples—and a dining room, as well as an auditorium where Asuncióner Mennonites met for church, a place for colony Mennonites to stay while in the city for medical appointments or shopping, or travelling into or out of Paraguay. A huge tree ringed with a sandbox loomed like beneficence in the centre of the courtyard, flowering bushes and potted plants graced the edges, and there were white benches and a large sitting swing where guests relaxed or visited or stared at other guests.

I liked the MennoHeim, its purposeful atmosphere of security, the city's noise and sensuality moderated and provoked into modest familiarity. The place was clean compared to other lodgings of comparable price, and the prices were reasonable. The hum of German and Low German was worth something too, and food one was used to, though I found the lack of manners upsetting at times. Rather than asking for an item at the other end of the table, people might stand up and simply reach for it.

When the boys were at the MennoHeim, their biggest thrill was the purchase of Fanta, for which they'd developed a passion, right out of the fridge in the dining room. But they weren't along this time. Helmut and I and the baby had come, him to buy the new truck, and both of us to get the girl's Paraguayan identification papers made. We would process her Canadian citizenship once in Canada. It had been a flurry of a day, from stop to stop with the papers and then some quick shopping and everywhere the child got smiles from officials and shopkeepers and *linda, linda*, beautiful, beautiful. She was rather obvious with her blue eyes and pale blond hair, the birth-black gone. She'd been terrific through it all, if wiggly, fingerprinted three times with the right thumb and once with each of the other nine digits. The poor fellow doing it had quite a time of it, getting the proper finger into ink and onto the relevant papers. What threat could she possibly be to the government to make such a production of it? But such were the procedures. And during siesta, washing diapers just to keep up, two at a time, and now the two I'd hung to dry earlier had been whipped away by the wind. Nothing to do for it but return to the room where I was greeted by the prettiest sight: my husband and daughter both asleep on their stomachs, both backs bare, one long and broad and taut, the other so small in comparison, as soft and rounded as a marshmallow.

We returned to the Chaco in style, in the new double cab Daihatsu, airtight and comfortable, all doors closing, and the boys had done well at their respective places, they hardly missed their parents, they insisted, even though I missed them terribly, and full of stories about what they'd done. It must have been more of a strain for them than they realized, though, the effort of being especially good when staying with others. Re-united in our home, they seemed to be fighting a lot and were snippy with me. I was informed, for example, that one of the other women in Yalve Sanga had her Christmas decorations up and our house was ugly and ought to be Christmasy too.

I heaved the sewing machine out of storage to make Christmas stockings to hang.

Now that we had a radio I sometimes listened to *Winke für Frauen—A Moment for Women*, produced for Mennonite women on the local radio station. The program often addressed the theme of *only* housewife, *only* mother, counselling acceptance of course, and reminding of those precious and tender moments with which one is rewarded for perseverance and a job well done. Which was fine as far as it went. I stored up these moments too, except that such advice often felt, in the face of my frequent flailing as mother, too sentimental as antidote. I required something more rigorous, astringent. But when the children's naptime arrived each day I was so relieved to have a break, I didn't work my thoughts and perceptions through. I could have been analyzing, strategizing for better effect, I sometimes reproached myself, but no, out of sight, out of mind, the time too precious, their siesta yielding to distance, to my own rest, reading, or catching up—uninterrupted—on some other urgent task. I strategized on the fly, decided the upswing in the boys' grouchiness was on account of us taking the girl along to the capital and leaving them behind. On the fly, yes, and when they grumbled that I spent more time with the baby than them, I explained why, in what seemed the zillionth reiteration, that she couldn't look after herself yet, and also, I was still nursing her. And then I gave them some extra attention. On the fly I noted that their unhappiness burst out when they were hungry or exhausted or sick so I fed them, put them to bed, comforted them. On the fly I reminded myself, *love covers a multitude of sins.*

Years later while re-reading the novel that came out of our Paraguay years, *Under the Still Standing Sun*, and once past the discomfiture a writer feels over earlier writing, the typos proofreaders should have caught, and my over-use of semi-colons, I was struck by the fatigue that characterized my protagonist Anna. Again and again, she was depleted of strength.

Then I remembered: I composed the novel when I too had often been depleted.

WHAT I READ those years in the Chaco was generally what came to me serendipitously or could be borrowed from the libraries of friends. I read *The Collected Stories of John Cheever*, strikingly good, though his American suburbs-and-backyard-pools settings were about as far from the Chaco as it was possible to go. A new couple had settled into Yalve Sanga, newlyweds, the groom from the Netherlands and the bride from Manitoba (she became a good friend) and from their combined library I borrowed *The Fire Dwellers* by Margaret Laurence, *In Search of Myself* by Frederick Philip Grove, and a biography of Jung.

The Laurence book was almost too much for me, the writing so powerful, though I couldn't articulate where the power was, for the images, though good, weren't unusually so, and much of the storyline seemed obvious, and Stacey didn't seem entirely real to me either, her name filmy and her person disappearing under the steady roll of words like the shoulder frill torn off her mauve nightgown. Yet it took an unshakeable hold on me as I read. It must have been the scenarios of Stacey as a mother, too close to my own, even if more hopeless and unrelenting in the book. "But how is it I can feel as well that I'm spending my life in one unbroken series of trivialities?" she said. "The kids don't belong to me. They belong to themselves. It would be nice to have something of my own, that's all. I can't go anywhere as myself . . ."

Laurence let Stacey utter her struggle for fulfilment over and over, and on and on. And though the ending provided a slight uplift of mood, she wouldn't give in to happily-ever-after solutions. To me the mother concerns were page-turningly real—her sense of what would happen to her children, her fears that she was "creating" them somehow but not creating them well. Fear darker than duty, flourishing deep in the mother core itself. Stacey knew what every mother knows, that to raise a child is to begin a relationship one can't end or fulfill to sufficient maternal satisfaction, and that the truth of all this was so serious and frightening it left no room for violet-hued Mother's Day doggerel.

And this was true for me as well, the scene in which Stacey imagined God asking her what she'd done with her life and all she could say in reply was that she'd loved her children.

IN THE MONTH before Christmas I typed my mother-in-law's *Lebensgeschichte,* life story. I'd accomplished something of a coup: I'd persuaded her to write it. I promised to type it and we would duplicate it as a Christmas present for her children.

Mama's memoir amounted to about twenty single-spaced pages. She didn't think she could do it; it was Papa, after all, who sat evenings noting in his notebook what he'd done that day, and he'd been the main letter writer too, but he was gone and I told her that her story was as important as his. "Dora asked," she said, as if to excuse what she'd done, as if to say she wasn't seeking attention but had to acquiesce to the whims of a daughter-in-law.

The *Lebensgeschichte* surprised me with its strength and confidence. I knew my mother-in-law as a good woman, warm and accepting, but elderly, in poor health, still sad at being a widow, not talkative. An impression of timorousness.

She described her girlhood sorrow when her doll with the beautiful china head was broken by a visiting toddler and when thieves stole the family's three fine horses. She told of fleeing as a family to Moscow to seek permission to leave because her father was in danger of arrest. There, on November 23, she fasted and prayed until, while praying,

> a calmness came over me and I was sure that we would be able to leave. On the night of November 24-25 the police told us that we could go. We left Moscow on the 30th of November.
> We reached the border December 1.

Eighteen days on the ocean, another eight in the small river steamer on the journey up the Paraguay River to Puerto Casado from where they went by train and ox cart into their assigned land in the Chaco, and then, for the first time in her life, she slept under the open sky. Rolling up their tarp the next morning, she saw a snake curled under it. She had never seen a live snake. She looked accusingly at her father, as if to say, "Where have you taken us?" She could never abide snakes—or rats. They dug themselves a *Keller*, a basement for cool storage, and one morning she spotted a rat in it. Her brother wasn't home, her mother as petrified as she was, and her father refused to help. She grabbed a slab of *paloblanco* wood and struck at the rat, screaming over and over, until she finally succeeded in killing it. She called to her father that she had beaten it to death. "No," he said, "you screamed it to death."

Mama said her parents didn't seem discouraged in the Chaco, though they may have hidden their feelings. Letters from uncles and aunts who were sent into exile in Russia made them grateful for their freedom.

When she reached her engagement and marriage, Mama's story meshed with her husband Heinrich's. He arrived in the third refugee group. His father died at the end of 1930, and then, scarcely four months later, his mother died in a lightning strike. He too was struck and was unconscious for some time. The parentless young man took over a farm in Schoenbrunn village and the couple married September 5, 1931.

She told of the work Papa did (thirteen years as head of the industrial plant, his subsequent *palosanto*-cooking enterprise, the ranch, and his work manufacturing and installing pumps). She told of houses she lived in, the births and weddings of her children, her various illnesses, including the midlife shock of cancer, and challenges they faced. "We battled a lot with ants and grasshoppers the first years," she wrote, in a typical understatement.

About mid-point in her pages, she reached the last months of Papa's life, and then, like a river reaching the sea, the detail widened, the emotion thickened. She described his death, her recollection of subsequent days, the long ongoing sorrow. She missed him still, the entire arc of her story made that clear, and why wouldn't she after experiencing everything she knew of hardship and happiness together with him for some forty-two years? What the story also made clear was that whatever else Mama was, she was certainly not timid.

HELMUT HAD overnighted with the crew but now he was back and the boys were jubilant and my spirit soared. It was always much easier parenting with two parents around, and he wouldn't mind getting up extra early to feed the neighbours' chickens, which we had agreed to cover while they were away. What he minded was the ailing bulldozer. Overheating, and once repairs were done, still overheating. He asked for advice, invited mechanics to examine and diagnose, studied and re-studied the page of specifications for that bulldozer model. It wouldn't run as it should. People who had contracted work were impatient. He worked from morning to night, tethered to his machines.

My Nivaclé helper arrived to clean the floors while I started the laundry. Washing, hanging, bringing in, folding. Lunch. More hanging and retrieving and folding. The dishes. A batch of cookies. The baby was beginning to eat solids and sleep less and wanted to play. It was the school holidays and both boys circled me often with "What can we do? Will you read to us?" But good grief, what was I fantasizing about in the midst of all this? We had made our decision not to continue in the Mission beyond next year, but sometimes Helmut threw out the idea of staying in the Chaco and venturing something else. We had our 100 hectares or so of Papa's ranch which was divided according to Mennonite inheritance practices after his death: half for Mama, half divided among the children. His ideas were a lit match, mine sparked from it like shooting flame. Say we bought a *Wirtschaft*, farm, I thought, two non-farmers trying to farm, which I would then write about—interestingly, of course. A Susanna Moodie of the Chaco. Recording the details of everything from the births of calves to the emergence of cabbages to the churning of butter, not to mention the price of milk and eggs. Local customs and traditions.

I snapped to reality. And when, dear self, I asked, would you do this recording? When would you have time to every day note what you see right in front of you, yellow daisies on the table perhaps, and the whitewashed walls? The walls would have to be whitewashed before Christmas, that was the custom, but busy describing this, how would the walls get whitewashed? Didn't Susanna Moodie, the English-born woman who settled in Canadian bush, have a servant or two? And why would you want to farm, when your most dreaded task this week was getting up early to feed the neighbours' crazy chickens? When you dreamt you were drowning in eggs?

And, I pushed some more, do you intend to lay this farming like dirt on the white cloth of your own culture and upbringing? Don't you know how snooty and ridiculous you'll look?

Thus I argued against myself, and all the while I kept getting whiffs of silo smell from the straw seat covers Helmut had purchased somewhere and set down by the door. The shots of pungent aroma should be farm enough.

"Look," I said to the married niece visiting from Neuland Colony. Strange sky in the south. A low purplish cloud on the horizon.

We were in the midst of tea and talk, made even lovelier because I'd devoted the previous week to a thorough pre-Christmas cleaning. I'd washed the windows and curtains and everything else I could think of to wash. My labour may not have been obvious to my guest, but I knew myself in a purged and rarified atmosphere.

Now I'd turned to the window as if to search for another topic of conversation. And there it was. I said "Look," and she looked.

"Looks like a dust storm," she said.

"Then I better get the diapers in."

I managed to pull half the diapers off the line before the wind and dust arrived. As I was closing the bedroom shutters a blast of it grabbed a panel out of my hand and nearly took off my head. I scrambled back inside, one hand gripping the salvaged diapers, the other pressing my ear where the shutter had hit. Then for the next long minutes—ten or fifteen it must have been—the niece and the children and I gazed through the glass living room windows into a dense grey cloud of Chaco topsoil roaring toward us at gale force speed. It parted around the house but rushed for entry too; the air inside the house greyed, we tasted dust on our lips.

My week of cleaning was totally undone.

When the storm finally ceased, we were drawn without discussion to the centre of Yalve Sanga where others had gathered to assess the damage. A large tree uprooted and fallen at a teacher's residence, just missing the house but blocking the door. A water tank blown over. The wind measure gauge indicated 100 kilometres an hour, but that was as high as the gauge could go, so who knew what the actual number had been.

The niece left for home and I went back to the house to dust and sweep. I scooped up the mounds of grey that mocked a whole week's work. I sighed and grumbled.

Later I heard that squatters along the *Ruta* had lost their homes to the wind. Perspective then: a week's work was not tragedy; my house had not blown away.

CHRISTMAS EVE. A LOAD of diapers agitated in the wash machine. They couldn't be left until after the holiday weekend. We ate supper and the boys opened their presents. They bounded off happily to play—while there was daylight—at "Daddy" with their new tractor and scraper and *stucker*, a bladed machine that cut up roots and trees, both miniatures of the machine station's tractor and scraper. They'd been singing *Feliz Navidad* on repeat for weeks and I knew they would be totally satisfied with their Chaco Christmas, meals at gatherings featuring manioc salads and beef roasted over white *quebracho* ashes, flies swarming in the heat, crickets chirping and chirping, sweet ripe watermelons for dessert instead of fruit cakes and pies. I, though, was feeling a little homesick—homesick for cold and snow, for greetings shouted by lips reddened in winter air, for the smells of pine and turkey and candles. Baubles on a cactus hardly sufficed to evoke my festive spirit.

The sun set; the dark was hot. Helmut cleaned the large water thermos and hung the diapers. We coaxed the boys into winding down for bed. The baby, who usually settled well into sleep by now, screamed when we put her into her crib and kept screaming, as if she knew the evening was special and she was missing it. Helmut tucked the boys in for the night and also went to bed. I picked up the girl, let her nurse some more.

The house was quiet now and the lights were off. I sat in the dark with the child, feeding, patting, rocking her. Singing. The small body in my arms grew heavy with contentment. Christmas Eve and the household was asleep. Well, why not? Yes, why not? I cuddled my baby as Mary must have cuddled hers. I was singing "This little light of mine" when I spotted a firefly bleeping its way along the floor in the living room darkness, its tiny light blinking on-off-on-off. Charting a course across the tiles, as if bidding me follow a tiny lantern to Bethlehem. I thought of Mary again, sore, bleeding, a red scrunched-up infant at her breast, Joseph washing or hunting for clothes or food, disposing of bloody straw. Someone had to cover those necessities. Sleep would definitely be required. Maybe like my Christmas there were fireflies by the manger, maybe shepherds sang *Feliz Navidad.*

AFTER CHRISTMAS, we had a mini-Christmas upon the arrival of a box of books sent by my aunt in Manitoba. The box had been opened, at customs we assumed, but the contents seemed untouched. We were grateful for that, and even more astonished and grateful for her generosity, the books worth $65, she'd noted on the mailing label, the postage costing $24. Which seemed a lot of money at the time.

Eighteen books—fourteen for the children. My aunt was a teacher and attentive to our children. The boys examined and exclaimed over every book. They launched a duet of please please please, will you read to us? It was evening and late, but, all right, we would start one as a treat to mark the occasion. They deliberated and chose *Runaway Ralph* by Beverly Cleary, about a mouse who lived in a run-down hotel in the foothills of the Sierra Nevada and drove a mouse-sized red motorcycle.

The postal surprises continued the following week with an armful of mail. The older boy got a parcel from his grandparents with the English Bible he'd requested for his birthday. He tore the package open and dashed off to his room, clutching his Bible and full of emotion. After lunch, he read to us. He read well. He declared he would read one chapter of the New Testament every day, starting with Matthew. I suggested he might start with Mark instead, because Matthew opens with a long genealogy. He agreed and began the Gospel of Mark, then realized how long a chapter can be and decided one section of a chapter per day would do as well.

His jubilation provoked a crisis for his younger brother, who could be heard crying in the bedroom. He so wanted to be at level with the older boy, to be *big*. "Everybody's always bossing me around!" he might say, or "You never let me make my own decisions." How was it that preschoolers said what I assumed I might expect of teenagers? And it wasn't fair, he said, that his brother could read and he couldn't. "All I can read is *Each Peach Pear Plum!*" Which was a picture book he'd memorized. The older brother's well-intentioned compliments didn't help. "That's not as nice as mine," he might say, about a drawing or some other effort, "but it's really good for a four-year-old."

The boy's weeping was a whirlpool of all these accumulated sorrows, and tiredness too. We comforted him and got both boys into bed for siesta. Then the rest of the mail suspended my schedule, as it always did, and Helmut's too, while we sat and read letters. There was a birthday card from my parents, just in time for my birthday the next day. For some reason—sheer happiness, I suppose, on account of so much mail and our seven-month-old daughter in her high chair looking innocent and goofy with noodles in her hair—the lines Mom had underlined in the card—*It seems like only yesterday That you were just 'so high'*—launched a rash of hefty tears. I was turning thirty-four and the girl who was "just 'so high'" had learned to clap her hands and my mother remembered birthdays and wrote letters, and I was poised between my mother and my daughter and loved them both and apparently it was a day for crying.

"Turn around twice," I blubbered, pointing at the girl, "and I'll be sending a thirty-fourth birthday card to *her!*"

Absorbed in the Christmas letters that had reached us in a heap, I forgot about the bread dough I'd mixed and kneaded before lunch and, unnoticed, it rose and rose and overflowed the pan. It had risen too much and the loaves caved when I set them into the oven. We ate them anyway. Like a cup of cold water, says the proverb, is good news from home. Or, like neglected but edible bread.

AM I WRITING about trifles?

If I warm to my defense, I can quote John Updike who said that the purpose of writing is to "give the mundane its beautiful due." Including, I would say, the quotidian details of domesticity. I may have wished to escape them often enough, but was committed to asserting their value as well. I was learning myself, always, into womanhood and it was women's stories I listened for and wished—then and now—to tell. When one reviewer of *Under the Still Standing Sun* said, in 1990, "Anna is clearly a budding feminist (within the modest bounds of her Christian-Mennonite environment, of course) who is not afraid to question and probe such issues as male domination, Mennonite nonresistance, pro-German sentiment in the Mennonite colony, and education and equality for modern Mennonite women," I was pleased. I wasn't calling myself a feminist yet because the word seemed to require too much explanation, but I liked that sentence.

My feminism expressed itself in two interests: in women's significance as people, their vital humanity and therefore equality, and in their agency, wherever it could be found. The official histories of the Chaco were told by men. *About* men mainly. It wasn't that I was trying for a version of history, I was interested in my Anna character for her own sake, but she lived through that history and I wanted to see it through her eyes.

I've probably gravitated to female characters in my fiction to learn from them for myself. How they crash against the limitations imposed by their environment, or move within them. My coming-of-age occurred at a time when the lives and roles of women were prominent discussion points in North American culture, when the great quiet mass of female Being stirred and said, *Stop thinking of me as lesser, stop thinking of me in stereotypical terms, I'm neither angel nor demon, but human.*

But I didn't mean Anna as any kind of lesson either. I was interested in how the women of the Chaco suffered, how they survived. If women's liberation was about agency, she was simply one example of how power could be inhibited or enlarged and extended.

WHICH IS ALSO NOT to say that women of the Chaco, for all their admirable qualities and courage, didn't sabotage themselves. Consider the letter to the *Mennoblatt*, 16 August 1983, from a writer identified only as "A housewife from Filadelfia."

> Opening your 12-page August 1 issue I stumbled over many long and no doubt worthy themes and titles. But in the midst of all this submitted and received material you left out the "Corner for Home and Housewife." Or did it happen on purpose? I think that the peace theme would have lent itself to much practical consideration also for the weaker sex and for those less educated, so we don't simply set the paper aside without reading it.

18. DREAMS AND *ZORN*

WE GOT A dog, a young dark-haired German shepherd cross with taffy-blond highlights. She was supposed to be a watch dog. Bark, at the very least. We could have used some barking the night Helmut was wakened by a sound, leapt to the window, saw someone walking off the yard. He rushed outside, couldn't find anyone. There were tire marks turning in and out at the driveway. When he checked the garage where he kept machine station supplies, nothing seemed to be missing except the hunting rifle. Though he wasn't sure he'd last put the gun in the garage or left it at the work site.

The boys were thrilled with the dog. They named her Tuffy, for their idealized tough-dog vision of a canine. They were annoyed when she was mostly frisky and friendly, when she "bothered" them. The idea of a dog, like the idea of a baby sibling, was different than the reality of babies and dogs. But they got used to her and loved her. And she seemed fond of them. If never much of a watch dog, she was good with the children, and especially careful with and even mindful of the baby.

Some while later, in heat and whining bitterly over the unaccustomed harassment from local dogs, Tuffy sprang into the truck box for a trip to Filadelfia, as if she knew it would give her a break. She stayed obediently in the open box until one of the last stops on a string of errands, where she jumped out and was gone.

We announced the missing dog over the radio and contacted the *Ordnungsmann,* the colony constable, with the details.

After some weeks, we heard that a German shepherd had been hanging around a certain house in Filadelfia. Sure enough: our Tuffy. She went nearly crazy with excitement to see us again. She was also pregnant.

In due course Tuffy bore four pups. She laboured in the garage and we stood in awe for some time, watching a pup emerge, watching how the young mother instinctively and immediately knew what to do with her offspring, solicitous for each, licking and nudging a newborn toward her with her teeth, even while clearly in pain and not yet finished with the birth.

She was fiercely protective later too. Anyone coming near her babies got a growl or show of teeth. With one exception. Our little human girl could touch, squeeze, even pick up the dogs. Tuffy tolerated anything she did.

Mid-February and harvest began in Yalve Sanga. Increase and industry pulsed in the air. A tractor hummed through the night in fields near our house, turning up the peanuts, and Indigenous families passed in wagons loaded with bulging sacks of cotton. Bits of escaped cotton fluff snagged on grasses along the roadway. The Enlhet store filled with people purchasing supplies with the money they'd earned at fieldwork.

School started again. Our son looked forward to seeing his friends. He returned at noon the first day enthused about his new teacher. "She's way better," he declared. "She has rules."

Although the Mission promised German instruction in language arts for him and another Yalve Sanga staff child now also attending Escuela Mariscal Estigarribia, nothing had come of it. A family with another school-ready child quit their Mission position on account of the educational question. Helmut and I wished a better resolution on the matter but found ourselves less concerned about it now that we'd decided not to extend our term.

The baby was standing up and walking along furniture, and her culinary tastes had widened to include dirt and insects. She amused herself for long periods, chattering away. The younger boy had become something of an Eeyore ("How did you sleep?"—"Not that good." "Did you have a good time?"—"Not that good"), though he was quite cheerful otherwise and spent hours playing with his tractor and other toys in the sand, or riding his bike, when it wasn't grounded with a flat. He had a vivid imagination, which he explained as seeing with his eyes closed. "It's because my eyes are turned around then," he said, "and facing into my head."

I asked him if he wanted to go to Canada.

"I'm more used to Paraguay," he said.

AFTER READING BITS of Carl Jung's biography in a book by Laurens van der Post, I began to record my dreams.

I dreamt I was at the house of a mission fundraiser, one of those confident public relations types. There was a repair shop in front of the house with a vehicle waiting to be fixed. Also a wringer washer. Someone was doing their laundry. It was a graduation service of some sort. I walked in nicely and was not self-conscious. The audience had to sit in alphabetical order. We sang hymns. A very fat woman with a baby and a fattish man were praised. "He planted 87 churches," the public relations man told me. I couldn't believe it. "You mean evangelized and someone did the follow-up?" "No, planted them." I wasn't impressed. I wanted to leave the group and be part of another one, somewhere else.

I dreamt that Helmut and I were travelling in Russia. In Moscow, it seemed. It was muddy. Worried about lodging, I was consulting a guidebook. We came to a beautiful onion-domed church, some two hundred years old. There were crude steps up to it, as if it was under construction. A huge tent-like structure had been built over the church to protect it. The building under the protective covering was small but lovely. It had radiant blue tones and seemed fragile.

I had no tools for dream analysis but thought these dreams might reflect my current disillusionment and critical spirit about the religious conditions around me, as well as my own religious aridity, my own gaps between saying and doing. I thought the latter dream might also be telling me something about the beautiful centre of faith. If the outside structure appeared rough and unfinished, deep within the core was wondrous.

I wished to think and speak in ways fresh and green but wasn't sure how. Besides, even fresh words, like meat and milk in the heat, quickly lost their freshness. Maybe I was cynical because Helmut and I hosted an English "sharing time," one of those sporadic efforts that folks in Yalve Sanga mounted for a bit of churchly life on the "mission station," and it had seemed a dud to me. I led it. Tried, that is. Tried to solicit expressions of how things were going personally, spiritually. There was next to no response. Only Helmut and my new Canadian friend gamely acted as if they were on course with the evening's intention. Maybe they pitied me. One of the clinic staff seemed miles away and only re-appeared at the end with a prayer request for "more love for the Indians." Another woman did her best, but the concept of "sharing" may have been too radical to her. The chief theologian of the group couldn't say much because he had a cold but he rallied at the end and gave us a short sermon. The important things we'd all missed, I supposed.

Perhaps the man who was attentive without participating was the most honest of us all.

How curiously bound together we were, such disparate people, simply by virtue of knowing English and working in Yalve Sanga.

But curiously disconnected too.

AND THEN, ON A HOT white Monday morning near the end of March, I steamed out of the house, over our backyard at an angle, along the worn sand-soil path across the field beside us, every step increasing in indignation—in *Zorn*, really, the German word for anger, which imitates its meaning by sounding like a treacherous bee—and there he was, the chief agriculturalist/administrator of Yalve Sanga, the very person I wanted to see, coming around the corner of the office building as if he wanted to see me too, though he was completely unsuspecting of what was about to occur.

I made a scene. I really let him have it.

It was, ostensibly at least, about the milk. For days Yalve Sanga had rumbled with rumours about the milk project coming to an end, the faithful Enlhet milkman weary, it was said, and planning to stop delivery. No other provision for worker families to purchase milk had been arranged.

About the milk, then, I railed at him. The no-milk, that is, about to be a big problem for families in Yalve Sanga who needed to have milk.

It was just the milk. In fact, I'd remarked to my journal the day before that though I wondered how the matter would be resolved, I was relaxed about it and noticing this, was pleased with myself, and I'd written this down too. Then Helmut told me something unkind the administrator had said and a bearish defensiveness on his behalf flared up underneath the problem of milk, and even further below flickered my knowledge of a disagreement the fathers of these two men had had decades ago. And then the milk project's demise heaved into view once more, like a log to the fire, and with it the Mission's seemingly utter disregard for workers and their children, be it their schooling or their daily drink. So yes, about the milk, but so much more fumed beneath what I dumped on him, not quietly, not calmly, there on the hard earth beside the building, the sun relentless over our heads—for wasn't he responsible for the station and *everything*?

Later I could scarcely remember what I said. It was loudly about the milk, though I know I concluded my speech with a final blow about the low level of Christianity in a supposedly Christian place—was the Spirit even present, I asked, as if the Spirit was his responsibility as well. I was vaguely aware of an Enlhet man at the periphery of my vision, a hoe or some implement in hand and his head raised and my words reaching him, of course, for they spilled like heat waves in all directions. He wouldn't have understood them, they were High German words, but the tone and raised voice would have spoken plenty. And there were others on the yard, and probably behind the open windows of the building, overhearing the fiery zing of my words, and then I was done and hurrying back to the house, my emotions not burnt down as hoped, not released, though I wasn't feeling quite guilty either, for the milk concerns were still legitimate, but deeply ashamed, and immediately so, at their manner of delivery. My entire body swelled red along the path homeward, conspicuous now to all Yalve Sanga, I felt, which minutes earlier had been going peacefully about its Monday morning business. Once home, I cried.

Two days after my outburst, after I'd apologized to the administrator though not yet forgiven myself, I got my first menstrual period in nineteen months. I'd been pregnant for nine, breastfeeding for ten. So the shift of hormones was a factor, though I'd given that possibility no forethought whatsoever. I generally experienced one or two days of premenstrual syndrome per cycle, when my nerves jittered and sparked, and I'd learned to be cautious with reactions on those days, but I'd been so long off the routine of menstruation, I forgot the way it ebbed and affected me.

Hormones amok: an explanation, then, but not enough to exonerate me to myself.

The boys and I, and Helmut too, were well into *The Horse and His Boy*, the third in the Narnia books by C.S. Lewis, the story of the talking horses Bree and Hwin and their humans Shasta and Aravis, who set out to escape the dark and southern kingdom of Calormen for the "free" and northern one of Narnia. Reading chapter by chapter over several weeks of evenings, this book had given us all plenty of new material and vocabulary for daytime thoughts and commentary. "Tisroc (may he live forever)," we teased, and the boys tossed Tarkhaan and Tarkheena into their play, and when one of them asked, "Where are you going, Dad?" he replied, to their delight, "Narnia and the North."

It didn't occur to us that C.S. Lewis may have drawn on stereotypes about civilizations like the Ottomans in his tale of the Calormenes and Narnians; we would hear about that decades later. Now we simply absorbed it as rousing adventure with a great read-aloud style, with distinctly charming or villainous characters and plenty of action, a book we adults enjoyed as well as the children, and if the boys picked up on its wisdom or made comparisons to real-life situations, well, that was a bonus. They had certainly both come to love Aslan the Lion, who was both great and good.

As for me, now I resonated with Bree: his prowess, pride, humiliation. Chased by a lion, Bree ran for safety while Shasta slipped off his back to help the other horse and her girl. He who held himself high as a war-horse and the veteran of a hundred fights simply galloped ahead to save his own hide. When the shame of this hit, it hit hard. Bree thought he'd lost everything.

"My good Horse," a wise hermit reminded the mortified Bree, "you've lost nothing but your self-conceit. . . . But as long as you know you're nobody very special, you'll be a very decent Horse, on the whole, and taking one thing with another."

Since the problem of milk for Yalve Sanga remained unsolved, it seemed only right—a kind of penance as it were—that I find a solution. Together with others, I was able to arrange for someone who regularly drove to Yalve Sanga through village Hohenau, some ten kilometres away, to stop for milk at a dairy farm several times a week and bring it to a central location, where those who needed it could pick it up. The price was reasonable, thirty guaranies a litre, and soon there was plenty of milk to be had—for drinking, for delicious ice-cream made from thick fresh cream, for cottage cheese. Enough to share. One of the bulldozer drivers, his young son with him, stopped by on a cool soggy day to speak with Helmut and the child peed through his shorts and looked so cold and wet and miserable, I didn't know what to do but I had milk and I thought it might help so I fetched him a cup full as if it was warmth. The boy wouldn't take it. I set the cup down on the floor beside him and his father picked it up and drank it all.

It's the Enlhet man, standing in the periphery of my vision on the day of my rant who draws my attention as I look back at this episode. I wonder if he spoke of it at his wood fire that evening, I wonder if the Yalve Sanga *indígenas* had assigned a name to me before that day, or if they gave me one then. (Though I'm not sure I want to know it.)

The mother of Abram Loewen, who wrote a memoir of his interactions with the Enlhet, *Frau Braun, die Lange, die übrigblieb*, was assigned the name *die böse Mutter*, the angry mother. Loewen grew up with Enlhet children in the 1930s when the Mennonites settled the Chaco. He learned their language. He learned *Spuren-Lesen*, reading of footprints. Through long association at Caraya, where he later established a ranch and the Enlhet had an encampment, and later in the Mennonite village Landskrone, which had been laid out on original Enlhet territory, he gained insights into their *Denkensart*, their way of thinking. He recalled his mother storming outside after some Enlhet women filled their bags with vegetables and fruit from her garden. She grabbed their bags, dumped the contents, and ordered them to leave. Thus, The Angry Mother, and thus his own name, Son of The Angry Mother. (Later, because of his prowess with a lasso, he was named The One Who Throws the Cattle, and still later, because he put a jaguar head over his ranch house, Jaguar Head.)

Loewen described the Enlhet view that a person who doesn't master themself dishonours themself. He told of old Piff disappearing from the encampment one day; all knew where and why he'd gone. Into the bush, of course, because he had a *Stockwut im Bauch*, rage curdling in his stomach, and instead of exhibiting it or letting it become destructive, he went away alone, gathered honey or berries perhaps, let "the loneliness of the thorny landscape" soothe him until his fury had passed. After that, the conflict or source of his anger could be addressed.

Loewen further described being reprimanded by an older Enlhet man at the Caraya ranch—a reprimand, but spoken quietly in a long, roundabout, self-controlled manner. Not only should the contours of the inner world be peaceful, but the outer should be a plane of dignity too. Mennonites told Loewen stories about *his* Indigenous, he said, but the *indígenas* had stories too, about *his* Mennonites. They thought the settlers uncivilized because they didn't seem to know common-sense ways to behave.

The Mennonites who settled the Chaco both appreciated and undervalued the Indigenous people they discovered living there (initially only Enlhet), both helped and used them, but the general attitude I picked up in my few years there was profound misunderstanding of their culture and disdain for their habits, especially in matters of cleanliness and property. The prospect of becoming "white Indians" was used as a warning to Mennonites in the early years, as motivation to keep washing and cleaning, to maintain school and church and music events, to form a news periodical, no matter how difficult the circumstances or surroundings.

I realize in retrospect how rudimentary my comprehension of the *indígena* worldview was. I wish that as non-Indigenous people working and living in Yalve Sanga and other Mission settlements, we'd been given more cultural training by those with long experience, anthropologists and the like, and by *indígena* teachers themselves. The original inhabitants, Abram Loewen claimed in his book, were *weltoffen*, world-open—open, that is, to what other groups had to offer in terms of spiritual power or "medicine." Were Mennonites open to learning from them? Did our neighbours possess medicine we needed for our ills, our wounds? Sometimes, Loewen said, he was "Indian enough" to control his impatience, but the next time, he admitted, he was *ganz unindianisch*, "completely un-Indian," and complained and scolded about everything.

That man with the hoe had listened and watched. If I'd known of Enlhet astonishment at Mennonites who lost their innermost selves, who hadn't mastered their anger, would it have shamed me into staying home with my *Zorn* and "leaving" for some metaphorical bush to work the emotion into quietness before bursting out to express it?

Another Loewen—Jacob Loewen, linguist and anthropologist—spent some time in the Chaco helping Mennonites know and relate to their Indigenous neighbours. In his ethnographic research, he wrote later, "the Indians confided that it was very difficult to live with the Mennonites because of their unstable innermosts."

19. REFLECTION

HELMUT'S OLDEST sister visited from Uruguay so we held a family gathering and had a family photo taken, Mama with her ten children, and then one with spouses as well. In Canada, two of my younger sisters got married, three weeks apart. On the days of their weddings, I figured out the time difference and imagined the discrete moments of it: the bride coming in, the ceremony, the reception. With my best imagination and heart, I was there. It was spring in the North and here, we'd advanced through autumn into winter. We marked the girl's first birthday with a candle and cake, and, as if she knew how momentous it was to be age one, she took her first extended steps across the living room, the boys cheering her on. Several weeks later we celebrated our younger son's fifth birthday with our friends, the Dutch/Canadian pair, who joined us for supper.

When I took the children's winter clothes out of the high built-in cupboard in their bedroom, the older son and I laughed and laughed. He put on his jacket and his arms dangled far out of the sleeves. He pulled on his long pants and the hems waved high above his ankles. How he'd grown! School was going well for him, and miraculously it seemed, he and the other Mennonite student of Yalve Sanga, a girl, were now getting German instruction three times a week from one of the teachers. The boy was so *begeistert,* enthused, about it, this teacher reported, she couldn't get over him at first.

The younger boy was growing apace. He was tall and lean and had completely lost his round, little-boy look. He knew the alphabet and quite a few sums, up to eight plus eight. "When I was little," he said, "I thought 1 + 1 = 2, 2 + 2 = 3, 3 + 3 = 4 and so on." Now that he was big, he knew better.

"Mom!" I heard him call numerous times a day, "I'm going hunting!" Helmut had purchased a sack of *Kugels,* clay balls, from some Indigenous boys who rolled them for sling shots, and now our son spent hours stalking around the yard with a tin of *Kugels* in one hand and his sling shot in the other. He would sneak as close as possible to the tree or wire where birds sat, take aim, let fly. The birds startled and lifted briefly into the air. Carefully he sneaked up again, and the hunt continued.

"Missed it by that much!" he reported, his hands just inches apart.

He also practiced shooting a tin can on a pole and one gleeful day succeeded twice, once hitting the pole and once the can.

Sometimes, hanging laundry or busy at the sink or kitchen counter, I stopped my work to watch him. Over and over, the hunt, its set-up, the shot, the near-miss, the next attempt. It fascinated me to watch my children when they were unaware of being watched, completely unselfconscious, acting for their own reasons. How intent and wonderfully vital they were. The way the older boy moved his tongue in his mouth as he concentrated on his workbook pages. The way the girl examined objects she discovered in her crawling about. Opening and closing cupboard doors, lifting excited arms to the two shiny metal vent circles under the sink. The younger boy with his slingshot and his birds or tin. Was it the children I saw, or were they reflecting something to me that had emerged into the world with me as well, a curiosity and focus surely everyone is born with but seems to un-remember too soon? These investigations, this childish and seemingly repetitive striving wasn't boring or "work" but of the human essence. Pleasurable. Joyous. The children liked being alive, and this was how they showed it. When I allowed myself time to observe them, like an investigation of my own, their expression—and modelling—of the essential seemed beautifully important to notice and emulate.

LIFE COULD HARDLY get better, could it? The bulldozer was working well. Only rain periodically brought the machine station endeavours to a halt. Helmut was busy supervising a procedure—chaining—which was new to the program though not new to the Chaco. A heavy cable was strung between two bulldozers that moved parallel along previously cut trails. The process was repeated with a chain in the other direction to remove the roots. When the uprooted bush was dry, it was burned. Chaining was a longer method of clearing land for cattle grazing but initially, in terms of machine hours, it was faster, hence cheaper.

Which reminds me of Miriam Rudolph, an artist working mainly as a printmaker, who grew up in Menno Colony in the Chaco. She moved to Winnipeg and later Edmonton to study art. Some of her recent work depicts bush, cows, people, and fences in a way that critiques deforestation for agricultural expansion; it expresses her sadness and dismay at the changing ecology of the Chaco and how this affects both people and landscape.

I admire Rudolph's pieces with a pin-piercing awareness that what Helmut and I did during his assignment with the machine station in Yalve Sanga in the 1980s contributed to exactly such deforestation. Cattle raising gained value in the local economy, exponentially, it seemed. Clearing bush for raising cattle and clearing for others on a contract basis encouraged Indigenous groups to participate in this shift. I would like to think that the blame for deforestation, which is ongoing, should be laid at the feet of rich, greedy ranchers whose holdings blanket the Chaco, but it's not that simple; all its inhabitants are entangled in this, in what has been won and what has been lost. We were in it too.

ANOTHER BOOK, AND ANOTHER, read in the evenings to the boys. The school winter break, when they enjoyed some days with cousins. An all-day excursion with other families to the Weber Kamp, a cattle ranch of some renown about an hour-and-a-half away, and to Mariscal Estigarribia, the small military town which was capital of the Chaco then, where the kids were allowed to roller-skate on the airport runway, no planes coming or going. A surprise visit from my friend and her daughters, a wonderful, harried week, five children underfoot. An all-day and overnight school excursion to Laguna Capitan for the older boy, including a visit to Fortin Boqueron, and later his reports of a good time, especially the visit to Boqueron where they toured the remains of trenches, bunkers, and graves from the first major battle of the Chaco War. Paraguay defeated the Bolivians there, though thirst was as deadly an adversary for both sides as enemy fire. José Félix Estigarribia, after whom their school was named, led the attack. The boy been coming home from school intoxicated with history, describing to us with great fervor Paraguay's "good" president, Carlos Antonio Lopez, and then his "bad" son, Francisco Solano Lopez, who wouldn't surrender in the Three Nation War until nearly every man in Paraguay was dead. The names clipped off the young scholar's lips with impressive precision. He repeated Francisco Lopez' dying words in Spanish ardently like a true Paraguayan patriot: *Muero por mi patria!* I will die for my country! Evenings I sometimes overheard him re-enacting some scene or another in the bathroom, mostly in Spanish, though I recognized bits about Mennonites and not fighting too.

Helmut and I began a morning ritual we continued for the rest of our marriage, namely, starting the day with *maté*. He was the first awake, put the kettle on, spooned yerba leaves into the *guampa*, drank a test infusion. On cold mornings, he made a fire in the fireplace. Sometimes he made the fire in the evening and if there was a *palosanto* log in the mix, it might still be glowing in the morning, exuding the sweet and slightly medicinal scent of its wood. When the *maté* was ready, he roused me and we drank in alternating fashion until each had had enough. We talked about the day ahead. He was a morning person but I'm not and the slow hot procession of liquid and caffeine and communication helped rouse me into full wakefulness.

We plowed through mud to Filadelfia one Saturday when officials from the capital had arrived to make *cedulas,* in another attempt to clarify the status of the boys and me. Helmut and the girl were born here, had their papers but what complications and penalties might the rest of us face at our departure? This time there were no demands I leave the country to make a new visa; the Fernheim mayor's office typed up certificates of residence for us, we were permitted to proceed, and finally, papers filled out, photos taken, all fingers fingerprinted, we had our *cedulas,* good for five years, evidence that we were here indeed and who we said we were. That we belonged in Paraguay.

All of us were now equipped with precious documents of residence, but in truth, we had begun to pivot to the end of our term, setting goals not for dwelling but for leaving. Helmut wanted to finish his role at the machine station well. I'd taken a break from the novel and attempted a play, but that was done, and knowing how quickly the remaining half year or so would pass, became acutely conscious of what I still needed from the Chaco in terms of myself and the book. What I still needed to see, take notes about, research, so I could re-write effectively in Canada.

I hired a niece to mind the children and do the housework for a week and spent a couple of days alone in Filadelfia. Spent them in the Archives, reading the 194-page typed manuscript by Dr. J. Postma about the *Völkische Bewegung*, the Nazi sympathy movement. The manuscript was controversial and supposed to be kept "under a lid," so I had to read it in the building. I read the reports and letters of an American dentist who worked in the Fernheim colony under the auspices of Mennonite Central Committee, who got himself rather heavily involved on the anti-Nazi side of the situation. For the first time, I had a chronological sense of those ideologically tense years, 1937 to 1944, years it had been nearly impossible to get people to talk about. The events and splits over ties to Germany, and Nazism, were referenced in the jubilee histories, yes, but the telling seemed pinched and severe—controlled by list-like cause and effect—compared to the loquacity of the colonists' reminiscences of early settlement. There was reconciliation—deep, significant reconciliation, apparently; the silence must have grown out of promises to put it behind them, not discuss it further. But why did reconciliation require dead air around what had happened? I wasn't turning up stones to frustrate beetles, I just wanted to understand the period. My fictional Anna lived through those years.

"The true history of Fernheim has yet to be written," the archivist confided. "The official history is very official and selective."

It was all fascinating but I was exhausted by the end of two days away. Hour after hour of non-stop reading in a complex German. I finished the Postma manuscript five minutes before Helmut arrived to pick me up.

I was also increasingly engaged with what was ahead of us in Canada. The months clipped along with a *just need to do this yet and then that* pace, they counted down, and though they were shot through with farewell, I was lining up wishes for the future like the children did for their birthdays, thinking home as anticipation now, hoping for some place where the children could thrive and be happy. We weren't sure if that would be Saskatoon, where we lived before Paraguay, or Winnipeg, where we lived before Saskatoon.

Helmut was calm about it all, except that one day he threw out a dandy: three options for staying. He listed them off. All were variations of some kind of bulldozer work and our undeveloped—except for some *picados*, trails, cut in—hundred hectares of ranch land. I groaned inside. I was adjusting to a return and, suddenly faced with the possibility of not returning, knew how terribly much I wanted to.

Once more we weighed the pros and cons. A Canadian friend in construction said the recession was still on, the drywall trade, which was Helmut's business, was currently uncertain and very competitive. On the other hand, our children—the biggest part of the decision—might be served best, since we were an English-speaking family, in Canada. We agreed that whatever decision we made now should probably be considered permanent. We didn't want to keep uprooting and re-rooting ourselves.

The suspense we found ourselves in because of our occasional indecisiveness sharpened our sense of both places and their possibilities.

Never had our previous home in Canada felt so real and enticing, but never, either, the awareness of what Helmut loved about the Chaco, what the children loved, what I had come to love. Here, or there, we would miss the other.

20. NORTH

THE HISTORY of Paraguay, in brief. The meeting of conquistador and Guarani, the Jesuit missions, the dictators: José Gaspar Rodriguez de Francia who closed the country off like a walled garden, Carlos Solano Lopez who opened it, his son Francisco who fancied himself a Napoleon of South America and led his country into a disastrous war with Brazil, Argentina, and Uruguay—the Triple Alliance War of 1864-70—and the bloodiest the continent had seen. Fine for him to cry *Muero por mi patria!* when there were scarcely any men left to hear it, when Paraguay had been crushed, would lose territory, would take decades to recover. In subsequent decades marked by revolution and instability, a stubborn nationalism persisted, because or in spite of the waves of continuous suffering. In 1932 the country readied itself for warfare again, against Bolivia this time, another 100,000 young men slaughtered between them. The Chaco War, also dubbed the War of Thirst. Which Paraguay won. The Russian Mennonites, having fled war and revolution, could hardly believe it when they once again found themselves in the middle of competing gunfire.

More political instability in the wake of that war, and presidents changing as often as the weather it seemed, until Alfredo Stroessner seized power in 1954 and held on to it for thirty-five years, the second-longest reign in modern Latin America after Fidel Castro's of Cuba.

There was an election in February 1983 while we lived in the Chaco but it scarcely registered with me. The Mennonite colonies seemed worlds away from Asunción and the so-called corridors of power, and besides, it was an election such as President Stroessner always conducted, winning by a large majority. He permitted a small opposition for the sake of democratic appearances but he was a dictator. I had the impression—and it was only an impression, I emphasize—that Mennonites appreciated the stability Stroessner maintained. Half-German, he approved of what he saw as Mennonite industry and efficiency. He generally left them alone to run their colonies with political structures of their own.

Did they know of his tortures and brutality? The full range of his paranoia?

"My life there was so small," I complained to expat friends in retrospect. "Inside the house. Not involved in anything else." But perhaps life for all Chaco dwellers was local in the extreme. Distance, isolation, separation in language and culture and religion. But I also knew that Paraguay was no staid, checks-and-balances constitutional democracy such as Canada inherited from Great Britain, which, if dull and relatively bloodless, made it seem the safest country on earth. This was another reason, frankly, if only articulated as fear and speculation—like a bet on where best to save our skins and the skins of our children—to hesitate about settling in the Chaco for the long term. What if things turned out like they had in Russia? What if there was revolution?

Which is why, when Helmut and I—back in Canada some five years—heard the news in 1989 that President Stroessner had been ousted in "a coup that reportedly left scores dead" according to the *Winnipeg Free Press*, we were glad on the one hand but shocked and frightened on behalf of our Fernheim family on the other. Would this usher in the dreaded upheaval of the so-called Mennonite success story in the Chaco?

I jotted a poem for them, called it "After the Overthrow of Stroessner (for our relatives)"

Someone in the crowd photographs the Paraguayan
president before his final jet. The picture is
shadowed, distant, and mute. We'll have to
imagine what configuration of melded colours
and faces he will lift along from his last
view of our lady the city, how he will spend
his recollections. Wishes and pity blur,
lines of exile fade across the sky. We are not
personally acquainted with slain bodyguards.

In the Chaco a father and son wait at lane's end.
Silent grey dust balloons and falls behind a milk
truck roaring to their village. Drought has left
the soil very wild. The men heard the news and now
the capital is closer than they once believed.

They need to see the driver, multiply thoughts,
diffuse slight tremors of fear, turn from watching for rain in case what has happened is true.

He assures them all is well, all is quiet.
The passing of rulers can be easy: insert other
names, find reasons, shake heads at people
in Asunción who danced. Time will tell whether
wounds, murder, a coup at dawn, undid the past,
or the future.

WHILE IN THE Chaco, my research skimmed over the larger Paraguayan history to closely examine the story of the Mennonites who settled the Chaco. And even more specifically, those who came after the release from Moscow in 1929. I read the informative *Strangers Become Neighbors* by Calvin Redekop, pored over the Fernheim histories and Peter P. Klassen's work.

While writing this memoir, I returned to that bigger Paraguay in other books. I read about the Jesuits—the Black Robes of Paraguay—and their missions. And who knew that Eliza Lynch, the Irish courtesan who was the mother of Francisco Solano Lopez' children, his first lady, though never married to him, had become the stuff of so much recent historical fiction? Irish novelist Anne Enright took her on in *The Pleasure of Eliza Lynch*, as did Lily Tuck in the 2004 National Book Award winner *The News from Paraguay*, though it wasn't a popular win. Tuck admitted in her acceptance speech that she'd never been to Paraguay, and then she was invited to visit, which caused a different kind of consternation in the country, for her portrait of Francisco Solano Lopez was far from flattering, and his coffined remains (or someone else's remains lying in for him) have the place of highest honour in the Pantheon of Heroes. Further, the book contained a fair bit of unflattering sex.

I thought Tuck's book a fine achievement, structured in sensually descriptive and tantalizing vignettes, but one book on Lynch and her surely half-mad Lopez sufficed. I re-read *The Honorary Consul* by Graham Greene, set across the river from Paraguay, which implicated the (unnamed) Stroessner regime. I followed travel writer John Gimlette on a rollicking tour through the countryside and history of Paraguay in *At the Tomb of the Inflatable Pig*.

The outsider view was refreshing, if exasperating when it came to what I knew. Take Ben Macintyre in his fascinating 1992 book, *Forgotten Fatherland*, about Elisabeth Nietzsche, sister of the philosopher, who founded with her husband a "pure" Aryan colony in Paraguay called Neuva Germania. Macintyre wrote there were 160,000 Mennonites in Filadelfia. Even dropping one of those zeroes wouldn't correct his massive error. And John Gimlette in his otherwise interesting book, who got the broad attitudes of the Chaco Mennonites right, I thought, but made silly errors like Salve Yanga instead of Yalve Sanga and approached Mennonites, as he approached many of his Paraguayan subjects, like a type of rare animal with customs as strange as the peccary's or armadillo's.

I began to read the complex fictional ravings of the dictator José Gaspar Rodriquez de Francia who called himself El Supremo, in Augusto Roa Bastos' apparently brilliant novel *I, the Supreme*, which was considered a barely-veiled attack on Stroessner when published; the author was subsequently disallowed from the country. I closed that book, eventually turned back to my smaller personal tale, the merely this and that within the tales of the past, remembering that I'd reached, in my narrative, the Chaco spring, a season of beauty and hope, and we were moving into summer, which would be hot, and we had finally stopped discussing the matter and taken a firm decision: we would not attempt our future in Paraguay but continue it in Canada.

Our children could have grown up in Paraguay, but they didn't.

A FAMILY GATHERING, probably our last, and we hosted it and I was nervous but it wasn't necessary, the women of the clan thoroughly pitched in, I was never alone with the work. As always, it was an all-day affair. At noon we ate barbecued hamburgers, coleslaw, pickled cabbage, fresh tomatoes, a bean and egg salad, and fruit soup or fruit salad for dessert. For *Faspa*, afternoon coffee, we had open face sandwiches with cheese or sausage or tomatoes—three mornings that week I baked buns so we would have enough—and sweets, which the others brought.

We totalled about fifty people. It was very hot. We had too little shade, only the *Schattendach* and castor bean hedge. The fruit trees were still too small. Nevertheless, I deemed it a good day. I sensed harmony within the family.

Mama wasn't at the gathering though. She was in the hospital, her pulse dangerously low. A pacemaker would correct the problem but she didn't want one installed. She feared a pacemaker would never let her die. "I want to go home!" she said, and she didn't mean home to her room in the *Abendfrieden*.

I WAS counting down. The weather was excruciating, into the high thirties and barely dropping for the night. The first draft of the novel was done, some 260 typed pages. Typing, re-typing every day, sleeping less, and somehow getting both it and the housework done. The archivist read it for historical accuracy and offered some helpful minor corrections but found no major point that wasn't right. "I'm amazed how you feel our history," she said.

A quick next-to-last trip to Asunción to get the girl's passport and to book our flights to Canada. A last illness, I hoped—the girl this time, feverish and listless. Probably chicken pox. While we were gone, a last holiday for the boys at the home of an aunt and uncle where they were treated like little celebrities. Their favourite activity was getting the cows for milking with their aunt and chasing them back. "We talked the whole time going and coming," the younger boy reported. This aunt had reams of stories for two inquisitive boys and they understood German well by now. She also left the breakfast things on the table, they could run in and help themselves any time they wanted, they said, with an overtone of reproach for my failure to do the same.

I was sewing, sorting, selling, packing in a whirl of heat. More letters from Canada arrived and put me in the mood for winter. We got some dental work done. The older boy picked up lice as a parting gift from school and shared it with the rest of us. We battled back and soon were rid of the critters, and grateful, surprised in fact that he went through two years at the school where lice were a perpetual problem and got them only this once.

The closing program at the Escuela Mariscal Estigarribia fell on an extremely hot day but the children performed their sports demonstrations and program as best they could. I accompanied the music classes on the piano. Tractors purred in the fields around Yalve Sanga. It was seeding time. We were invited for meals and visits to say good-bye, though I preferred the word *Aufwiedersehen*, until we see you again.

Helmut was also doing last-minute things. He was pleased overall with how the work had gone. He'd had a few changes in crew, but was proud that the machines had been driven two years with only Indigenous drivers, which he was told couldn't be done. Until he took over there had always been a white driver in the crew as well. Since he had promised my parents he would write at least once, he wrote his letter now. "To see these young men . . . be responsible for an expensive machine gives us satisfaction," he said. Each man, of course, had his own story and there had been many significant discussions. "To get to the bottom of things, it takes much time. Many concerns are being dealt with around the fire when all is quiet except maybe for a fox or the sound of an owl."

Then, we closed the door of our Yalve Sanga house. We would move into Mama's house in Filadelfia for another series of last meals with siblings and friends. We heard rumours that the Mission was close to finding a replacement for Helmut as machine station manager. I hoped his family would like the house as much as we had. And my husband was passing on good workers and a bulldozer newly painted in bright yellow and running well again after its re-welding and latest repairs.

The boys sat beside Tuffy, petted her, talked to her, and cried. One of the crew drivers had asked for her. When we called to the boys, though, that it was time to go, they jumped up and climbed into the truck, smelling of sunshine, dirt, and dog. We could have stayed, we loved it enough. But this was the human obstacle: you can be in only one place at a time. Both staying and leaving required forgiveness and strength, and leaving had its conveniences: let others manage the unmanageable of this environment now. I could cast off its challenges and keep in my heart what I would miss.

In Filadelfia, our girl got sick again and our younger son broke his arm, but nothing seemed a surprise, it was life. And then it was time to get ourselves to Asunción. It had rained and the *Ruta* was slippery, until we reached the paved part of the highway. This rain seemed a fitting farewell from the region itself, so unpredictably predictable, the press of heat and dust one day, the hazard of muck and sliding adventure the next.

We had scheduled several days of relaxing at a camp with friends, but soon these days were done and before we knew it, it seemed, we'd managed the gauntlet of baggage and personal checks at the airport and were strapped into airplane seats and lifting away from the red soil and lavish green of the capital, Helmut and I and the boys and the girl he called his Paraguayan "clear profit," our little joke at what we were paid, bringing nothing of value away with us but our precious children (nut brown from two years in the sun) and tied-tighter connections with family, good memories, many experiences, and a manuscript draft tucked into a case—all of which were, in fact, of immeasurable worth—and then we were up, looking down at the city, and the plane rose and flew over the river and though we weren't sure of the route, we imagined that the blur of grey-green far beneath us was the Chaco, a place we made home but were leaving nevertheless, and we looked as long as we could until what was both vast and intricate to us was closed away by distance and cloud. If anyone on the ground had looked up and mused about who was travelling above, I would have had to tell them that we five were already absorbed with the small details of modern flight, the tight quarters, tray tables up and down, activities pulled out of carry-on bags, all of us tucked close and together for the hours ahead that were neither Here nor There, except that we were going north.

Acknowledgements

The epigraph for "Learning geography" is from Joanne Epp's poem "On finding a friend's obituary" in her chapbook *Nothing but time*, Seven Kitchens Press, 2020. Used by permission.

The essay by Timothy Taylor cited in "In the house of my pilgrimage" can be read at www.timothytaylor.ca/the-mobile-age-part-one-modernism/.

The photographs in "In the house of my pilgrimage" are from the author's collection.

Parts of this book have been published in various journals or anthologies, some in a slightly different form:
- "Notes toward an autobiography" was written while the *Mennonite Girls Can Cook* website was gaining followers and fame and two writer friends suggested a Mennonite Girls Can Write collection. Although that project didn't happen, this piece appeared in a food-themed issue of *Room*, Vol. 40.1, 2017.
- "Return stroke" was shortlisted for the Edna Staebler Personal Essay award and appeared in *The New Quarterly*, summer 2016. An abbreviated version was presented at Mennonite/s Writing VIII, 2017

and then appeared in *Journal of Mennonite Studies*, Vol. 36, 2018.

- "On the memory set" appeared in *The New Quarterly*, winter 2020.
- "Mother and child" appeared in *The New Quarterly*, spring 2018, and in the anthology *Body & Soul: Stories for Skeptics and Seekers*, edited by Susan Scott, Caitlin Press, 2019.
- "Burial grounds" appeared in *Prairie Fire*, spring 2020.
- "Reunion" appeared in the fall 2020 issue of online journal *Persimmon Tree*, fall 2020.
- "How I got old" appeared in the anthology *You Look Good for Your Age*, edited by Rona Altrows, University of Alberta Press, 2021.